Dumb Beasts and Dead Phi

Dumb Beasts and Dead Philosophers

*Humanity and the Humane in
Ancient Philosophy and Literature*

Catherine Osborne

CLARENDON PRESS · OXFORD

OXFORD
UNIVERSITY PRESS

Great Clarendon Street, Oxford OX2 6DP

Oxford University Press is a department of the University of Oxford.
It furthers the University's objective of excellence in research, scholarship,
and education by publishing worldwide in

Oxford New York

Auckland Cape Town Dar es Salaam Hong Kong Karachi
Kuala Lumpur Madrid Melbourne Mexico City Nairobi
New Delhi Shanghai Taipei Toronto

With offices in

Argentina Austria Brazil Chile Czech Republic France Greece
Guatemala Hungary Italy Japan Poland Portugal Singapore
South Korea Switzerland Thailand Turkey Ukraine Vietnam

Oxford is a registered trade mark of Oxford University Press
in the UK and in certain other countries

Published in the United States
by Oxford University Press Inc., New York

First published 2007
First published in paperback 2009

British Library Cataloguing in Publication Data

Data available

Library of Congress Cataloging in Publication Data

Data available

Typeset by Laserwords Private Limited, Chennai, India
Printed in Great Britain by the MPG Books Group, Bodmin and King's Lynn

ISBN 978–0–19–928206– (Hbk)7
ISBN 978–0–19–956827– (Pbk)7

10 9 8 7 6 5 4 3 2 1

To the memory of
Dick Beardsmore

Preface

Dumb beasts and dead philosophers. This much they have in common: that we find it hard to be sure how effectively we are communicating with them. They do not speak to us in our language.

But is this our fault or theirs? Is it they who have nothing to say, or we who have no means to listen? It is easy to suppose that because other animals 'lack language' (as we put it), they must have nothing to say to us. But the impression that they *lack* something, a faculty that *we* possess, is created entirely by our anthropocentric perspective. Perhaps, if language were the only way to communicate, then lacking such language might be equated with having nothing worth communicating, though even that seems unsafe as a general inference. In practice, language may be a restriction as well as a facility, since language users, accustomed to reading or hearing truths expressed in words, may find it hard to recognize communication conveyed by other mechanisms.

Our dependence upon verbal discourse, preferably couched in a language that we understand, restricts our capacity to understand what is not expressed like that. So perhaps it is our disadvantage to be language-confined, to be unable to hear what others can hear, unable to read what others can read. If there is communication without words, who is better placed to comprehend, those who do or those who don't talk only in language? Do we close ourselves to forms of communication that we once had fully in our control—once, before we learned to talk? At the risk of sounding pathetic, we need to remind ourselves that there are many things, human things included, that can be conveyed by other forms of communication besides the systems of vocal sounds or written signs that make up what we call human language (or the artificial sign language substitutes, which are derivative from natural spoken forms). Human communication is much more extensive than what we narrowly call language. Or, if we extend the term 'language' to cover the non-linguistic methods of imparting information and sharing thoughts within a social community, then language is a much more widespread form of communication, with a much greater variety of quasi- or non-propositional structures, than we often suppose when we talk philosophy.

With the dead philosophers we may be more willing to concede that they have things to say to us, which we are badly placed to understand. They write in a language—though, if they are long dead, it is not ours. They speak of things we recognize, but often in terms that clash and jar with our conceptual map. They seem to utter claims that belong to our debates, yet what they say may shock or sometimes irritate us. Often we close our ears and try not to hear, lest we be corrupted.

The bulk of this book consists of a range of studies that attempt to open our ears to hear what those dumb texts can still say to us. These detailed studies are preceded by an introduction which embarks, by way of a discussion of some poems by William Blake, on a rather general outline of the position I want to defend. I have chosen to begin with poetry, and have not tried to engage directly with specific texts in meta-ethics, although my questions are meta-ethical ones, about what it means to get something right in ethics: some may feel that I have failed to situate the discussion adequately in the context of recent work in that field. If that is so, I apologize. However, my main point is to argue that we can learn from listening to poetry and stories, and that arid argument is not always (or perhaps ever) the way to grasp moral truths—such as coming to understand what it is to take a humane attitude, and not a sentimental attitude, towards the other inhabitants of the world we live in. It is on those questions that I hope to cast some light, by way of the dumb texts examined in Chapters 2–9.

Acknowledgements

I have been working on topics in this area intermittently over many years, during which I published one or two preliminary papers, on related themes to those covered in the chapters of this book. In particular, some material that I discuss in Chapters 2 and 6 was also a focus of my attention in a paper that I published in 1990,[1] but there I was sketching the historical and cultural implications of the texts I was discussing, and now I am talking about how we come to draw moral lines between ourselves and other kinds. Part of Chapter 9 extends ideas I treated at a rather superficial level in a paper on 'Ancient vegetarianism' published in 1995.[2] Chapter 7 draws upon conclusions that are more fully defended in my paper 'Aristotle on the fantastic abilities of animals' published in 2000.[3]

As always, much water has passed under the bridge. Since I first became interested in this topic, I have spent ten years working in Swansea, three years in Liverpool, and three years in Norwich; my children have grown up; and the work is scarcely recognizable as the project it once was. I have benefited immensely from live discussion of my work both at home and elsewhere. I am sure that it is the better for the many marks it bears of those with whom I have had the good fortune to work and to converse in the intervening years. Various bits of the book have been exposed to fruitful discussion with seminar and conference audiences, at Swansea, Liverpool, and Norwich, and also in the wider world, including meetings of the Southern Association for Ancient Philosophy, the Patristic Conference, and the B Club. A conference on food in antiquity in London and a seminar in Nottingham provided useful opportunities to try out ideas at an early stage of the work.

[1] Catherine Osborne, 'Boundaries in nature: eating with animals in the fifth century BC.', *Bulletin of the Institute of Classical Studies*, 37 (1990): 15–30.

[2] Catherine Osborne, 'Ancient vegetarianism', in *Food in Antiquity*, ed. John Wilkins, David Harvey, and Michael Dobson (Exeter: University of Exeter Press, 1995), 214–24.

[3] Catherine Osborne, 'Aristotle on the fantastic abilities of animals', *Oxford Studies in Ancient Philosophy*, 19 (2000): 253–85. The copyright for this is my own.

A preliminary version of the whole manuscript was read by two anonymous readers for the Press, and I have revised it in the light of their insights and helpful suggestions, and in response to suggestions from three readers who assessed the proposal at an earlier stage. I am sorry that I have not been able to follow up every idea or meet every criticism (for reasons either of my own incompetence or because they would have made the book a different book), and I hope that if those kind and helpful readers are reviewing this finished work, they will be indulgent over my failures. Richard Sorabji and Angus Ross, between them, read the whole of the finished manuscript in the final stages of revising it, and passed me a wealth of useful comments, criticisms, and encouragement, of just the right sort for that stage of the proceedings. I also owe a particular debt of gratitude to Richard Sorabji, not only for this but for many enlightening exchanges in the past.

My current university, UEA Norwich, generously allowed me to take a full year of research leave, starting only four months into my first year of employment there. I am also grateful to the Arts and Humanities Research Board for funding the second half of that time, which allowed me to complete the manuscript on schedule.

Not all the dead philosophers who figure in this book are so very long dead. Here I must mention in particular R. W. Beardsmore, whose profound and humane intelligence was inspirational to students and Faculty alike, in Swansea in the 1990s (and in Bangor before that). For some years before Dick's untimely death in 1997, we were required intermittently to list the Department's plans for the upcoming Research Assessment Exercise. Among the planned works we used to list was a co-authored book, by Beardsmore and Osborne, on animals. In the proposed book, I was to explore the ancient philosophers, and Beardsmore was to work on the contemporary material relating to animal minds and morals. It was to include his legendary paper called 'Do fish feel pain?', long promised, but never delivered, to the departmental seminar.

RAE plans don't always materialize. The co-authored book didn't happen, and this isn't quite what it would have been (if it ever could have been). Perhaps it was never more than a myth. However, I think that there are still some traces of conversations with Dick, about animals and other things, and I'd like to dedicate what I've written here to the memory of Dick Beardsmore's unforgettable irony, in gratitude for what he taught me—about moral philosophy and bluegrass music, about guinea pigs and Saab engines, about literature, art, loyalty, courage, hope, determination, despair, self-sacrifice, and all the other things that really matter, in life and in death.

C J O

Contents

PART I

Constructing Divisions

1

Introduction: On William Blake, Nature, and Mortality

The Beautiful Vision

> To see a World in a Grain of Sand
> And a Heaven in a Wild Flower,
> Hold Infinity in the palm of your hand
> And Eternity in an hour.[1]

This first puzzling quatrain which introduces William Blake's *Auguries of Innocence* is widely known. The other 128 lines of the poem, less often quoted and very rarely transcribed in full, comprise sixty-four rhyming couplets, mainly in the form of two-line proverbs. Here Blake imagines a world in which cruelty and insensitivity are abhorrent, and offences against wild creatures have terrible consequences.

The consequences that Blake asks us to envisage are not natural disasters but moral ones:

> A Robin Red breast in a Cage
> Puts all heaven in a Rage.

> A dove-house fill'd with Doves & Pigeons
> Shudders Hell thro' all its regions.

> A dog starv'd at his Master's Gate
> Predicts the ruin of the State.

---

[1] William Blake, *Auguries of Innocence*, 1–4.

A horse misused upon the Road
Calls to Heaven for Human Blood.

Each outcry of the hunted Hare
A fibre from the Brain doth tear.

A skylark wounded in the wing,
A Cherubim does cease to sing.

The Game Cock clip'd & arm'd for fight
Does the Rising Sun affright.

Every Wolf's and Lion's howl
Raises from Hell a human soul.

The wild Deer wand'ring here and there
Keeps the Human Soul from Care.

The Lamb misused breeds Public strife
And yet forgives the Butcher's Knife.[2]

Although the structure of the formulae makes it look as though Blake is appealing to consequentialist considerations to discourage cruelty ('You'd better not do this, or that might happen'), the nature of the consequences shows that, for Blake, morality is not shored up on a foundation of self-interest or utilitarian benefits. When he suggests, in lines 15–16, that some cherub ceases to sing whenever a skylark is wounded, he is not citing something else that is harmful besides the offence to the skylark, such that if there are no cherubim we need not worry about skylarks. Rather, he is pointing to the inherent offensiveness of the deed: it is harmful because to kill a skylark *is what it is* to silence one of the cherubim. We have to learn to see it as such, in order to see what kind of offence is committed in cases of wanton cruelty to wild things. With his simple-minded 'penny proverb' formulae, Blake tries to persuade us to see things from the point of view of 'heaven': to be enraged by what puts heaven in a rage, to take delight in what is delightful to heaven itself.

Blake's poem does not seem to offer the kind of persuasion that would convince a philosophically minded person to change his or her views. There is no attempt to show *why* we should see the death of

---

[2] William Blake, *Auguries of Innocence*, 5–24.

a skylark as tragic; nor does Blake tell us what is the source of the absolute external judgement of value implied in the claim that something 'Puts all heaven in a Rage'. He does not explain how he knows this for a fact, nor what kind of fact it is. It is hard to see how these proverbs could be effective against someone who took a more grudging view of the value of non-human lives, or who thought that right action was to be judged by the calculation of overall utility, not by some postulate of heaven's anger. If we look for argument in Blake's vision, it is lacking.

But that is not to say that there are not other forms of persuasion, besides academic arguments, that are also philosophical. One might, in fact, want to say that some apparently non-rational techniques are more suited to engineering the kind of change of outlook that Blake is interested in producing. Sometimes it is more effective to resort to poetry or story-telling in order to offer a way into an alternative view-point. Yet the reader who clings to argument and rational debate is in danger of remaining blind to such alternatives—blind largely because of those very blinkers that refuse to see what can only be shown and not proved.

Blake asks us to bring our moral sensibilities into line with some absolute standard, the viewpoint of heaven. Moral sensibility, he suggests, involves having our emotions in good order, which means being enraged, offended, and upset by things by which we should be enraged, offended, and upset, and delighting in what merits delight. Indeed, surely Blake is right that moral vision consists in seeing things as offensive when they are offensive, and as wonderful when they are wonderful. But we need to be brought to see which things are wonderful, and, if there is a truth out there about which things are wonderful, and it is not up to us, then moral vision will demand a kind of cognitive awareness of some truth, and an alignment of our sensibilities with the sensibilities of heaven (to use Blake's picturesque language). In other words, correct emotional responses will include a response to or recognition of real values, something objective about the events or circumstances that are to be judged. The emotional response involves an evaluative judgement, a kind of cognitive awareness of something: namely, the genuine offensiveness, or beauty, of the things in question. Hence we might want to say that moral judgements involve emotional responses with cognitive content,[3] though that content need not be propositional, as I hope to show in Chapter 4.[4]

Blake clearly envisages that moral attitudes will follow once we learn to see things aright. If we come to see things as worthy of care, we shall care for them as such. Indeed, surely that must be so: to care for something just is to find that its concerns matter to us. Blake points us to the hunted hare, the wounded skylark, and the badly treated horse, and asks us to see the difference between kindness and cruelty, between humane and inhumane kinds of killing, and between justifiable use and unjustified abuse. These are sensitivities that do not appeal straightforwardly to natural features of the creatures in question, for the person who is content to leave the lamb to starve, or to whip the horse to death, perceives exactly the same biological specimen before him as the person who decries such action. Blake asks us instead to see how other moral agents (heaven and the angels, providence and the personified moral welfare of the community) react with horror at such deeds. Only by learning to react with horror like that can we become humane people.

Moral learning, then, is not to be equated with scientific or biological learning, since the facts we need to master are not simple facts of biology. Blake's humane vision clearly does not dawn when we master a new set of value-free truths about biology, or if we master a set of maxims to prescribe or limit action (even if Blake's formulae sometimes look, unhelpfully, like maxims to memorize and act upon). No utilitarian or consequentialist

---

[3] The cognitive content of emotional judgements has been the focus of a number of recent studies, including work on ancient thinkers, Stoics in particular. For scholarly work on what the Stoics' position was, see Richard Sorabji, *Emotion and Peace of Mind: From Stoic Agitation to Christian Temptation* (Oxford: Oxford University Press, 2000), and for a defence of cognitivism on the Stoic model, see Martha C. Nussbaum, *Upheavals of Thought: The Intelligence of Emotions* (Cambridge: Cambridge University Press, 2001). There is a risk, however, which is particularly evident in Nussbaum's treatment of this question in relation to animals, of taking it for granted that the requisite cognition must be a propositional attitude, and hence must be implicitly structured as a proposition, so that in order to ascribe emotions to animals one must attribute the same propositional beliefs to them as would found the corresponding reaction in us. In Nussbaum's case, these are cognitive appraisals of the significance of something *vis-à-vis* one's own goals and projects. Nussbaum, *Upheavals of Thought*, p. I, ch. 2. See further below, Ch. 4.

[4] To my mind the account that Nussbaum gives of the cognitive processes involved in the animal's appraisal of the situation stretches credulity. When I use the terminology of 'seeing', such as 'seeing' a certain action as offensive, I do not mean to imply that a complex proposition is involved. In order to observe offensiveness in a situation, one does not need to think 'x is offensive', or even 'this is offensive'. One reacts to the offensiveness: one judges it disagreeable—much as one might react to a noxious smell, burning heat, or a dazzling light, only in this case the offensiveness will be morally painful, not physically painful. A certain kind of discernment of a property deserving a negative response (at the cognitive rather than the behavioural level) just is what it is to judge that something is offensive. See also Ch. 4, n. 12.

persuasion can ever bring one to see the world in the way Blake urges us to see it, unless one has first learnt to value (or decry) certain kinds of consequences. So moral development, we might say, will be about learning what to value, which consequences to decry, what to weep for, and what to love, not about calculating the net results of some *already given* values.

In moral judgements, then, nature seems to be the object of our attention, not the subject of it. Nature itself does not tell us what to value—by 'nature' here I mean the kind of information about the natural world that goes into biological taxonomy, and the results of empirical experiments on animal psychology and behaviour.[5] Different observers, and different communities of observers, see the natural objects around them in one way or another: some see them as a resource to exploit; others see them as a gift to love and cherish. Neither of them seem to be making a factual mistake about the natural capacities of the objects they are observing. Nothing in the biology can tell us that one of those attitudes is a more accurate estimate of what is before us, laid out for our attention, because what is there can, in fact, be treated either way. There is nothing about a mortal human being that ensures that we cannot enslave her, rape her, take her livelihood, or murder her children. On the contrary, without some artificial precautions, she is wholly vulnerable to all those things and more. Nature provides no protection against such atrocities. That is why they are so common. And that is why so much legislation and social engineering is expended on trying to minimize the risks. Equally, there is nothing about lambs that makes them immune to abuse; nothing about foxes that makes it impossible to set dogs upon them, or to tear them limb from limb for fun.

Yet when we look upon those kinds of cruelty and abuse, we often use the language of necessity and impossibility. 'You can't do that to an innocent

---

[5] I am invoking a simple-minded contrast here between nature (external, objective facts about the natural world independent of human value judgements) and the value-laden attitudes to them that are fostered by art, literature, and human culture. Perhaps this distinction begs the question, and it may be that we do not have any access to such supposedly 'objective facts'. We may also wish to dissociate ourselves from any such ideal of objective science seeking objective facts (so we may have a value-laden attitude to the project of discerning value-free facts about nature). But my claim is not (I think) seriously disturbed by these worries. My suggestion is that the attitudes fostered by art and culture are not dictated by external objective facts of nature, but are a way of seeing those facts and placing value on them. The fact that these attitudes are, in a certain sense, up to us does not, however, prevent them from being objectively right or wrong. But they are right and wrong in a different way from the way in which our beliefs about biological facts may be right or wrong. The latter could be corrected or confirmed by recognized methods of empirical research; the former could not (but could, in some cases, be rectified by reflecting on a poem such as Blake's, for instance).

person,' we say. And then we try to justify that claim by drawing attention to some quasi-empirical biological facts about the innocent creature whose suffering we find offensive. 'She's a rational being'; 'It feels pain'; 'They have a potential for self-awareness'. The reasoning looks odd. For it appears that we are trying to appeal to value-neutral natural features, things that biology could discover, as though things like that could provide answers to questions about what we should or shouldn't do to our fellow creatures. Given that nature makes rational beings just as vulnerable to cruelty as others, and given that it is clear that creatures that can suffer are naturally more vulnerable to suffering than things that cannot suffer, what mistake are we making when we try to say that you *cannot* inflict suffering on a creature that is capable of suffering?

In one sense perhaps we are making some mistake, at least when we try to take this limping attempt at justification to be something that it is not. When we decry cruelty with words like 'cannot' we are typically asking the hearer to come to see the world as we do (for in *our* world, perhaps, it is true that one *cannot* do that: 'cannot' because of a range of psychological and moral constraints, for one is personally incapable of, say, choosing to inflict suffering on another creature gratuitously, and one cannot do so without remorse, or without failing to adhere to the things that matter most, and so on). So we express our horror in the terms that come naturally to us: we describe the offensive action as an impossibility, and we think that our vision is obvious and is written unmistakably in the nature of things—because it seems to us to be a correct expression of how things naturally are. And just as Blake asked his hearers to see that heaven was angry and to learn to feel angry in the same way, so we ask our morally insensitive fellows to acquire the sensibility that is expressed in our outcry 'You can't do that!'. If we think that it is genuinely the case that the other person can't do it, of course we are mistaken, because they can do it, and they are doing it. They do not feel the horror and will not feel the remorse, and they are not failing to uphold any of their own personal values or commitments. In a kind of factual sense, it simply is not true that they 'can't do that', in the way it is true for ourselves.

Yet perhaps we shall still want to say that there is a sense in which they 'can't do that' and get away with it, because there is something seriously missing in their understanding of the situation. Nor do we leave it, when we see that the other person has no scruples where we have scruples. Like Blake, we then go on to try to persuade the person who does not share our sensibilities to come to see the vulnerable creature as something to care for. Perhaps this can best be done by the kind of expressions that Blake provides, expressions that show that the sensitivity required is to the *moral evaluations* that are missing—heaven's verdicts about what matters—not to some supposedly objective empirical facts of nature, or to some naturally harmful consequences that haven't been assessed correctly. But by default, and through lack of poetic understanding, we often find ourselves tempted to try some more pragmatic appeal. We resort to a naturalistic form of argument. We try drawing attention to features that we think might weigh with those who are blind to moral considerations: we try to appeal to consistency—for instance, to the idea that one should treat alike things that have like capacities. We try to force people to concede that if they treat other human beings in a decent way, that must be because of what human beings are by nature (rational, or sentient, or whatever). And then we try to get them to reason to a similar consideration for other creatures that share some of the same capacities. We delude even ourselves into thinking that it is because of some natural abilities that we take such things to be precious, and that our fellow humans deserve care (or 'have rights') in virtue of being something naturally special—sentient, self-conscious, or rational, say.

In that project, too, we must surely be mistaken. Why should we think that the value of a human being derives from his or her rationality, for instance? Surely there is nothing especially noble about rationality as such—far from it. Where it exists at all, rationality is often a source of deeply unpleasant and cold insensitivity, or of unyielding pig-headedness. Such obstinate rationality stands to be condemned and despised, not admired or prized. It is often those times when emotion, intuitive empathy, and gener-ous sensitivity triumph over rational calculation that human nature reveals its better side—though that is not to say that every intuitive or empathetic response is a fine one. Nor, evidently, does a person's value derive from any other natural feature of the individual, whether it be looks or physique or intelligence. Such things are not intrinsically valuable in themselves—at least not in the way that would be needed for them to make their possessor an object of unconditional moral respect—, [6] while their instrumental value

---

[6] It might be tempting to think that good looks, a fine physique, and intelligence are aesthetically pleasing in themselves, so that it would be as great an evil to have the world devoid of such fine things as to have it devoid of small blue butterflies or the works of Vivaldi. But the issue here is not whether intelligence is, *ceteris paribus*, a good thing in itself, but whether it makes the individual or species that

is invariably morally ambiguous, since they may be put to good or evil uses. Yet, to the eyes of affection, all these things may come to seem beautiful, even wonderful and fine. When such gifts are properly appreciated, and properly used, they become valuable (in the hands of the one whose gifts they are, and in the eyes of the one who sees the world aright).[7]

So what we are really trying to do, in bringing another to share our moral viewpoint, is to teach him to see value where we see value, to pay attention to what we find merits attention, and to direct his care and love towards what we find worthy of care and love. Frequently we—both philosophers and ordinary unpretentious folk—try to do this by pointing to uncontroversial facts in nature that we think are the things that justify our take on the world. We do this, first, because we take it for granted that our evaluation of things can be read off in their very nature (for that is how it seems to us), so that we suppose that someone who accepts the relevant biological facts must accept the moral truths that seem (to us) to follow from them. And second, we suppose that someone who lacks moral vision will learn to see what matters by being directed to look again at things that already count as important for him (such as facts of biology, say, or utilitarian consequences, or self-interest). Yet it is probably just this false evaluation of what matters that most needs to be shifted, not reinforced by suggesting that it is factors such as those that underpin our own evaluations, if there is to be a shift in the person's moral outlook.

Suppose we have a beautiful vision of the world. We cannot bring someone whose vision of the world is a grudging one to see it as a thing

---

possesses it intrinsically superior, not just instrumentally (as the necessary means for preserving the beauty and intelligence that would otherwise be lost), but as an end in itself.

[7] I have not mentioned the capacity for speech here. Raimond Gaita identifies the capacity for speech, equated with the possibility that things might go deep or have some meaning for us, as the crucial mark of human life, which makes someone a limit on another's will. (This is a theme in both Raimond Gaita, *Good and Evil: An Absolute Conception* (Basingstoke: Macmillan, 1991) and many of his other writings, including *The Philosopher's Dog* (London and New York: Routledge, 2002).) This focus on speech may be an attempt to pick something that is more obviously morally relevant, and more clearly valuable, than the candidates mentioned above. But I think that, in so far as it has anything to do with the capacity for speech as such, it suffers from the same problems as the other candidates—in particular the moral ambiguity of its uses; while if it is not about speech as such, but about what (often or sometimes) goes with a capacity for speech, then the identification of speech as the criterion of value seems to rely upon a more basic idea: namely, that some of the deeper sides of human experience are morally significant. This does not, however, give us a natural moral division that coincides with the species boundary between humans and other kinds. On Gaita's emphasis on the significance of the capacity for speech, see Alex Segal, 'Goodness beyond speech', *Philosophical Investigations*, 27 (2004): 201–21.

of beauty by re-describing it in terms of that grudging vision. For then it will just be the same grudging and valueless world that he inhabited before; then, as before, the things that attract his attention will be the same pointless things, without grace and without beauty. Perhaps, then, poetry and art, rather than science and argument, are the kinds of things that can change our sense of which features of the world demand our attention and our love.

True Values and Relativism

Suppose we hear what Blake has to say, and thereby come to see the world as a thing of beauty, deserving of care. Suppose we feel that we have grown out of the grudging values of self-interest and externally imposed obligation, and come to a more mature perception of what it is to act in a humane way. So we have changed one set of values (the grudging values we used to endorse) for a new set of values, Blake's beautiful vision, the ones he ascribes to 'heaven'. Is there no more truth to our new, humane attitude than to the grudging one we held when (as we see it now) our moral vision was undeveloped? Is value simply relative to the perceiver, so that our sense that we have changed for the better is nothing but our current preference for what we now believe is good? Is our commitment to the genuine and exclusive truth of heaven's moral vision just an illusion? Perhaps there is no neutral reason to prefer that beautiful vision, that cares because it sees in the object of care a thing of joy, and to prefer it over the grudging vision of utilitarian or deontological outlooks? My answer to these sceptical questions is 'No', because there is a kind of second-order evaluation here, which is not vulnerable to the charge of relativism, although there might remain a sceptical doubt as to whether we could prove that the caring outlook is superior to someone who does not already see that it is so.

This needs some clarification. We have two levels of moral judgement involved. At the lower level we ask, for instance, whether the welfare of farm animals overrides considerations of profit, and we find that some individuals see farm animals as fellow creatures and objects of care, so that it is natural to conceive of their welfare as a matter of moral significance that can limit the extent to which we use them for profit, while others see farm animals as an investment in resources for a factory production process, so that welfare is a consideration only in respect to the risk of diminishing profits when the animals are below optimum health. These two attitudes seem to stem from alternative assessments of the motives and values that should weigh with us in deciding what to do, and they don't seem to be settled by appeal to the biological facts, such as what kind of conditions cause an animal distress.

But there is also a second level of moral judgement, a judgement about which assessment of the motives and values that should weigh with us is the better (or right) one. Here we can attempt to stand back and ask which of two outlooks is better. At this point we are not judging from within a particular outlook, but trying to adjudicate between different outlooks. Of course, one might hold that one is never in a position to do that, or that when one does so, one is in no position to show that one's adjudication is correct—and in particular, that there is no way to prove, to someone who does not already endorse the better outlook, that one's favoured outlook is better. Once again it seems that poetry and stories will be the only way to bring someone else to see why a certain outlook is missing out on something of real value, or that another one is more perceptive of what really matters. Nevertheless, even if this fact cannot be shown in terms that could convince a scientist, a philosopher, or anyone who hates poetry, it is at this level, I am suggesting, that there is indeed a truth to be known that is not relative to a perceiver.[8]

In this way there need be no hint of relativism in the *evaluation* of the true moral vision—that is, in the second-order evaluation of which outlook is the better one. Even though holders of the true moral vision see value where others do not see it, even when they have been brought to see all the relevant empirical evidence, it may still be better to see it there than elsewhere. The location of moral value, I am suggesting, is in the outlook of the person who has a developed moral vision: in his perception of things under a certain description that others do not share (and are the worse for not sharing). One take on the world is better than another: the finer description is a better one, the humane attitude is a better

---

[8] That is to say, some things that do matter to us perhaps shouldn't matter to us. Other things that don't matter to us perhaps should. This is not to say that the things that should matter to us do, willy-nilly, matter to us, even though we are not aware of it and act as though they did not (though that would be one way that we might sometimes want to explain things—as, for instance, Socrates explains it in conversation with Polus in the *Gorgias*). It is to say that some people genuinely do fail to attach any significance to some things, when those things should be among the most important if their lives are to have any genuine meaning.

attitude—morally better. If others do not see the world as precious, that is a misfortune for them, even though they have made no mistake about how the world is and looks for them. They have, however, missed out on what is most crucial in life.

That last paragraph may seem obscure or opaque. To clarify what I mean, it may help to compare the situation with regard to appreciation of music or art. If one comes to an unfamiliar genre of art with limited critical awareness, or with preconceptions from another field, one may be initially unable to see which features in the unfamiliar work are salient in passing judgement on its merits. We may disapprove of the work for the very features that a more educated critic admires. The critic's task is to bring his public to see the work in a new way, so that the features that make it great strike one as admirable, not distressing. Thus the critic finds himself drawing attention to features that were already there to see (or hear) in the work when it was first encountered, but by re-describing them and encouraging a new outlook, he persuades the viewer to alter his attitude to those features and to revise his evaluation. It makes sense to suggest that when we learn to appreciate Tavener's music, we discover what it is about it that is superb (not that we have a private value system in which things that have no intrinsic value come to look valuable to us), and that when we come to a humane appreciation of the world around us, we discover what it is about nature that is precious (not that we adopt a private value system in which things that have no intrinsic value come to look valuable to us).[9] To miss out on that is to miss out on something worth understanding, though it need not involve failing to notice any physical feature of the work of art, or of the objects of biology. I mean something of the same sort when I say

---

[9] The first of these looks like a classic case of what Raz calls the social dependence of value, such that one has to become an aficionado of the genre in order to appreciate which items in that genre are good of the kind. Then it would not be dependent upon a private value system, but one shared by those who understand contemporary music, in which certain techniques come to look valuable—and to be brought to see those things as valuable would be to enter the practice. But it seems unhelpful to hypostasize values as though they were metaphysical entities brought into being by social practices (or, in some cases, existing independently of any social practice) rather than focus on the practice of valuing, and ask which evaluative practice is the superior one—which Raz tries to address by appealing to further values such as freedom or the 'value of people' that are not merely within a social practice but are somehow independent and serve as the standard against which we judge the generic values. Joseph Raz, *The Practice of Value*, ed. R. Jay Wallace, The Berkeley Tanner Lectures (Oxford: Oxford University Press, 2003), 33–6. This is perhaps an attempt to explain what I am here calling the superiority of one practice of valuing over another, but cashing it out with reference to more of the mysterious entities called 'values', this time values that exist independently of any valuers.

that those who miss out on the better moral outlook miss out on something that is most crucial, something most worth understanding, in life.

Against Human Flourishing

When I say that such moral blindness misses out on what is most crucial in life, do not think that I mean anything to do with what is called 'human flourishing', or with any human goals—as though we were to suppose that humanity or human life were something naturally worth valuing for its own sake. I do not mean that the better vision is better for pragmatic or utilitarian reasons. It is better because it is more noble, more admirable, finer, more beautiful, and *because it sees a beauty that is really there*. These are moral virtues not pragmatic ones. If this appears like a virtue-based account of the locus of moral value, it must nevertheless not be assimilated to those popular but debased forms of Aristotelianism that assume that the measure of virtue is determined by whether it contributes to a successful human life—or, indeed, to any other kind of project that is to be assessed by non-moral, pragmatic, criteria of 'flourishing'.

Typically, a virtue-based account of moral value will have problems with some kinds of self-sacrificial virtues, if the explanation of their merit is supposed to be found in a simple-minded pragmatic notion of human flourishing. By contrast, I have no wish to explain away the sacrificial nature of genuine altruism.[10] For my purpose, an attitude counts as a noble one if it is a thing of beauty, and it may be a thing of beauty even if its effects upon the agent's own life, or indeed her own species, might be devastating; even if it entailed the destruction of her world and of all her worldly projects.[11] Indeed, that is precisely when it is a thing of beauty. Morality may be at its most beautiful when it is wholly and ungrudgingly self-sacrificial. Human flourishing may be—should be—the least of its concerns. So if

---

[10] Aristotle explains self-sacrificial altruism at *Eth. Nic.* 1169²18–29, including death for a good cause at ²25. As I read it, this does not try to reintroduce self-interest as the motivation for apparently self-denying actions, but rather explains how the well-motivated person can coherently choose the fine but self-destroying action, because what is fine presents itself as an overriding goal. The fine action is what motivates the virtuous person beyond any other more tangible benefit.

[11] It will not, of course, destroy the one dearest project: namely, that of acting for the best, choosing the noblest way. Rather, I am thinking of the person who goes to a self-sacrificial death, or chooses a hard way of life, with deep regret, even despair, for what they and others dear to them will lose as a result. Compare Sophocles' portrait of Antigone (lines 801–943).

we need to package my proposals with some classic doctrines, I suspect that it is probably better to drop my account of what makes for moral goodness not into the Aristotelian carton, but into one marked 'Platonism'; for such moral vision involves seeing a beauty and a goodness in things that others see as worthless—a beauty and a goodness that are a vestige of the goodness and true beauty that we all long to realize in ourselves and in the world. And once things are seen in that light, they become the objects of passionate devotion, and the attempt to preserve and realize the vestiges of beauty among the things of this world is then a matter of extreme altruism. For the Platonist, virtue involves total attention, taken to extremes, and not the moderate self-interest characteristic of contemporary Aristotelianism.

Perhaps it sounds surprising to talk of *seeing a beauty that is really there*. If the beautiful vision is one that sees a beauty and preciousness that is really there, and this is one of the things that makes this vision better than the one that fails to see the beauty in things, why is it not a natural fact or feature in the world that is perceived? My point is that our perception of the world is partial, and structured by evaluative commitments; it is a kind of favouritism. When we focus on good qualities at the expense of weaknesses, or on positive features at the expense of negative ones, these qualities are not more correctly perceived than the negative qualities that the grudging agent sees: each of us looks out at the world and sees it with a selective focus. The question then is: which selective focus is morally superior, the one that reveals the prejudices of love or the one that reveals the prejudices of callous self-interest? Neither is superior in factual truth value, as regards the natural features of the objects observed, but one is true to something like a moral truth—that love is a better attitude than callous self-interest, for example.[12]

Mortality

Others before me have tried to formulate a position along these lines, and indeed I am not the first to explore these questions in relation to the supposed ethical significance of the divide between humans and other animals, and to use that as one of the tests against which to put theory

---

[12] A selective preference for seeing goodness and value in others may sound naïve and gullible if it is applied in situations where there is evil and corruption. I do not mean to say that this vision will turn a blind eye to corruption: on the contrary, it will be as passionately offended by evil and ugliness as it is devoted to beauty and goodness.

on trial.[13] My purpose in this book is not to address other recent thinkers directly—or, at least, not to do so at great length or in great detail—but rather to turn back to the dead philosophers of the ancient past, so as to distance myself somewhat from the constraints of the current debates and to think with a clearer head. Conversion, I suggest, can be achieved better by returning to square one and retracing the way we first came, but picking out a clearer path to a different end, rather than by repeatedly checking just the last set of false turnings at this end of a long and seductive wrong road.

Nevertheless, we might permit ourselves a brief diversion by way of Raimond Gaita's reflections upon mortality, which will, in due course, take us back to Blake's gentle vision with which I started this chapter. In chapter 3 of *Good and Evil*, Gaita emphasizes the place that ordinary expressions of horror, disgust, and appreciation have in conveying the depth and seriousness of genuine moral understanding.[14] He exposes the inadequacy of the suggestion (typically made on behalf of Kant) that we might re-express what is deep in our appreciation of other human beings in terms such as 'treating them as rational beings'.[15] To show what is missing in such a reduced moral vocabulary, Gaita reflects on a passage from Shakespeare's *Henry IV Part One*, which had previously been used as an example by Alan Donagan in *The Theory of Morality*.[16] The question here is whether Falstaff, in *Henry IV Part One*, displays respect for even the most worthless among his fellow men, according to the Kantian motif of unconditional respect for rational beings. Donagan identifies Falstaff as a Kantian; Gaita disputes Donagan's Kantian reading of the passage and suggests instead that Falstaff expresses pity and fellow feeling for the worthless rascals in his charge. Each

---

[13] The works of Cora Diamond and Raimond Gaita are probably the most well known and closest neighbours to my project in terms of their philosophical position (see e.g. Cora Diamond, 'Eating meat and eating people', *Philosophy*, 53 (1978): 465–79, repr. in *The Realistic Spirit, Representation and Mind* (Cambridge, Mass.: MIT Press, 1991), 319–334, and Gaita, *Philosopher's Dog*). Martha Nussbaum and Stephen Clark have (like me) used ancient material as a source of enlightenment (e.g. in Nussbaum, *Upheavals of Thought*, and Stephen R. L. Clark, *The Moral Status of Animals* (Oxford: Oxford University Press, 1977)); but I shall intermittently mark my general disagreement with their respective positions on a range of issues in what follows. In addition, Daniel A. Dombrowski has written both about Stephen Clark's contribution (*Not Even a Sparrow Falls: The Philosophy of Stephen R. L. Clark* (East Lansing, Mich.: Michigan State University Press, 2000)) and on the ancient material directly (*idem, Vegetarianism: The Philosophy Behind the Ethical Diet* (Wellingborough: Thorson's Publishers, 1985)).

[14] Gaita, *Good and Evil*, 24–42.

[15] The chapter also criticizes the inadequacy of the utilitarian project to reduce moral language to talk of utility and harm, but my focus here is on Gaita's discussion of Donagan's Kantian reading of Falstaff.

[16] Alan Donagan, *The Theory of Morality* (Chicago: University of Chicago Press, 1977), 240.

thinker sees in Falstaff an exemplar of the perfect moral attitude to one's fellow human beings. I shall dispute both readings, and instead suggest that Falstaff is as cynical as Prince Hal about the value of his recruits. Yet that cynicism is also a kind of realism about the worth of human life.

In the passage from Shakespeare, Falstaff, who has recruited a band of worthless rascals by conscription to fill the empty ranks in time for the forthcoming battle, declares to Prince Hal that the men are good enough for the purpose:

FALSTAFF. Tut tut; good enough to toss; food for powder, food for powder. They'll fill a pit as well as better. Tush man, mortal men, mortal men.[17]

Donagan cites Falstaff's speech with approval, because he observes that Sir John is defending the value of his assembled band of scarecrows and beggars against Prince Hal's verdict that they are worthless and good for nothing. Donagan wants to contrast Falstaff with Prince Hal, as regards their attitude to the recruits. The Prince (Donagan insists) 'is a man of self-esteem: securely convinced that his plan of life is worth carrying out and confident that he can carry it out; and he accurately registers that Falstaff's scarecrows have no plans and no confidence', and hence he has no esteem for them.[18] Donagan sees in Falstaff's response ('Tush man, mortal men, mortal men') a rather different attitude, which does not dismiss the men just because they have no life plan and no self-worth.

Perhaps Donagan is roughly right about the Prince, though we might want to put it more baldly. The Prince is interested in the recruits only as a means to an end. He accurately registers that Falstaff's scarecrows are untrained and incompetent as soldiers, and he considers them worthless for the immediate purpose. By contrast, Donagan would have us believe, Falstaff, though he likewise has no great esteem for his men, thinks that even his dishevelled rascals are at least that: mortal men. For that reason alone, he thinks, they merit respect in Falstaff's eyes: 'Yet, for all his misdeeds, Falstaff respects other human beings as he respects himself, irrespective of esteem. Respect in this sense has no degrees.'[19]

So, Donagan implies, whereas Prince Hal sees no good in men for whom he has no esteem, Falstaff, a good Kantian at heart, respects the men despite their inadequacies. Hence he ticks Hal off for failing to see that a human

---

[17] Shakespeare, *Henry IV Part One*, IV, ii. 71–3.   [18] Donagan, *Theory of Morality*, 240.
[19] Ibid.

being, a fellow mortal, must always be granted respect just for that. This Kantian message Donagan reads into that one phrase 'Tush man, mortal men, mortal men'.

In his discussion of the passage, Gaita disputes Donagan's Kantian interpretation of Falstaff, and replaces it with one of his own. On Gaita's reading, Falstaff's response is not a Kantian respect for rational beings, but an expression of pity and fellow feeling.[20] Gaita, like Donagan, holds Falstaff up as the model of a moral agent, a man who sees in even the scum of mankind an object of pity and fellow feeling. Once again, following Donagan, he locates this accent of pity in the characterization of the poor fellows as 'mortal men'. We can grasp how Gaita must have heard that phrase in his mind when he says, 'To speak this way of "mortals" is to speak in the accent of pity, and this accent is both expressive and constitutive of a sense of human fellowship.'[21]

To be sure, Gaita is again right (as was Donagan) to see that Sir John is momentarily defending the value of his recruits against Prince Hal's disgust. But the example was sadly ill-chosen in the first place, whether as an illustration of Kantian respect for rational beings or as an illustration of Gaita's ideal of pity and fellow feeling. Only a moment before, in his soliloquy before the entry of the Prince on the scene, Sir John had been expressing the very same estimate of the worth of these wretched men as the Prince is now uttering to his face. That is, of course, the passage to which Donagan alludes when he observes that Falstaff has no esteem for these men. So his cynical retort to the Prince now, when challenged about the poor quality of his recruits, is to observe that the men are only being recruited as cannon fodder ('good enough to toss; food for powder, food for powder'), and hence the worthless rascals that he has assembled are as good for that purpose as any finer soldiers. There is no question here of ultimate respect, or of pity: Sir John is assessing their instrumental worth, just as much as Prince Hal was. But, Sir John wrily observes, in the circumstances the requirements are minimal: the recruits need only be the kind of thing that can be thrown into a communal grave ('They'll fill a pit as well as better').

For this purpose, Falstaff grimly observes, the only relevant qualification is that one be mortal, fit to die. Hal's desire that the recruits should have been finer specimens is pointless. 'Tush man,' says Sir John, 'mortal men, mortal

---

[20] Gaita, *Good and Evil*, 27.   [21] Ibid.

men.' For him too they are just a means to an end, material to fill a pit. Their mortality is what makes them suitable for that purpose. So Falstaff's defence of the value of these rascals is not an expression of unconditional respect for the rational being as an end in itself, but an observation that any human being, however unprepossessing, can always be used as a mere means to something, if only because, being mortal, he can be killed for some end.

Both Donagan and Gaita move too quickly from their recognition that Falstaff is defending the value of his miserable recruits, on the grounds that they are at least mortal men, to supposing that his—Falstaff's—defence is an expression of *their own* personal commitment to the unconditional worth of a human being, no matter how disreputable. That is, Donagan reads there, in Falstaff's exchange, a recognition of those wretches as other rational beings who also die; Gaita reads there an expression of pity and an unconditional limit on our will, though he resists the idea that 'rational beings' adequately captures the kind of attitude that he has in mind. Both thinkers equally fail to enter into the spirit of a conversation that is entirely alien to the moral outlook of either thinker, in so far as it is a conversation premised upon the unscrupulous assumption (shared by both characters in the play) that the recruits are simply there for one quite unromantic purpose, to die in the Prince's campaign against the Percies and Owain Glyndwr. They are being assessed for their suitability much as cattle might be assessed for their fitness for breeding or slaughter.

It is ironic that it is precisely because Falstaff's men are mortal that they are not a limit on another's will in any sense at all. Hal and Falstaff are entirely free to send these hopeless mortals into battle, and to feel no remorse for that action at all. Human beings, like other animals, are vulnerable, and they can be abused without any sanctions.

Yet there is, nevertheless, something to be said about Falstaff's attitude, when we do succeed in entering into the spirit of his cynical response to the Prince. Perhaps, if we were to read Gaita in a more generous spirit, we might think that this was how he found an accent of pity there. For Falstaff might be said to be reflecting upon the horrors and pity of warfare—reflecting on them bitterly and cynically, but reflecting all the same—in the observation that the men he is recruiting are, after all, destined shortly to be tossed into the firing line and then into the grave, and that when matters stand thus, there is indeed no difference between a fine and brave, well-equipped and well-trained soldier, on the one hand, and, on the other, some wretched piece of humanity that had no hope besides the desire briefly to escape the gallows. I doubt that we should say that Falstaff pities his men. In fact, he surely despises them, and he intends to use them as 'food for powder' without regret. But he does see the truth about the pointlessness of such human lives, and he sees the futility of wars that waste lives, especially if they waste lives that had some promise (as these ones, thankfully, have not).

We might say that Falstaff's attitude is one of pragmatic expedience, and that he lacks any moral conscience regarding the wastage of these unprepossessing lives. That attitude, I would imagine, is not one that is likely to endear him to us. Engagingly, however, he does avoid exalting humanity into some special place of honour, as though just any human life were somehow precious and pitiful, just because it was human. His attitude to his recruits is that they are precisely worthless, but that since he has a worthless end in store for them, it is no pity whatever that they should be sent that route.

Why should we think that human life is of some supreme and over-whelming value? Is it because human achievements are (sometimes, or often, say) of great value? The Kantian, like Gaita too, must resist that claim, since it invites the utilitarian response that if the value of a human life is instrumental, measured by its chances of yielding great achievement, then a life that has no such promise of achieving anything great is of no value at all. So Gaita is surely right that the moral response cannot be respect for something splendid about human nature, but must be more in the form of a kind of pity, for humanity's smallness, its frailty, and its inadequacy for the tasks that it sets itself, and for the moral demands that are so far beyond its abilities. Had Falstaff been moved by moral scruples, he would perhaps have pitied those men—as one would also pity other small, unprotected creatures destined to be sent to their deaths for the sake of someone else's futile ambitions to power—and he would have sensed that their lives posed an unconditional limit on his will. But that is to see things in a moral light, and nothing can or could conceivably force Falstaff, or any other potential moral agent, to grant that things are so if they do not yet see that they are so. For the attitude that feels pity at sending such men to their deaths is just one view, perhaps one that is more noble and more selfless than the view that it matters not a bit, given how hopeless their lives are. But it does not emerge just from seeing what a human being is like. Nothing in life as such commands our pity, and human life is generally pitiful more for its vain pretensions and hopeless delusions of grandeur than for its spectacular pre-eminence at anything particular.

Blake's Fly

In *Songs of Experience*, William Blake famously reflected with pity on the death of a fly he had squashed without thinking. The poem has puzzled commentators because in the second half Blake compares his own life to that of a fly, and seems to find nothing to human life that is more significant than the behaviour of the fly.

> Little Fly,
> Thy summer's play
> My thoughtless hand
> Has brushed away.
>
> Am not I
> A fly like thee?
> Or art not thou
> A man like me?
>
> For I dance
> And drink and sing,
> Till some blind hand
> Shall brush my wing.
>
> If thought is life
> And strength and breath,
> And the want
> Of thought is death,
>
> Then am I
> A happy fly
> If I live
> Or if I die.[22]

Is it still Blake speaking in the last two stanzas? If so, he seems to see no tragedy in death, and concludes not only that he is himself no different from the fly, but equally that there is nothing to be regretted in his death any more than in that of the fly. Yet the meaning remains the same if we read the last two

---

[22] William Blake, 'The Fly', from *Songs of Experience*.

stanzas as voicing the fly's imagined response, not Blake's own assessment.[23] For now, too, the fly assures us that his own (and therefore Blake's death) is of no consequence. For the loss of life, 'when some blind hand/Shall brush my wing', merely terminates thought, and in the absence of thought there is no sorrow or regret. What more is there to life? What is there in death? Death just is the end of this round of trivial behaviour: we dance, we drink, we sing, until death deprives us of all that. And the hand that does so is, we understand, blind: it is not the will of God; it is not significant. Our death is just as trivial as Blake's thoughtless brushing away of the fly.

Either way, the poem achieves its effect by reducing the significance of human life and human death. Blake deflates our sense of the value of human activity by comparing it with the fly's pointless activity ('summer play'), and he deflates the significance of human death by comparing it to the thoughtless squashing of an insect. The poem is at the same time compassionate yet unsentimental about the fly; it does not try to pretend that its death is a tragedy that calls for much lament. Yet at the same time it debunks a range of human delusions, delusions about consciousness beyond death, and delusions about the care with which God chooses the moment to call us home. Suppose that when we die, there is just a cessation of thought? Suppose that the moment of death is purely contingent? Then there can be no more to mourn in human passing away than there is in the case of the fly.

Read like this, the song which seems to start with such a sense of contrition for the careless treatment of the little fly ends up with a more realistic appraisal of the situation. The fly is, after all, unaware of any harm, and is not unhappy in its death. But the finished version of the fourth stanza leaves us with a question about the significance of human life and death, for we are invited to ask whether the difference between life and death is just the difference between awareness and lack of awareness, and no more than that.[24] The reasoning is hypothetical: if that is all there is to it, then I shall be as unconcerned about my death as a fly is about its death. But is that all there is to it? The question seems to leave room for the possibility that we might have projects that are more significant than mere

---

[23] For this suggestion, see David Wagenknecht, *Blake's Night: William Blake and the Idea of Pastoral* (Cambridge, Mass.: Harvard University Press, 1973), 109.

[24] The first draft of the song (found in the Rosetti Ms) reads: 'Thought is life/And strength and breath ...' without the 'If'.

summer's play—indeed, perhaps that we *should* aim for something greater than the achievements of a fly. But that is to say not that human life is unconditionally something fine and deserving of respect, or that all casual loss of human life is a disaster, but rather that human life has as little worth as the life of a fly unless we make something of it, something that would, after all, make it regrettable to die before one's time. It is open to us to feel compassion, pity, and regret for the waste of a life that was destined to achieve nothing. But we cannot be obliged to rate it higher, just because it was a human life, than the same life wasted by a fly.

Of course, Blake is not suggesting that we should pluck the wings off flies, or that we should look on while wanton boys play cruel games, comforting ourselves with the thought that the flies lack any conception of their death, and have no self-esteem and no plans.[25] Least of all is he advocating that we should think that way about human beings who lack a life plan and any sense of self-esteem. Rather, he is recommending a realistic limit on the meaningfulness of mourning the unpremeditated death of a fly—a constraint beyond which we would stray into sentimentality. And he is recommending a realistic shattering of our delusions about the relative value of human life—a constraint beyond which we would stray into anthropocentric pride.[26] The poem leaves no justification for cruelty or callousness in either case. But it does recall us to reflect on what, if anything, could allow us to congratulate ourselves for the superiority of our lives, or to feel that our death is something more dramatic than that of the fly.

One candidate, of course, might be our capacity for some deeper kinds of selfless love, including compassion towards our fellow creatures.[27]

---

[25] Blake stresses the difference between wanton cruelty or mistreatment and justified humane employment of the lives and labour of the beasts, in *Auguries of Innocence*. Some of the relevant couplets are quoted above, but see also lines 33–4:

> The Wanton Boy that kills the Fly
> Shall feel the Spider's enmity.

[26] The popular term is 'speciesism', but since the associations of that term (and the analogies that go with it) are abhorrent to me, I shall repudiate it in favour of more traditional vocabulary that does the job better.

[27] Here I do not mean a mere genetic capacity, as though humans were naturally superior because they possess an innate capacity for learning to be kind, gentle, and affectionate. An unrealized capacity is nothing to be proud of. Indeed, an unrealized capacity for goodness is something to be ashamed of, if the opportunity to develop such sensitivities has been provided but rejected. So, as before, we should say that the locus of moral value is not in human nature, which has the capacity to be horrendously cruel, insensitive, and false, but in the moral attitude of one who makes the best of human nature—not by nature and not for show.

2

On Nature and Providence: Readings in Herodotus, Protagoras, and Democritus

On the day that Adam went out of the garden he offered frankincense, galbanum and spices, as a food offering of soothing odour; and so he did every day in the morning, at sunrise from the day he covered his shame. And on that day the mouths of all the wild animals and the cattle and the birds, and of everything that walks or moves, were shut, so that they could no longer speak (for up till then they had all spoken with one another in a common tongue). And he sent out of the garden of Eden all creatures that were in it; and they were scattered to the places naturally suited to them, according to their kinds and species. And Adam alone, as distinct from all the wild animals and the cattle, did he cause to cover his shame.

Jub. 3: 27–30

This extract from the Apocryphal book of *Jubilees*[1] is part of a longer passage reflecting on the consequences of the Fall, and of Adam's expulsion from the Garden of Eden. The author suggests that various divisions, in what was formerly a harmonious and undivided natural world, were initiated as a direct result of the Fall. These divisions affect five kinds of relationship. First, the relationship between humanity and God has changed: Adam now makes a daily food offering of spices to God which was apparently not required in former times.[2] The second consequence, not apparent in the

---

[1] *Jubilees or the Little Genesis: Ethiopic Version*, ed. R. H. Charles (Oxford: Oxford University Press, 1895); I am quoting from the English translation in *The Apocryphal Old Testament*, ed. H. D. F. Sparks (Oxford: Oxford University Press, 1984), 1–139. The original (now lost) was in Hebrew, and is usually dated to the second century BC.

[2] According to the account in *Jub.* 3: 15–16 describing Adam's activities while still in the Garden of Eden, none of the fruit is set aside for God, but all for the man and his wife.

passage quoted but evident in 3: 24, is a loss of equality in the roles of men and women. Woman becomes a child-bearer, dependent on and subject to the man;[3] she also receives a name, just as the beasts had been named by Adam before the Fall.[4] So Adam is now 'master' of the wife who was to have been his 'partner'.[5]

As a third consequence, the bonds between humankind and the product-ive earth are severed: the land he now tills does not co-operate with Adam's needs, but resists; the invention of the weed inaugurates mankind's hatred for the world in which he lives.[6] Fourthly, mankind is newly marked out from the beasts by the use of clothes and the sense of shame that goes with this,[7] and by the use of speech, which the other animals lose on leaving the garden.[8] The old communion enjoyed by all the inhabitants of Eden is disrupted once Adam can no longer communicate with the dumb animals, and they cease to know their names. Finally, as a fifth area of division, the beasts themselves are set apart from each other as they leave the Garden of Eden and take to their different natural habitats.[9]

A sixth source of disunity, though not an immediate consequence of the Fall, is a development in the subsequent period of increasing evil. Humans and animals gradually abandon their original vegetarian diet (universal both in Eden and for some time after the expulsion from Eden) and start to devour one another.[10] In this period creatures come to be seen as meat and non-meat, edible and inedible, nice and nasty.

The author of *Jubilees* distinguishes in this way between the original act of creation which built innocent variety into the created things that were to occupy the Garden of Eden, and the post-lapsarian outlook of fallen creation, which turned that variety into division. After the Fall the differences that had previously played no moral or ethical role assume a divisive significance. The harmony of Eden is ruptured, and the world becomes a place full of frontiers and boundaries.

Differences may exist without being observed; they may be observed without being divisive; and on this view, the use and abuse of natural differences to make a divided world is seen as the result of evil, a falling away from God's perfect world. The writer of *Jubilees* explores humanity's feelings and attitudes towards God and towards the rest of the created

---

[3] Cf. also Gen. 3: 16.   [4] *Jub.* 3: 33; cf. 3: 1–2.   [5] Cf. *Jub.* 3: 3–4 and 2: 14.
[6] *Jub.* 3: 25; cf. Gen. 3: 18.   [7] *Jub.* 3: 20–2, 26, 30–1.   [8] *Jub.* 3: 28.
[9] *Jub.* 3: 29.   [10] *Jub.* 5: 2; cf. Gen. 1: 29–30; 9: 2–3.

world, explaining why we attach significance to the natural distinctions that are picked out in this way.[11]

Thinking about the way in which *Jubilees* links our perception of divisions in the world to humanity's fall from grace can prompt us to observe that the way we divide the world up is not directly derived from natural variations there in our environment, but reflects our ethical take on that environment, or our culture's ethical take on it. It appears that we see divisions where we have been taught to make divisions. Where we have learnt to see similarities, we see similarities. Ethical reflection will then be less about discerning divisions that are there in reality, and more about which ones we are to put there—that is, which differences we should count as meaningful for determining what we should do, and which, if any, we should learn to erase.

Culture has to do with the drawing of lines—between us and them, between what can and can't be done, between which things can be eaten and which cannot, and how they are to be eaten. Not all the divisions that we recognize as significant are chosen as a result of self-conscious ethical reflection. Much is built into our cultural background: we grow up in a world which divides us from them, and we learn to distinguish clean from dirty, nice from nasty, friend from foe, tame from wild, and edible from inedible among the things around us. Only later do we come to ask ourselves whether those divisions are well made. But it would be a mistake to think that to have one's divisions well made is to have them in accordance with nature, as though nature without culture or without human judgement could inform us as to which differences count, and which do not, for human practices and just dealings with the rest of creation.

In this chapter we shall look briefly at some thinkers from the fifth century BC, in particular Democritus and Protagoras, who raise questions about the providence of nature and humanity's place in it. Is humanity as well or less well endowed than the other animals? What are the consequences of seeing things one way or the other, for our understanding of our moral place in nature? Long before the development of systematic biological taxonomy, which emerges only with Aristotle, these thinkers are dividing up the world, and using the perceived differences to construct an account of what

---

[11] It is worth noticing that the distinctions noted (God/man; man/beast; man/woman; weed/crop; beast/beast; hunter/prey) do not include divisions between human communities by race, colour, or breeding.

is justified and what is not justified in humanity's dealings with the beasts. These are not merely reports of how society does construe the divisions in nature; they are also used in constructive theories by which the thinkers aim to alter their readers' perception of what matters in moral terms. But let us begin with a glance at Herodotus, the famous fifth-century historian of the Persian wars, whose account of the even-handed nature of providence will set the scene for the more revisionary theories presented by Protagoras and Democritus.

Herodotus: On the Providence of Nature

In book 3 of his histories, Herodotus presents a long digression concerning the lifestyle and culture of a range of exotic peoples who provide resources to the Persian king though they are not themselves subject to Persian rule. Among the tribes found in India, for instance, there is a cannibal tribe which kills and eats anyone who falls sick, and another tribe that eats only a certain kind of grain and never kills animals.[12] There is also a tribe that hunts for gold with the aid of some particularly large ants who (so Herodotus says) throw up piles of sand containing gold dust.[13]

In the midst of this disquisition on Persia's sources of supplies, in chapter 106, Herodotus stops to reflect on the provident ways of Nature. His first observation concerns the fact that Nature provides such a spectacular array of superb creatures at these rather exotic ends of the earth. Secondly, he remarks on Nature's attention to ensuring both that no species ever dies out and also that no species becomes too numerous. These thoughts concerning Nature's careful attention to regulating the population are prompted by a traveller's tale concerning some 'Arabians' who allegedly encounter infestations of indigenous winged snakes in the trees from which they have to collect frankincense. They are obliged to smoke out the offending creatures in order to gather the frankincense. Herodotus suggests that if the population of these winged snakes were not kept in check, it would become impossible for the human race to survive. But Nature, in her providence, sees to it that the snakes do not multiply effectively, for

---

[12] Hdt. *Hist.*, 3: 99, 3: 100.

[13] Ibid. 3: 102–5. The report is noteworthy partly because Herodotus appears to be absurdly misinformed about the anatomy of the back legs of camels.

(so Herodotus tells us) the female bites off the head of the male as soon as he has once impregnated her, and the young gain passage from her body by gnawing through her belly. In this way, we understand, they render the female incapable of bearing further broods of young. This evidently ensures a relatively poor rate of reproduction, and this is supposed to reflect Nature's concern that the world should not be overrun by such creatures, since doubtless it would be not just frankincense that would be hard to find if it were.[14]

So, Herodotus informs us, Nature ensures that no species will die out, and to this end she adjusts the fertility of different species so as to ensure a suitable supply. Creatures that are of a timid nature and those that are vulnerably edible reproduce in greater numbers; those that are more fierce and predatory produce fewer offspring.[15] Herodotus does not imply that Nature's providence is directed particularly at the well-being of mankind. The benefit clearly extends to all species equally, whether they are eaten by humans or by other kinds, and whether they are beneficial to humankind or not. The hare, for instance, is remarkable in being more fertile than any other beast, according to Herodotus. This is evidenced by the fact that it alone can conceive again concurrently, while already pregnant from a prior mating.[16] Nature grants this privilege not because the hare is particularly valuable to mankind, or for any other purpose, but simply to ensure the survival of hares, because the hare is prey to a multitude of species of animal, birds and beasts as well as humankind.

Lions, on the other hand, Herodotus recalls, produce only one cub in the lifetime of each lioness, since at the time of giving birth the lioness sheds her womb as well, in tatters and useless from the damage done to it by the lion cub's claws. No doubt the similarity between this (fanciful) piece of pseudo-natural history and the alleged reproductive habits of the winged serpents of the Arabian gum trees has prompted Herodotus to engage in these reflections on Nature's providence.[17]

---

[14] *Histories* 3: 108.

[15] The same idea appears in the myth attributed to Protagoras in Plato's *Protagoras*, 321b 5–6 (see below p. 31). Cf. also Arist. *Part. an.* 696^{b}23–4.

[16] Aristotle too attributes this characteristic (superfetation) to the hare (though he does not think that the hare is alone in this), *Gen. an.* 774^{a}31.

[17] The myth about lionesses producing but one offspring in a lifetime is not repeated by Aristotle (who, by contrast, is struck by a decline in lioness fertility over a lifetime, resulting in reduced numbers of live births at each pregnancy). *Gen. an.* 750^{a}30–^{b}2; 760^{b}23–7.

The principle is clear. It is not that lions (or for that matter, the Arabian gum tree flies) are selected for extinction, or even for reduction in numbers, as we might have expected had providence been directed at the well-being of mankind in particular. Nature cares for lions as lions, even though they are a threat to people, and Nature cares for hares as hares, not just as food for lions or people.[18] Herodotus's account of providence in nature clearly thinks in terms of species, and sees nature's preservative role as operating at the species level, rather than at the individual level, but it is an impartial preservation that does not favour one species above another.

Protagoras: Plato's Myth

In Plato's *Protagoras* we encounter Socrates in dialogue with the fifth-century Sophist Protagoras, notorious for his relativism about truth. Plato puts Protagoras in the spotlight for that aspect of his thought in the *Theaetetus*, but in the *Protagoras* the focus is a little different. The issues are political and educational, rather than epistemological or metaphysical. In particular, Plato devises for his fictional character Protagoras a myth about the origins of human political communities—a myth that is probably modelled on work by the historical Protagoras.[19] In this myth, Plato's Protagoras tells of the origins of the human race along with the other animals, in order to explain the distribution of social skills and morality among the human race.

Protagoras first envisages a primeval time when all the animals were naked and defenceless, before they emerged from the earth where they were gestated. At this point the demigods Prometheus and Epimetheus are given the task of distributing the means of protection to enable the species to survive. Instead of sharing the task, however, Prometheus lets

---

[18] Herodotus's solution to the potential population explosion of lions is clearly rather too drastic, even to maintain a tough species at the top of the food chain. But the context makes it clear that he believes he is describing a procedure that ensures stable populations, not declining ones.

[19] Pl. *Prt.* 320c–322d. This is not first-hand evidence of the historical Protagoras's views, nor even purporting to quote or paraphrase a work by Protagoras. I think it probable that there is an authentic work of Protagoras known to Plato that has inspired the dramatic structure of the dialogue. For support for this view see Catherine Osborne, 'Socrates in the Platonic Dialogues', *Philosophical Investigations*, 29 (2006), 1–21, and the cautious optimism of Cynthia Farrar, *The Origins of Democratic Thinking* (Cambridge: Cambridge University Press, 1988), 80; but for a less optimistic view, Joseph P. Maguire, 'Protagoras…or Plato? II: The *Protagoras*', *Phronesis*, 22 (1977): 103–22; 111–20.

the foolish and acratic Epimetheus (meaning 'Afterthought') take charge of the distribution.

Like Herodotus (whom we considered above), Protagoras suggests that the non-human animals are equipped in such a way that no species is threatened with extinction. Epimetheus had a range of equipment to hand out, and different creatures received different means of survival: some got weapons and armour for aggression or self-defence, others got mobility for swift escape from predators, and there were various kinds of protective foot-coverings, insulation against the elements, and so on. Like Herodotus, Protagoras includes prolific reproduction for species vulnerable to predators.[20]

The story is partly, as in Herodotus, an aetiology for the provident arrangements in nature. But it goes on to explain that by the end of Epimetheus's profligate dispensation, when everything had been used up, humans had been forgotten altogether and were left still naked, homeless, cold, hungry, and without any resources against either the elements or the wild beasts.

Now Protagoras turns to the second phase of the story. Here Prometheus steps in to provide humans with a different kind of resource: namely, the use of fire and the arts, both stolen from the gods. This second, Promethean distribution serves to explain two observable facts (or to make those facts seem worth observing and morally significant). First, it draws attention to the radically different methods of survival typical of humans by contrast with the beasts. Humans survive by technical skills (including the use of fire) and tools, which substitute for other species' natural equipment. And second, it suggests a certain affinity between humans and the gods, since humans are the only species to develop religion and articulate speech.

This second phase in Protagoras's story contributes relatively little of relevance in Plato's *Protagoras*, where the myth serves as part of an attempt to explain the social and political virtues. That subject features in the third and last distribution described in the myth. So what is achieved by dividing the earlier part into two distinct phases, the first done, over-generously and impetuously, by Epimetheus, and the second, furtively, by Prometheus? By these two moves Protagoras effectively adjusts our perception of our place in nature, to offer a picture quite different from what we found in

[20] Pl. *Prt.* 321b.

Herodotus. Nature is no longer an omnicompetent mother figure who supplies every species with what it needs (as in Herodotus's version). Instead, humanity emerges as nature's forgotten child, bereft, unprotected, and left to beg for whatever charity it can get. Even the resources that we use for our daily survival are not our own, but were by rights the exclusive property of the gods, which we struggle to retain, outwitting the gods, as well as other species, by any means we can. Thus, Protagoras transforms our moral status in the natural world: our war on the rest of nature comes to seem like a justifiable struggle, undertaken in self-defence, against unfair odds. Now it seems that we can apply any techniques we can invent, whether fair or foul, to the task of securing our advantage at the expense of the other animals, since the poverty of our natural endowments leaves us so unfairly threatened. And if we must ignore or evade the gods, or try to get away with dishonest behaviour, this is justified because our very survival depends upon cunning, stealth, and craft.[21]

Finally, in the last phase of the myth that Plato puts into his mouth, Protagoras explains the origin of co-operative social skills, which enable human individuals to form a collective society. This final stage in the distribution is quite different again, although again it is a protective measure to save men from extinction. This time it is sanctioned by Zeus. Humans are endowed with moral sensitivities as a universal gift, distributed by Hermes on behalf of Zeus, so as to ensure that all humans have an innate aptitude for moral thinking, including (at a minimum) a sense of fairness and of shame.[22]

The communal life of the city-state is the final stage in the project to reduce the threat from wild beasts. The gift of morality, or political skill, is pictured as a survival tactic for a threatened species. Its god-given status leads us to believe that the gods really intend us to win, or at least to

---

[21] Evidently Aristotle saw the moral impact of this portrait of humans as ill equipped relative to the rest of nature. He protests against it at *Part. an.* 687ᵃ23–5, where he attributes it to 'those who say that humankind has not been set up well, but is the worst equipped of the animals (for they say man is unshod, naked, and has no armour for defence)'. Aristotle points out instead that the ability to remove one's shoes, employ different kinds of cladding, and change the weapons and tools that one holds are positive advantages, and that nature has so designed the hand to be perfect for the use of tools. It seems clear that he sees the Protagorean story as an ideological falsehood directly opposed to his own teleological view of nature's work. See below, Ch. 5 n. 42.

[22] The two capacities are called *dikē* (justice or law) and *aidōs* (shame or discretion). As I go on to argue, these moral sensibilities (which Protagoras suggests are crucial to social life) are fully compatible with a cultural relativism about what the given standards—to which one becomes sensitive—might be.

survive, in our war against the beasts, and hence adds to our sense that we are justified in pursuing that war.[23] Correspondingly, since the moral sense is just a tool in the fight against the beasts, there is no scope for extending moral consideration to the beasts or for seeing constraints of justice in respect to our capacity to inflict suffering or even extinction upon other species. No: humanity's moral sense is there for a purpose. It is provided simply in order to allow humans to win the war against the beasts more effectively.

In Protagoras's myth, moral thinking is a survival tactic—though it is significant that it is bestowed from without. Humans do not have the resources to realize what they need, we are to understand. Nor can they work out a solution for themselves. And even if the gods can see what morality is for, humans themselves do not perceive their moral scruples as being designed to achieve self-interested goals. In that respect Protagoras's motif differs from social contract-type accounts of how a moral community might grow *naturally* out of a Hobbesian state of nature.

Protagoras's myth is interesting for two reasons. First, it is interesting for its method. As we have noticed, it engineers an ideological shift in the listener's self-perception: it encourages us to see ourselves not as top species but as the weaker, disadvantaged group in a struggle for survival, and thereby it prompts us to adopt a more aggressive moral outlook. We come to think of ourselves as justified in pursuing tactics of stealth and aggression in self-defence against other kinds. This method of revising our preconceptions may belong to an authentic portrait of the way that the Sophist Protagoras manipulated his audience's values. It is significant that he uses a story to do the work.

Secondly, Protagoras's theoretical position is interesting because it appeals to the idea that a moral sense is a good thing—for utilitarian reasons—and fundamental to the human way of life, without committing Protagoras to any independent truth in the moral values that humans learn to feel sensitive about. One can be a Protagorean relativist about moral values, yet maintain that a sense of right and wrong is a useful means of achieving various results that could not otherwise be achieved. Although the agents operating in the social sphere may need to believe that their moral values

---

[23] There is no suggestion that we are given a single set of moral values with independent value or truth. Rather, we are given what we need in pragmatic terms, some way of agreeing about how to live together in peace.

are true, Protagoras the theorist, looking at the institution of morality from without, does not need to claim that the society's values are true, or that there is any such thing as truth in relation to values. For the system will work just as well without a notion of truth, so long as everyone is satisfied that they are all working to the same notion of fairness, and that others respect what they conceive to be their rights, whether the system is, in fact, fair or not.

For instance, Protagoras's story need not be in a position to show, say, that slavery is wrong. It need not be able to prove, or even to think, that it is actually better to have a morality that considers it unfair to enslave others. Of course, it would be essential that in a society that did use slaves, people should see the system as fair (for all human societies depend upon being able to draw distinctions between actions that are just or fair and actions that are unjust or unfair). But provided that a society is functioning well, and is content with the notion that some people (say, those on the losing side in war) deserve to be enslaved, the relativist will have an adequate account of what he means when he claims that all human societies depend upon their members having a basic sense of fair treatment. Members of a slave-owning society will hold that some do and some don't deserve to be free. And they will see it as wrong for those who should be slaves to be treated on a par with those who should not. Their sense of what is fair will be just the same as the sense of fairness invoked by a member of a society that disapproves of slavery, except that the considerations that enter into deciding whether someone is entitled to freedom will include different factors, factors such as their past history and the status of their parents—factors that the other, non-slave-owning society denies are relevant. Similarly, just as one society's sense of what is fair may see fairness where others see injustice, so too one society's sense of shame may see as shocking things that another society (or someone who believes in absolute values) might admire as noble and virtuous.[24]

Part of Protagoras's technique in adjusting our outlook on the world was, as we saw, to suggest that the human race is, by nature, weak and rather less well-endowed, by comparison with the other species.[25] Questions

---

[24] Compare here the dilemmas faced by Huckleberry Finn (Huck feels ashamed of his desire to save the runaway slave, because it goes against what he has been taught is just. He thinks of his natural instincts, to loyalty and friendship towards the black man, as a kind of weakness and failure to adhere to correct, upright moral principles).

[25] The basis of the story of Prometheus's theft of fire on behalf of mortal men appears in Hesiod (*Theog.* 561–9 and *Op.* 50–3), but Hesiod thinks of man's primitive life (before Prometheus's

about natural superiority and inferiority were evidently a topical issue for Protagoras and his contemporaries.[26] Anaxagoras too, like Protagoras, suggests that we gain advantages over the beasts by means of skills that are a uniquely human accomplishment, and a further comment on the same lines is found among the fragments of Democritus.[27] Like Protagoras and Anaxagoras, Democritus contrasts the relative strength of the beasts and the relative weakness of human resources. But instead of remarking on our use of intelligence and technical skills to survive, despite physical weakness, Democritus claims that we are not, after all, any better at the technical skills either. In fact, Democritus claims, humans are actually less able than the beasts in most skills:

Perhaps we are foolish to admire animals for their learning, but Democritus asserts that we are their pupils in all the most important things; the spider in weaving and mending, the swallow in building, the song birds, the swan and the nightingale in imitative song.

Protagoras had suggested that mankind is disadvantaged only physically, but has some distinctive advantages over the other animals in matters of skill—thanks to the interventions of, first, Prometheus and then, Zeus. Democritus denies that skills are exclusive to man. We are not even very good at them.[28]

   We do not know whether Democritus went on to explain how we are still successful in the survival lottery. Notice that his examples, so far as the quotation goes, are exclusively of practical skills. He does not mention the capacity for thinking, communication, or cunning. Nor is it clear whether Democritus's thoughts formed part of an ethical discussion, reflecting on rules of justice in relation to other kinds.[29] But what is clear is that all these fifth-century thinkers, Anaxagoras, Protagoras, and Democritus—whether

intervention and before the arrival of Pandora) as a golden age in which life was easy and humans lived in peace (Op. 90–105, 109–26); Protagoras, by contrast has reversed the motif to create an idea of progress from an age of strife towards one of greater ease.

   [26] These thoughts are not unique to Protagoras, but can be traced in other Presocratic thinkers of the same generation, including Anaxagoras, fr. 21b and a fragment of a lost play by Euripides, fr. 27 Nauck (see my fuller discussion in Osborne, 'Boundaries in nature').

   [27] Fr. 154, quoted by Plut. De soll. an. 20 974a.

   [28] On animal skills see Richard Sorabji, Animal Minds and Human Morals: The Origins of the Western Debate (London: Duckworth, 1993), 86–7.

   [29] But see further below (Ch. 8) for Democritus's reflections on the moral rules about treatment of animals.

independently or in reaction to each other—were using comparisons such as these, between ourselves and the other beasts, as a tool to think with. They used these stories and pictures about where we fall short, and where we excel, in the natural kingdom as a way of marking out 'us' from 'them'. In this way they focused attention on certain features which they saw as important for the human lifestyle and survival. And in doing so, they persuade their readers to place themselves morally *vis-à-vis* the beasts, either as weaker or stronger, advantaged or disadvantaged.

But what is also clear is that when one engages in argument along these lines, to prove either that humans are better than the beasts or that they are not, one is always picking out and focusing on those features that answer to the point one wants to make: we come to see ourselves either as inferior or as superior, depending on what aspects of our lives we think are most significant. But the two are not really distinct: which aspects of our lives we come to think are most significant will depend on whether we see ourselves as the superior species or the inferior species, and whether we classify ourselves as essentially similar to the other inhabitants of this world, or essentially different from them.

We can come to see ourselves as just one kind among equals. Or we can come to see ourselves as something marked out as favoured. Which way it looks to us will depend on whether we are treating characteristics that we share with others as definitive or putting the emphasis on the characteristics that we don't share. But it is not a clear-cut question which characteristics we should be said to share. For any characteristic, we might decide that we do share it, or that we don't share it, depending on how finely we divide the mesh in the imaginary table of what characteristics there are to be distributed: for it is not clear whether we should say (with Democritus[30]) that spiders have the same skill as us (weaving), only they do it better. Someone else—say, Protagoras—might urge that if the spider appears to weave, it is surely not weaving as we know it.[31]

---

[30] Fr. 154.

[31] Perhaps this sounds too sweeping. Surely there must be some characteristics which we clearly don't share with some other species, provided we compare ourselves with a species so dissimilar that its lifestyle seems incomparable. Do fish breathe? Does the amoeba see? I think (perhaps controversially) that as soon as we ask these strange questions, we are forced to start apologizing for the anthropomorphic biological categories in terms of which the question is asked. But in any case, these distant cases will not be the ones that matter when it comes to assessing whether there is a continuity between ourselves and the more complex mammals whose lifestyle looks (from a certain perspective) plausibly comparable.

Such disputes can hardly be resolved by checking the facts; for neither thinker disputes the existence or details of the activities that we identify as weaving among humans, or the activity of web building among spiders. The question is, then, whether the web-building activity is the same skill as the weaving activity, so that the skill is indeed one that is common to man and beast, or whether the weaving skill is a distinctive kind of craft, subtly different from the web-spinning skill of spiders, and—like all crafts—one that is exclusive to humans. This question, to which we come by pursuing Democritus's thought (that we are in many cases inferior to the beasts in performing the very same craft-like skills), is no different from questions that arise in current debates about the mental capacities and linguistic abilities of animals. For instance, when we ask about language, we have to decide whether the parrot's ability to utter articulated speech counts as the ability to talk: do we share the capacity for speech with parrots, or not? The answer will be 'Yes' if by speech we mean producing articulate utterances, of correct grammatical form, that convey meaning to the listener. In this sense my computer also has a capacity for speaking, which I keep turned off. The answer will be 'No' if we think there is something more, like intentional content, in proper human speech. But then we have begged the question by first cutting the capacity for articulated speech into an exclusively human variety and one that is shared with non-human imitative utterances. And if we move on from the parrot's speech, which most will grant lacks some crucial aspect of human language use,[32] we can ask the same question about the sign language that is drilled into chimpanzees. Is that the same kind of language as human language? It has some features in common and some that are not common (even to the sign language of the deaf among humankind).[33]

So are there two kinds of ability to talk, or three, or four? Which sort must one have to count as distinctively human? It seems that we can

---

Do cats think? Do chimps tell jokes? Do dogs feel shame? Does the foetus appreciate music? These are not so easily resolved without controversy.

[32] What is the crucial missing ingredient? The question is actually not easily resolved, for there are some characteristically human uses of language (playground games, nursery rhymes, and certain kinds of repetitive routines in prayer, comedy, or other playful role-play contexts) that involve parrot-like mimicking of otherwise meaningless utterances. Could we envisage a tribe of human beings whose communicative routines consisted solely of playground game chants with no external referent or truth value?

[33] On these issues see the fuller discussion below, Ch. 4, and also Sorabji, *Animal Minds*, 80–6.

subdivide apparently similar practices and skills so as to generate whatever premisses are needed to support the desired conclusion. Do we thereby succeed in proving that the human race does, or does not, share the crucial abilities with the neighbouring species? Or do we just arrive at the result that we started from?

Conclusion

Protagoras's story about the origins of human society is a rich and fruitful source of reflection for our purposes. When we compare it with Herodotus's reflections on Nature, we see how thinkers can appeal to what might appear, at first sight, to be value-free observations about the varied distribution of resources in nature, and yet draw from them two quite different moral lessons.

By reading the natural world through Herodotus's optimistic description, we come to see Nature as provident, equipping us all alike with survival factors. That way we see our place among the beasts as that of one species among equals, all of them well endowed, all of them equally important and valuable in the larger picture. That larger picture is of a world of unrivalled beauty, artistry, and balance.

Alternatively, one can read the variety of nature through Protagoras's more pessimistic myth and see there an unfair world, one in which we struggle to keep alive. There nature emerges as a botched job, governed by absent-mindedness rather than design. Whereas in Herodotus's story we admire and wonder at Nature's forethought and inventiveness, reading Protagoras's description we become bitter and angry at our poorly thought-out provisions. We see ourselves as deprived. We become determined to fight, in order to keep our end up, and we reckon ourselves fully justified in all kinds of aggressive behaviour towards other species, because they are either rivals in our patch or potential predators.

In Protagoras's myth morality becomes a necessity, not a virtue. It is given instrumental value, and is distributed by the gods not for its own sake but for its benefit to our chances of survival. Once we have read Protagoras's myth, we cease to admire noble deeds as a manifestation of the human capacity to do splendid things and to undertake altruistic and self-sacrificial challenges for their intrinsic beauty and value. Moral behaviour takes on a new significance: we see its contribution to peaceful living as its justification, and we start to see moral behaviour as just another manifestation of an essentially self-interested strategy for avoiding untimely death—a Darwinian tactic for the preservation of the genes. Although morality appears in Protagoras's story as a gift from the gods, the gods do not choose to promote it for the greater good of the wider world. Their concern is only with preserving humankind, not for bettering the world as a whole. The beauty of creation is not their concern: only human well-being. So human virtue no longer comes to seem for us to be the crowning glory in a wondrous and ravishingly beautiful natural order. It becomes instead just a means of grasping a petty advantage over rival species in a universal but disorderly struggle for domination.

Thus we can get two different moral messages from observation of the same facts. And Protagoras shows us, too, that by telling such stories we can manipulate the beliefs of others and bring them round to a new way of seeing the natural world and their responsibilities in it. Yet, although Protagoras himself, the historical Protagoras or the Protagoras of Plato's dialogue, may have invited us to choose a relativist vision of the world, I want to suggest that this is not the end of the story. Protagoras himself might want us to believe that his way of seeing the world is just as valid as any other. And he might go on to suggest that the only measure of whether one's moral outlook is right is whether it delivers survival advantages for our species (or for our friends, or for ourselves).

But we need not accept the relativism, or indeed the instrumentalism, just because we accept the observation that one's world is structured by one's cultural or philosophical outlook. We may grant that moral outlooks can be changed, and that the stories we tell can make us see the divisions in nature in different ways; it may be true that Protagoras's myth can persuade us that we should view our fellow creatures as rivals and threats, not as equals and friends. But it need not follow that there is no independent value against which one vision of the world counts as better or worse than another.

But equally, if we say that one way of dividing the world is better, this does not mean that it is closer to the way nature is really divided, or that we have to locate divisions that are real and not perceived. The value of one way of drawing the divisions relative to another need not be its truth or its correspondence to the way things really are, in some independent value-free structure of things. Protagoras might be right that the correct way of dividing nature into 'us' and 'them' is not written into nature's structure, and that the moral rules for what we can and cannot do are not to be discovered by closer observation of the distinctive structures and capacities of the brains or spinal cords of this species or that. That is, one outlook is not more true to a physical reality out there in nature, for the morally significant divisions are fixed by our outlook, not by 'the way the world is' independently of us.

Yet it might still be true that one outlook is, in a real sense, better—morally better—than another outlook. The value of the morally better vision of the world cannot be cashed out either in terms of its better fit with how things are in fact—for several different kinds of vision can make perfectly good sense of how things are in fact—or in terms of its utilitarian benefits for the survival of the species—for it is possible that the superior outlook would be one that did not yield survival advantages but jeopardized our species in the interests of some other, more noble goal. If we are to explain what the value of such an outlook must be, on the realist project I am recommending, it would be cashed out in terms of its *beauty*, its nobility, or its intrinsic loveliness. I do want to call such a superior vision a truer vision of the world, but it is a notion of *moral truth* which captures not a correspondence with some physical facts about the things in the world that are available independently of the moral outlook. It refers, rather, to the precise alignment of one's own vision to the perfect ideal, the genuine morally perceptive take on what is around us.

The world looks different when viewed from such a true moral perspective. It looks more beautiful and more lovely. It inspires devotion, not appetite; it demands giving, not taking; nurture, not destruction. What we learn from Protagoras is that if we believe in such a world, we should not try to say that it is 'true' on the specious grounds that such a view of the world captures the physical reality how it really is, free from all value judgements. Rather, we must say that it is how it really should be seen, with the appropriate value judgements in place: it is how it should be seen at its best, because that outlook is true to, or approximates to, a moral ideal—that is, not to a set of empirical facts about what is out there in the natural world, but to a set of moral facts that are perceived by a well-trained moral sense.[34]

But how do we distinguish the better from the worse vision? How can we match our vision of the world to the ideal and come to think rightly about the moral significance of natural differences? In the next part of the book we shall look at thinkers who encourage us to see continuities between ourselves and other kinds.

---

[34] I have favoured speaking as though the true moral vision did not correspond to the way things are independently of us, because I mean to say that it is not a matter of correspondence with empirical facts of biology. But it is equally correct to say that the perfect moral vision does correspond to something out there in the world, if by 'what is there in *the world*' we mean what exists in some morally structured ideal reality of the sort that Plato described when he talked of what is really good. Then to have one's view of the world approximate to reality is to have it come close to a vision of moral truth, and to have that vision inform one's evaluative attitude to things around one. This reality is indeed independent of us, and is in that sense an external set of facts 'in the world'. The structure of the metaphysics is realist in so far as the moral facts are not subjective, but independently true.

PART II
Perceiving Continuities

3

On the Transmigration of Souls: Reincarnation Into Animal Bodies in Pythagoras, Empedocles, and Plato

We saw in the last chapter that we can come to see ourselves as advantaged or disadvantaged, privileged or deprived. Which way we view our place in nature will depend on our attitude, and on how we have learnt to classify, identify, and evaluate the resemblances. The structure of our world *reflects* our value judgements, rather than *dictating* what value judgements we are to make. We can come to see our fellow creatures as like us, as 'fellow creatures', by dwelling more emphatically on the aspects of their lives and capacities that resemble our own, and by affirming how little their deficiencies or differences count among the things that we take to matter for morality. Alternatively, one might come to think that the differences matter a great deal, and that the resemblances count for little.

That question, how much the differences are to count for morality, might look as if it is a different question from the question whether there are such differences, and that it could be answered later.[1] Perhaps we could start by asking what differences there are. How do the species differ? This looks like an uncomplicated task for biological science.

However, nothing is so simple. Even our answers to the simple question whether there are differences between these or those natural kinds, and

---

[1] As I suggested in the last chapter, different individuals may find that different things count as important, so that they will disagree on how much a certain difference should count. The disagreement may not be settled by any argument that appeals to factors both would recognize. But yet one may be a morally better evaluation, and it is that which provides the standard for how much a certain factor should count. This is where the realism outlined at the end of the last chapter comes in.

what they are, turns out to be coloured by our moral outlook. Indeed, arguably it is not just coloured by it; for the question seems to make no sense in the abstract. What differences would we be looking for? Which ones would count as differences? For what purpose must they be different? What is the difference between an elephant and a pillar box? What is the difference between an elephant and a bumble bee?[2]

So it seems that evaluative judgements are integral to our grasp of what is around us. First, we see resemblances or differences depending on what factors we take to be important for a particular question (and different questions may yield different answers as to whether we are or are not relevantly similar in some respect). And second, when we are asked to see resemblances, we may or may not find that such things carry any significance for us. Why should we be moved by finding that sharks probably do (or probably don't) have a take on the world that is recognizably like our own? Does anything follow from that? We cannot read off from the existence of some resemblance any truth about whether that resemblance should count for us.[3] And if we see it as something that is to count, that is because we have already taken a certain attitude towards the moral issue. It is only when we have already granted that the ability to feel pain counts as significant that we shall accept that it counts as significant in the treatment of sharks—or (alternatively) we might come to think that the ability to feel pain is significant because we have first come to believe that the treatment of sharks is important. Perhaps even the value we place on rational consistency, which we may find hard to question, is itself a prejudice that is founded in a system of values of our own.[4]

---

[2] On the implicit essentialism of most forms of classification in biology and elsewhere, see the various papers by John Dupré in *Humans and Other Animals* (Oxford: Clarendon Press, 2002), and particularly *idem*, 'Is "natural kind" a natural kind term?', *Monist*, 85 (2002): 29–49, repr. in *Humans and Other Animals*, 103–23.

[3] In effect Richard Sorabji's avowed conclusion in Sorabji, *Animal Minds*, 216–18, is that relevant similarities (or morally relevant differences) are what should count in working out our obligations to other kinds, and that where we treat human beings one way, if the animals are relevantly the same, we should treat them similarly. The more particularized demand for 'morally relevant' differences is appropriate, but already alerts us to the problem: which differences count as morally relevant differences?

[4] It has recently been observed that people with doctorates in philosophy are more likely to be vegetarians on ethical grounds than any other group, whether highly educated or less educated (Julian Baggini, 'Degrees of concern', *Philosophers' Magazine*, 23 (3rd Quarter 2003): 35–9, based on a survey of readers of *Philosophers' Magazine*). It would be unwise to infer, I think, that philosophy makes us more moral, or more sympathetic to irrational animals (graduates with philosophy Ph.D.s were less opposed than other people to medical research on small mammals, e.g.). More plausibly, philosophy makes one more obsessed with rationality, consistency, and the need to have grounds for unequal

In this chapter we shall consider a collection of thinkers from the sixth to fourth centuries BC who suggested that we have close psychological similarities with other animals: they claimed that the minds of the beasts into which we can be reincarnated after death are in fact the very same kind of minds as our own. Pythagoras and Empedocles also claimed that we needed to avoid killing and eating the animals into which human souls can be reincarnated. There is a coincidence between the claims about continuity of mental functions across species boundaries and the claims about heightened moral obligations towards members of other species. But which way round did the reasoning of these philosophers go? Did they first observe a similarity or identity in the mental functions of the beasts, and then conclude that we ought to respect them for that reason? Or did they first develop an unusual respect for the beasts and then devise a theoretical foundation that appealed to a notion of identical souls? I shall suggest that it was the latter. The claim that these beasts have human souls, and that they are related to us as close family members, is an *expression* of a distinctive outlook on the world, in which one can come to hold such creatures dear and find oneself as one of them (but temporarily in human form). The theory does not ground the moral advice; rather, the moral outlook generates the theoretical justification.

Reincarnation Theories

There is a thematic resemblance between the myths of reincarnation put forward by the Pythagoreans, including Empedocles, and Plato (in some of his dialogues). Souls of individuals circulate (or transmigrate) from body to body, and can reappear in the bodies of other creatures. Since the soul remains the same (the same individual) from one life to the next, this has the consequence that the soul of animal x (say, my current dog) is the same individual soul as the soul of human being y (say, my deceased grandfather, or William Shakespeare).[5] So long as there are no constraints on who can

---

treatment of different species. Yet consistency is clearly a complicated matter, and the relevance of any supposedly telling similarities must clearly be presupposed or demonstrated before one can deduce the rationality of vegetarianism.

[5] It seems to make sense to say that several different individuals (Socrates, Pythagoras, William Shakespeare) have the same soul, so the identity of the individual is not the same thing as the identity of the soul. See further below, n. 40.

become what, it seems that we can then generalize and say that all dog souls are potentially human souls, and so are all worm souls, all frog souls, and all wasp souls. It is not just the ugly toad that might be your handsome prince in disguise.

Now it does sometimes seem to us that the souls of dogs, wasps, and worms lack a few of the more refined capacities of our human friends. But this may turn out to be only apparent. That is, it may be either a result of *bodily* deficiencies, which contingently restrict the soul's ability to fulfil its potential—the toad's cold lips and croaky voice make it hard for him to express his devotion in quite the stylish way that the handsome prince once would have done—or it may be a temporary incapacity on the part of a soul suffering from moral corruption, in such a way as to inhibit its understanding. As a punishment for neglect of philosophy, the dullard may have been banished to the body of a centipede, whose whole effort is devoted to working out which leg to move first, leaving no time for pure contemplation of the number 10 in the abstract.

In this way a Pythagorean could consistently maintain that the soul is essentially the same soul, retaining all the fully developed human capacities, even though in its present condition, reincarnated as, say, a worm or a bird, it is unable to display the latent characteristics it possesses. And it follows that to claim that the similarity between species lies in the soul rather than the body allows for a far more radical identity between human and animal souls, a similarity that is not confined to minimal stimulus response or pain sensation of the sort often invoked in modern attempts to include the beasts in the same moral sphere as human beings. By contrast, the radical identity envisaged by a reincarnation theory such as this includes not only the minimal animal responses but also all the finer sides of human moral and intellectual understanding. It may be quite impossible to determine what latent capacities the centipede or worm might be temporarily unable to realize, but that is irrelevant; a Pythagorean might still want to claim that each one has all the potential of a human embryo, though none of the opportunities.

Pythagoras

Our earliest evidence for Pythagoras's teaching comes from a fragment of the sixth-century poet Xenophanes, and for present purposes I shall confine myself to a discussion of this passage.[6] The passage known as Xenophanes fragment 7 tells of a supposed occasion on which Pythagoras found someone beating a puppy, and told him to stop:

> Once he was present when a puppy was being beaten,
> they say, and he took pity and spoke this word:
> Stop! Do not strike it, for it is the soul of a man who is dear.
> I recognized it when I heard it screaming.[7]

It is wholly unclear from the context whether Xenophanes is poking fun at Pythagoras (for his sentimental attitude towards the beasts, perhaps, or his far-fetched ideas), or whether he is an admirer of Pythagoras. But either way we may find in this fragment one possible interpretation of the Pythagorean doctrine about animals. The doctrine of reincarnation, on this view, entails avoiding cruelty to animals, or at least cruelty to those animals who are one's own friends in disguise.

Why did Pythagoras think it wrong to beat the puppy? We are told three things. (1) He felt pity (ἐποικτῖραι); (2) he said it was the soul of a man he knew, or a friend (ἐπεὶ ἦ φίλου ἀνέρος ἐστίν ψυχή);[8] (3) he said he recognized it when he heard it screaming (τὴν ἔγνων φθεγξαμένης ἀΐων). It seems likely that the immediate reason for Pythagoras's objection to beating the puppy is the fact that he feels pity for it, and that the reason why he feels pity for it, while others might not, is explained by what he recognizes it as.

But what is it that he recognizes it as, and how does that explain his pity for it? Here the detailed interpretation of the fragment leaves us in some doubt. Pythagoras (according to the story) plainly claims that it is the soul of a man, indeed the soul of a 'dear man' (φίλος ἀνήρ). But it remains unclear whether just *any* man is a 'dear man' and hence pitiable if beaten, or whether it is only because it is a man known as a friend or relation to Pythagoras.[9] Does he mean 'Don't beat

---

[6] There is some other early evidence, including two mentions in Herodotus, but these add nothing of any philosophical interest on the subject.

[7] Diogenes Laertius quotes these lines in his life of Pythagoras, and it is on his authority that we understand the lines to be about Pythagoras. The identification is not controversial, and I shall assume that it is correct. Diog. Laert. *Lives of the Philosophers*, 8. 36.

[8] The man is said to be *philos*, which means at least that he was a member of the same social group, and that Pythagoras would have obligations to befriend him, and would expect reciprocal friendly behaviour on his part. It need not mean that there was any affectionate relationship.

[9] The term *philos* is often used, from Homer onwards, of close members of the family, and Pythagoras might have a theory to the effect that all human beings are kinsmen and hence belong among our 'dear

it because it is my friend', or does he mean 'Don't beat it because it is a man'?

Some solution to this ambiguity might be forthcoming from the claim that he recognizes the voice, were it not the case that this line carries the same ambiguity. It is unclear whether Pythagoras recognizes the voice as that of his friend, or whether he recognizes the voice as that of a man. Perhaps the story has more point if it is the former. If the point is that he recognizes his friend, this implies that he finds the creature pitiable in so far as it is his *friend*. Animals in distress become objects of moral concern in so far as they might be human *friends*. Morality with regard to humans and morality with regard to animals would doubtless be on the same footing, but in both cases one would cite the fact that it was a friend, not its species, to justify why it deserved to be well treated.

Thus it seems more plausible to suppose that Pythagoras means that he pities the puppy because it is a *friend*, rather than because it is a *man* and hence a friend.[10] Perhaps its status as a human soul is important if that is what allows it to qualify as friend or foe. Pythagoras was friends not with a puppy but with a man, and he is then friendly towards the puppy because it is the same person. However, its human status is not in itself enough to elicit a kindly response, for had his relations with the human individual been hostile, then Pythagoras's response to the puppy would surely have been different. Pythagoras does not seem to be saying that all animals need to be treated with kindness, even if it is true that they all have human souls and should be treated like human beings.

But is it actually possible to treat other animals just like human beings?[11] The distinction between friend and foe implicit in Pythagoras's response to the puppy seems to raise a problem. For we take it for granted, with normal

ones' for just that reason; but equally, *philos* can be used of all those to whom obligations of kindness apply because they are our neighbours and allies—as opposed to strangers (*xenoi*) or enemies (*echthroi*), to whom different kinds of obligation apply.

[10] The second alternative begins to look a little incoherent, in that the notion of a 'friend' starts to look vacuous. For suppose that Pythagoras pities the puppy out of fellow feeling for the whole of humanity (such that all human souls are 'dear'). Then all animals should be treated with kindness, just in virtue of their beloved human souls. And, surely, this should extend to all fellow human beings too. All men must be *philos* just because they are human, presumably, and Pythagoras would have to treat all alike as friends, not foes. If the puppy merits kindness merely in virtue of being human, then so must any human being. But then what is it to be *philos* if there are no individuals who can be enemies? And why pick out that puppy as opposed to any other?

[11] The question arises similarly, and no more acutely, in the treatment of non-sentient things, plants and inanimate parts of nature.

adult humans, that they are themselves moral agents, whose actions will be governed by a moral outlook sufficiently like our own for us to make sense of the distinction between friend and foe. Thus we may decide, for example, that certain sanctions are appropriate against individuals who fail to recognize the moral conventions. Or we might conclude that pressure should be put on children, in order to instil acceptable kinds of behaviour. These sanctions are justified because we presuppose that human beings grow up capable of understanding what it is to behave well, and we take it that they can choose to treat us well or badly, or to be friendly or unfriendly. If they do not choose to behave well, we may then consider ourselves morally justified in treating them harshly, or indeed may even find ourselves obliged to do so. We may find that we must go to war, or administer penal sentences, or withhold privileges that we should normally consider to be essential to a decent way of life.

But in the case of the beasts such sanctions will hardly make sense. We may feel that some antagonism against slugs or bacteria is justifiable on grounds of self-defence, but not as punishment to avenge these creatures' failure to respect our rights, or as training in the expectation that they will adopt better manners in the future. Hence it seems impossible to make sense of the notion of treating the beasts as friends or enemies, in exactly the way we treat our fellow humans as friends or enemies, unless we first presuppose that they too could display the appropriate kind of moral sense, the absence of which we find blameworthy in normal human beings.

Strikingly, however, Pythagoras himself can readily surmount this difficulty, because his theory suggests that the beast is indeed just the kind of thing that can be friend or foe. If each animal possesses a fully human soul, each can be treated as a moral agent like a normal human being. Still, we shall need some way of discovering whether the creature holds friendly or unfriendly feelings towards us. But it does, apparently, make sense to think that it might do so, in the same way as it makes sense to ask such questions about a person (if, for instance, it makes sense, to think, of a person, that one is not sure whether she is with you or against you).[12] Perhaps,

---

[12] It seems that this does make sense, and it is not hard to imagine a context in which just those doubts can enter a human relationship. There might seem to be a worry about whether the same doubt figures meaningfully where one has none of the normal kind of human communication, but this is surely importing exactly the species-bound assumptions that Pythagoras is removing. Why not? Just because we assume that there is no means of communicating friendly or hostile feelings between man

on Pythagoras's theory, we should not blame the animal for the *physical* limitations arising from the inadequate body that it occupies; since it cannot speak, for instance, it might be unreasonable to complain that it failed to say please or thank you politely. But behind the outward features Pythagoras locates a fully human soul that can be said to be morally virtuous or vicious. We cannot then infer from the disabilities of its physical make-up that it is morally or intellectually deficient.

If we reconstruct the Pythagorean story in this way, it focuses wholly on the individual soul and its personal moral character. It is not that some particular species of animal is said to be our friend or foe (as we sometimes say that the dog is man's best friend, or that the fox is sly and cunning). Pythagoras can simply ignore distinctions of species, since they make no difference to the identity of the individual soul. He asks us to invite the animals into the same moral sphere as the humans, and to judge our response according to whether the individual is personally hostile or friendly, whether it belongs or does not belong to our social group.

Empedocles

Empedocles lived and wrote in Sicily some eighty years later than Pythagoras. In his poetry we find a revival or survival of something very like Pythagoras's belief that reincarnation places human souls in other kinds of creature. Empedocles too imagines a dramatic situation in which one fails to recognize a friend or loved one in disguise, this time in a situation where the problem is not cruelty to animals but animal sacrifice. When you go to the altar to slaughter a fitting victim for the gods, into whom exactly are you about to plunge the knife? Might it be one of your own family?

Here are the relevant lines from fragment 137:

> Taking up his own dear son, though changed in form,
> the father, great fool, cuts his throat and offers a prayer. ...

and beast, and hence no means of withholding, concealing, or misunderstanding such information? But plainly communication of this kind is both normal and fallible. Often it is easy to tell whether the dog is friendly or hostile, but sometimes the effusiveness of the friendly barking is alarming. Generally a domestic animal can distinguish friends from strangers with remarkable acuteness—though there are cases where a dog who has suffered traumatic ill treatment may be unable to recognize good will, for instance.

And in the same way son taking up father, children their mother,
they bereave them of life and feast on their beloved flesh.[13]

But what exactly is Empedocles talking about? Animal sacrifice, obviously;
and the fact that animal sacrifice involves the slaughter of things that have
(according to Empedocles) a human soul, even though you might not think
so. But the references to members of one's own family make the passage
ambiguous.

Empedocles might mean that whenever you slay a beast for sacrifice, it
is inevitably a member of your own family in disguise. That is a possible
account if we suppose that all human souls are akin, perhaps due to their
common origin at the start of this present world order.[14] Alternatively, he
might mean that some (but not all) cases of sacrifice are going to turn out
to be murder of one's own kin, in the normal sense of kin (where that
picks out some people as kin, as opposed to others who are not). This is
the reading that I shall assume in what follows.[15]

What is evident on either interpretation is that the worshipper is unaware
of the identity of his victim. On the one hand, he may be unaware that
his victim is human. But that is not apparently the essential issue in this
text. More importantly, he is unaware of whether his victim is his own
child. The worshipper is a 'great fool' (μέγα νήπιος), one who commits
a horrendous deed in all innocence, as a result of ignorance of the true
significance of what he is doing. Indeed, the irony of the whole event is
that he *thinks* he is doing the right thing, when, if he only knew it under a
correct description, he would recognize that what he is doing is terrible.[16]

Why exactly is it terrible? Murdering one's own kin and eating the
members of one's own family are clearly supposed to be far worse than

---

[13] Empedocles, B 137, 1–2, 5–6.

[14] There is support for this idea in the notion that all *daimones* (souls) were united in the unity
of Love before a primeval outbreak of strife and consequent 'fall' into incarnation. See Empedocles,
B 115. Interpretation to this effect in Catherine Osborne, *Rethinking Early Greek Philosophy* (London:
Duckworth, 1987), 119–223.

[15] The difference is significant because, on the first reading, I am kin to every potential victim, and
therefore I have a direct moral obligation to treat it as kin; on the second view, I am kin only to some
potential victims, and I am obliged to treat all of them as if they were my kin due to my ignorance of
how to distinguish one group from another. See further below.

[16] On the parallels with tragedy, particularly the unwitting crimes against the family in the Oedipus
story, see Catherine Osborne, 'Sin and moral responsibility in Empedocles's cosmic cycle', in *The
Empedoclean κόσμος: Structure, Process and the Question of Cyclicity*, Apostolos L. Pierris ed. (Patras:
Institute for Philosophical Research Patras, 2005), 283–308.

murdering and eating just any human being. Empedocles' theory of reincarnation would entail that all or most living creatures are human souls, but these verses make out that the victim is more than just another member of your own kind. It is, or may be, *your own mother.* The offences against your own family are supposed to be peculiarly abhorrent. What matters here is your close relation to the victim, the idea that you and it are next of kin.

On the other hand, there are indirect consequences for how we have to respond to animals in general. If killing and eating your own relations is wrong, then killing and eating any animal will be risky, so we shall have to avoid all killing, but not because killing an animal is itself wrong *under that description.* The forbidden deed is killing and eating *your own relations,* not killing and eating *animals.* As it happens, we have to refrain from killing animals, because they are our parents or children, or because we do not *know* which of them are our parents or children. The veil of ignorance is crucial; it creates the moral problem: if the father could recognize his child, he would not be doing what he is now doing. Indeed, it seems that it is only because of our ignorance that we need to be told what we must not do. If we could *see* what we were doing, we should find it abhorrent: 'Will you not cease from the cacophony of slaughter? Do you not see that you are devouring one another in the heedlessness of your minds?'[17] Empedocles' task is precisely to raise the veil of ignorance and reveal the true horror of what we could not see.

So Empedocles' way of seeing things does forbid the slaughter of animals,[18] but not, apparently, on the grounds that they are human, or because they are like us in some way, but rather because we cannot tell whether they are members of our family. What holds me back from killing you or any other creature is not some fact of biology—the fact that you are of the same species, or that you possess the same characteristics or faculties. Rather, fear, distaste, and love hold me back: fear that you might be someone dear to me; or, in cases where I can see who my relations are, love holds me back—for if I see that you are someone dear to me, I shall have no desire to sacrifice you.

---

[17] Empedocles, B 136. Notice the appeal to the listener to change his or her moral perceptions ('Do you not see ... ?') and his or her choices ('Will you not cease ... ?').

[18] It rules out the slaughter of those animals, and perhaps plants, which might possess a human soul. That class might not include all living things. Empedocles seems to envisage transmigration into some, if not all, plants (B 117, 127). The prohibition on slaughter applies to the killing and eating of flesh (cf. B 139), but eating some plants, notably beans and bay, is also apparently forbidden (B 140, 141).

As a follower of Empedocles, then, one will continue to discriminate between loved ones and strangers in one's treatment of other people, and one will also add the beasts to the circle of loved ones. Where we cannot tell who is a loved one, we are compelled to behave in the same way to all, but not all for the same reasons. With one's own kinsfolk, the reason is that they are kin, and one finds it repellent to kill them. No further explanation is needed. With others the reason is that they are indistinguishable, and one cannot tell whether they too are one's kinsfolk. Gentleness towards others who are not one's kin is derivative, a kind of precaution against error. It does not depend upon supposing that all those whom one treats the same way merit equal moral consideration for their own sake.

As with Pythagoras, so for Empedocles too, it does not follow merely from reincarnation as such that all animals must be treated alike. Nor indeed does it appear that human beings themselves, *qua* human, are objects of concern to us, neither for that reason (that they are human) nor for any reason to do with their being biologically or psychologically like us. Instead, kinship grounds our concern over the treatment of other creatures. The abhorrence that we are to feel is not so much against *eating flesh* as against *sins towards our own kin*. The fact that any occasion of eating flesh might be an unwitting case of eating our own kin is sufficient to prevent us from eating flesh. But eating flesh does not appear to count as abhorrent in itself.

It is true that Empedocles evidently included at least once in his poem a couplet in which someone is lamenting some past errors regarding diet:

> Alas that the merciless day did not first destroy me
> Before I devised with my lips ghastly deeds in respect of food.[19]

It is plausible (as Porphyry implies when he quotes these lines) to think that the ghastly deeds have something to do with the eating of meat. Nevertheless, it might still be that the sin lay not in the meat eating as such, but in something peculiarly foul about it. Empedocles chooses an emotive word for food ($\beta o\rho\acute{a}$) which is normally used of carnivorous beasts, often eating raw human flesh, and then also for acts of perverted human

---

[19] The text translated here is the one provided by Porphyry (*Abst.* 2. 31) and is known as B 139. An alternative version (reading 'claws' in place of 'lips') appears as lines d5–6 of the Strasbourg papyrus. If these are versions of the same pair of original lines, it is not clear which is the better text.

sarcophagy, including Thyestian banquets.[20] If the lines refer to normal human domestic fare, and not to another life in which we ate as beasts, then Empedocles is assimilating the apparently civilized human diet to a perverted or offensive devouring of forbidden things. Ghastly deeds are concealed in superficially decent eating habits. So it remains possible that animal sacrifice and the eating of flesh would, in itself, be unproblematic in Empedocles' eyes, if that were all that it were. But once we are aware of who we are, we find that what we are actually doing when we eat meat is devouring flesh torn from the bodies of our own children. We find ourselves in a horrific Thyestian banquet. So perhaps it is that horror that we are to lament: namely, the day that we first partook of the flesh of one of our own kin.[21]

So for Empedocles, the desire to abstain from all kinds of meat seems to be motivated by a fear of offence against one's own kinsfolk. It is not a fear of offence against other living creatures; nor is it a prohibition on the taking of life. Such things would, apparently, be inoffensive were it possible to ensure that there was no kinship relation between the agent and the victim.

Plato: The *Timaeus*

Some seventy years later reincarnation returns again in several of the writings of Plato. In the dialogue called *Timaeus* Plato has the main speaker, a man called Timaeus, deliver an elaborate account of the creation of the world, together with an explanation of why it is made as it is. According to this account, the world is made by a divine craftsman, the Demiurge, who makes everything to be the best possible. One of the things that he has to create is souls: souls for ordinary creatures and a soul for the world itself (which is also alive and has its own soul, the world soul, which accounts for its movements and functions).

---

[20] See e.g. Aesch. *Ag.* 1220 and 1597 (of Thyestes' meal) and Soph. *Ant.* 1017 of the consumption of human flesh by carnivorous beasts. The alternative reading 'claws' in the papyrus text of these lines suggests that the occasion lamented might be in a previous incarnation as an omophagous beast.

[21] Perhaps it is safer to eat other humans, then, if we can more readily identify and avoid killing our kin when they are in human form? This too, however, is risky; for some humans may be our kinsfolk reincarnated, and those would not be immediately recognizable any more than one reincarnated in an animal body.

First the Demiurge makes the world soul to an elaborate formula. Later he makes the individual souls for the creatures that live in the world, which are constructed to exactly the same formula, so that they have the same structure as the soul of the world. Part of the individual soul is made by the divine craftsman himself, and that part is of exactly the same sort as the world soul.[22] But after the Demiurge himself has finished work on these immortal bits of the soul, he then oversees the work of some lesser gods, whose task it is to prepare a further part of the soul, a mortal part, to be joined to the immortal part that was made by the Demiurge. The new, mortal part which is not present in the world soul, is responsible for emotions and desires.

Having both the mortal part of the soul, made by the lesser gods, and the immortal part made by the Demiurge, the souls of ordinary living creatures now have the full range of psychological capacities typical of normal mortal creatures. The same lower gods also make bodies for the mortal creatures.[23] So ordinary animals differ from divine beings in having the mortal parts as well as the immortal parts of the soul, but within the range of mortal animals nothing marks out one kind from another. All animals have the same kind of soul with the same set of capacities.

At 39e Timaeus announces that there are to be four kinds of living things in the world: gods, beasts that fly, beasts that live in water, and those that go on dry land. He classifies the animals according to their habitat, not according to their possession of different faculties of soul, and there is no special class for human beings. Humankind must belong in the general class of animals that have feet and live on land.[24] This is consistent with the pattern throughout Timaeus's discourse, which makes no significant distinction between the human and the animal soul.[25] For the sake of completeness, Timaeus urges that every region should have its complement of living creatures. Earth, land, sea, and sky should all be populated. And mankind is just one of the things that is assigned to the land. Without the full range, the world would not be complete, he says; but man is not any more crucial to the design than any of the rest, it seems.

---

[22] Pl. *Tim.* 41de.   [23] Ibid. 69c.   [24] Ibid. 40a.

[25] By this I mean that the soul is basically of the same type, with the only difference being that the destiny (whether it becomes a male human being or one of the lesser kinds of creature) is determined by how good it is of its kind, and particularly how rational or intellectual it is. The degrees of rationality are not (as I understand it) *given* differences of natural kind, but rather the result of malfunctions or voluntary preferences on the part of the individuals. See further below, n. 28.

On the other hand, Timaeus does not mean to say that we humans *are* animals. On the contrary, all animals are human. The only soul that the Demiurge and his lesser gods create is the human soul; every soul at its first incarnation is born as a male human being.[26] The capacities that this soul possesses, both intellectual and appetitive, are designed to provide for the requirements of a satisfactory human life.[27] These capacities do not seem to be *lost* so much as ignored, distracted, and under-nourished, in the subsequent incarnations as they fall down the *scala naturae*.[28] This implies that in a certain sense the aims and goals of humans and animals will turn out to be identical, if the goal is a satisfactory life, and a satisfactory life is one that allows us to achieve our full potential and exercise our best faculties. We all have all the faculties, so for all of us the best life would be one in which the intellect could play its full role, as well as the senses, emotions, and appetites. Whether we are humans, sparrows, or slugs, it seems that we would be fulfilling our potential and living a perfect life, in accordance with what is best in us, only if the divine and intellectual capacities of our soul were unhindered (or only minimally hindered) by the necessary appetites of our mortal nature. Since the nature of other kinds is the same as human nature, that nature will be fully realized only in the best of human lives, if that is a life in which the intellect has a chance to flourish.

There is, then, for Timaeus, no fundamental difference between men and women, or between men and animals. Women and animals are simply those of us who fail to live up to our full potential; we are nature's under-achievers, though the reason seems to be that we find ourselves in bodies that make it extremely hard to achieve better. Certainly we entered female or beastly bodies only after we had failed to achieve much the first

---

[26] Pl. *Tim.* 41e–42a.

[27] Ibid. 42ab, 69cd. The first of these passages seems to imply that the sensations and desires necessary to bodily life were provided in the original immortal soul; the second passage implies that a second mortal soul was provided to supply these appetites, and moreover that these appetites were on the whole disruptive and must be located well away from the intellectual faculties. This is just one of a number of puzzling ambivalences in the *Timaeus*.

[28] Timaeus is clear that disorders of the soul in humans are due to disorders of the body, and are not strictly damage to the soul (86b–87a). The subsequent incarnations as lower forms of animal are due to malfunctions of the soul in human life (90e, 91d–92c), which must, as shown, be due to the body, and the dysfunction of the soul in these animals is therefore presumably due to a similar malign bodily effect on the soul. Timaeus implies that one can go up or down the scale depending on one's exercise of the higher intellectual functions, so that these must be potentially present, but dysfunctional, at every level of animal life (92c).

time round (when we were men and had ample opportunities), but even the disorders in male souls seem to be the result of bodily corruptions.[29]

Plato's *Timaeus* is a cosmological text. It does not enter very far into any of the moral issues implied by its divisions of kinds and species. When Timaeus discusses the nutritional arrangements for the body, he envisages that the food required will be plant food.[30] In this context he allows that plants also count as living creatures, but of a different sort, in that they lack parts of the soul that other creatures possess; namely, those that are concerned with belief, reasoning, reflection, and self-awareness.[31] In fact, we now find that there are more kinds of soul than we had originally included: there are immortal souls, mortal ones which have both cognitive powers and appetites, and plant ones which have no intellectual ones but do have sensitivity to pleasure and pain, and appetites.[32] Timaeus does not say whether plants are provided for nourishment because animals must not be killed, but it seems likely that he would be committed to such a view.

Suppose we ask why the animals are not for eating. On Timaeus's story, the animals have the same souls as we do. In fact, they just are some of us. For whatever reason—or for no reason—we don't eat each other.[33] And perhaps, since we do not eat each other, we would not wish to eat other animals either if we came to perceive them as included in 'us'. It seems to me that Timaeus's story is inviting us to widen the class of 'us' so that the animals are included.

Family Resemblance

I have focused in this chapter on a number of thinkers who claim that human *souls* are interchangeable with animal souls in some way. Others might draw attention to the similarity between human *bodies* and those of animals.[34] Yet, given the striking differences between some animals' bodies, an argument to the effect that animal bodies are broadly similar would be

---

[29] Pl. *Tim.* 42b–d, 90e–92c.   [30] Ibid. 76e–77c.   [31] Ibid. 77ab.   [32] Ibid. 77b.

[33] On the irrelevance of looking for the reasons why we do not eat people, see Diamond, 'Eating meat and eating people'.

[34] Theophrastus offered an argument based on this factor. Theophrastus, F531 FHSG, quoted at Porph., *Abst.* 3. 25. The quotation may come from Theophrastus's lost work *On Animal Intelligence and Character* or from his *On Piety*. See Theophrastus, *Sources for his Life, Writings, Thought and Influence*, ed. William Fortenbaugh *et al.*(Leiden: Brill, 1993).

asking us to shift our estimate of which differences count as significant.[35]
With souls it is different. Some aspects of the soul may seem to be hidden,
or not deducible directly from the behaviour of the body. This leaves
space for supposing that creatures whose bodies are somewhat different
may have identical personalities and identical mental lives, lives which are
not adequately recognized and understood from the observer perspective.
In this space philosophers have the scope to revise our attitude to other
animals by suggesting that there are no differences at all, at the psychological
level—not just that there are no morally relevant ones. Indeed, it is ironic
that Descartes, whose radical separation of soul and body made it least of
all likely that one could infer the mental life of a creature from its physical
equipment, was so remarkably sure that animals had no mental life.[36]

Pythagoras, Empedocles, and Plato are among the philosophers who take
apart the body and the soul in this way. Their theories of transmigration
of souls allow them to claim that even when we share no obvious bodily
organs with another kind of animal, yet those creatures may still have a
soul just like our own. This is more than just the thought (familiar to
our ears)[37] that there is something special about things that are *alive*. The
equivalent of that thought, in the language of ancient thought, is to say
that there is something special about 'ensouled things' (*empsucha*)—that is,

---

[35] Not all investigations of bodily features function like this. Some contemporary studies on whether
certain animals have the capacity to feel pain appeal to bodily features such as the presence of a
backbone or a central nervous system comparable to our own; but in such cases these bodily parts are
merely serving as evidence in support of the claim that the individuals share some of our psychological
capacities, particularly the capacity for suffering. The psychological capacity is attributed to the animal
by inferences from the bodily organs. The argument for moral obligations rests on premises about
the mental life of the creature, not on the physical features from which that mental life was deduced.
On issues concerning pain, see esp. Bernard E. Rollin *Animal Rights and Human Morality* (Buffalo:
Prometheus Books, 1981), 31; Stephen R. L. Clark, 'The reality of shared emotion', in *Animals and
their Moral Standing* (London: Routledge, 1997), 121–38, 133; Richard W. Beardsmore, 'If a lion could
talk', in *Wittgenstein and the Philosophy of Culture*, K. S. Johannessen and T. Nordenstam ed. (Vienna:
Hölder-Pickler-Tempsky, 1996), 41–59; 53–8.

[36] On Descartes, see further below, Ch. 4.

[37] The stress on living things is particularly apparent in thinkers who emphasize the idea of 'interests'
or goals: e.g. Paul Taylor, *Respect for Nature: A Theory of Environmental Ethics* (Princeton: Princeton
University Press, 1986), for whom the important feature of a living thing is that it has a goal in life, and
hence we can say that something is good or bad for it. Compare also Rollin, *Animal Rights*, 40–1. It
remains unclear to me how it can follow, from the fact that an organism has a perceived purpose, that
it is morally right to promote that purpose (unless nature as a whole is a morally perfect agent, in which
case all of nature has a moral goal, and there is no reason to restrict our concern to the benefit of living
organisms). See Rollin, *Animal Rights*, 40, for the (opaque if not bizarre) idea that the spider's *telos* is its
own, 'imposed on it by nature' (by contrast with the car, which has its *telos* imposed on it by someone
else). The question as to how goals are purposive and whether natural ones are more purposive than
those of art seems to be even less clearly distinguished in these writers than in Aristotle.

creatures who have soul, *psuchē*.[38] By contrast, the stronger claim made by the Pythagoreans, Empedocles, and Plato is that the other animals possess not just *some* kind of soul, with a different range of mental and physical functions, but *exactly the same* kind of souls as we have. It is worth noting that reincarnation theories do not necessarily attribute a full mental life to the soul during its beastly incarnation. There may be some functions missing, so to speak. So the assertion that the soul is still a human soul (but disguised) is not based on observation of corresponding behaviour, or of corresponding cognitive capacities or the like. It is actually an assertion that has no empirical support whatever—unless we grant Pythagoras his myths of earlier lives that he remembers.[39]

There is a problem, however, with the notion of *exactly the same kind of soul*. Surely, if the soul were identical in all respects, that would amount to personal identity or cloning, so that the individuals would be not just two of the same kind, but the same person again.[40] If we take the members of a species as a paradigm of what it is to have the same kind of soul, we evidently tolerate a great variety of abilities and interests. Some people are musical, and others are not; some have better memories; some are more aggressive than others.

What level of similarity do we demand, then, if the soul is to be classified as of 'the same kind'? What is it to have a human mind, if not all human minds are the same? Perhaps we suppose that (in a normal healthy example) a certain range of distinctive capacities are evidently there, at least to some degree, if only as a potential that might be realized in favourable circumstances. However the argument now begins to look circular. Which faculties one takes as the definitive characteristics will depend on how wide

---

[38] This can include plants, which, according to Aristotle, have the basic kinds of soul (the nutritional and reproductive functions) but lack the more sophisticated functions of perception, locomotion, thought (see e.g. *De an.* 2. 3, 414²31, and further below, Ch. 5). It is unlikely that Aristotle is innovating wildly here: he alludes to his predecessors' similar views about plants as living things (*De an.* 410ᵇ22–4), and Plato ascribes an even fuller range of life functions, including sensation, to plants (*Tim.* 77a–c).   [39] Diog. Laert. 8. 4–5. See n. 40 below.

[40] If we were trying to secure personal identity over successive incarnations of the same individual soul, then we might be looking for exact replicas. But that does not seem to be what is intended in any of the reincarnation theories. It is not clear that all the same personal characteristics need to be retained in the return of the same *soul* into a fresh person. Pythagoras is said to remember his past lives as Aethalides, Euphorbus, Hermotimus, and Pyrrhus the Delian fisherman, but there is no suggestion that these individuals were clones or replicas of each other. He remembers being five different people (whatever that might mean). The story is from Diog. Laert. 8. 4–5. Cf. also Plotinus's discussion of the question of what makes a person an individual if it is not that they have a different soul, *Enn.* 4. 3. 5; 4. 4. 2.

the resulting class is to be. If the soul counts as the same simply in virtue of minimal sensation or ability to react to stimulus, virtually every living thing will be the same in the relevant respect; but if we include the more complex responses, the class will be more restricted. It evidently remains unclear what *ought* to count as 'the same'. So the apparently factual attempt to draw bounds round what qualifies as the same turns out to be implicitly evaluative. If the answer is supposed to solve a moral problem, it turns out that the moral question of what is to count as the same has to be solved first. We have to start with some moral assumptions about what capacities count as relevant for classification, and hence what counts as 'the same'.

Anyway, it is surely naïve to suppose that the species can be classified, independently of our judgement, in virtue of objective differences in their capacities. How we classify the animals and plants that are the subject of biology will depend upon the needs that the system of classification is required to serve. The same goes if the classification is supposed to have a bearing on morality. A biological taxonomy, designed to help the scientist to compare and contrast patterns of behaviour among the specimens under investigation, will not provide any account of how the world is to be divided up morally. There is no reason to suppose that the lines of division drawn up for a taxonomy of species include any differences that are morally relevant. We should need to embark on another comprehensive taxonomy if we thought that moral divisions could be made on the basis of differences in intellectual or psychological capacities.

On the other hand, perhaps we should not be looking for a taxonomy at all. The Pythagorean and Platonic texts that we have just examined seem to problematize the idea of a definitive taxonomy for dividing up members of the animal kingdom into classes, whether for the scientific classification of species or for moral purposes. Plato gives us a taxonomy according to the habitat that a creature occupies, and he builds a set of value judgements into that classification by suggesting that one gets closer to the earth the more disabled one's intellectual powers.[41] But this only draws attention to the fact that we have to start with the evaluative categories 'up' and 'down', or 'higher' and 'lower', and then read the animal species as imbued with value-laden divisions on that basis. For we do not know independently that

---

[41] Pl. *Tim.* 40a. Cf. also Pl. *Soph.* 220a.

centipedes are more lowly than birds.[42] Plato assigns the weaker intellects to the centipedes and worms because he despises the weaker intellects, and because he thinks that worms are low on the *scala naturae*. The two value judgements combine to build a value system into the Platonist's view of the natural, despite the rejection of any substantial difference between the souls of humans and other animals.

Pythagoras, Empedocles, and Plato set out to persuade us to see our fellow creatures as members of our own family, creatures with the same capacities and origins as ourselves, though perhaps sadly degraded and corrupted. But they were expressing the conclusion of their arguments, not the reasons for them. Their claims were based on a revised moral understanding of how the world is divided. It was from that basis that they deduced something fresh and challenging about the psychology of the beasts. They did not first discover something about the souls of the beasts and then work out what their moral outlook should be.

Learning to See our Neighbours

In this chapter we have glanced at a few examples from a recurrent tradition in Greek thought which claims that the souls of beasts and the souls of men are indistinguishable in kind. Such a claim seems to be systematically accompanied by an unconventional concern for members of other species, as we have seen. All these thinkers suggest that maltreatment, slaughter, or eating of the other creatures who have souls of the same kind will be constrained by moral scruples comparable to those that apply to our normal human relations.

To generate these attitudes to other kinds, evidently it would not be sufficient to show that a creature is something rather like us, a living thing with a soul, with motives and with purposes. That view, after all, was shared by other Greek thinkers, including Aristotle, for example. It is and has been widely endorsed by many people before and since, in this and other cultures. In itself it does not entail a revisionary moral stance. It is perfectly possible to hold that animals have intelligent and sensitive souls, and that

---

[42] Pl. *Tim.* 92a.

they struggle to achieve their goals as we do, but that we are still free to ride them, cage them, use them, eat them, or breed them, in ways that would horrify us if the creatures were human beings. Indeed, cultures that permit slavery assume the same about some human beings, without revising their estimate of the proper treatment for free-born human beings. So biological arguments about the psychological functions of a species seem to count for little.[43] And what is more, arguments based on the idea that a creature has goals and interests seem to apply equally to plants, in so far as those organisms too can be said to have unconscious goals and to suffer harm when maltreated or deprived of the things they need in order to flourish.

So biological classifications provide no uncontroversial tools to determine the moral divisions. Similarity (and indeed genetic or evolutionary kinship) seems to emerge everywhere we look, and we are hard pressed to offer excuses or explanations for our need to draw firm lines. We find ourselves tempted by the idea that something else must count, besides the possession of life, soul, and interests, if there is to be a radical change in our attitude, and if this is supposed to occur at the division between animals and plants or between animals and human beings.

But we should not succumb to that temptation. It arises because we wrongly suppose that biological similarities are what ground our moral rules. The Pythagorean tradition can help us to see that it is our moral outlook that grounds our perception of similarities, and hence our classification of what is dear to us and what is distant, what is similar and what is alien. To change whom we see as kin, we must first change our moral outlook. These thinkers give us a story to explain how souls can transmigrate and how we might all be kin, but the story is there to defend and promote a revisionary moral outlook. It cannot be discovered to be true independently of that moral outlook.

---

[43] Notice how Aristotle, who gives a psychological justification for the practice of slavery, generates his biological account (about the lack of some factor in the naturally slavish soul) from the moral perception of what one can do to the individual slave. See further below, appendix to Ch. 5.

4

On Language, Concepts, and Automata: Rational and Irrational Animals in Aristotle and Descartes

Besides the moralists' quest for morally significant differences between humans and other species, philosophers have always been intrigued by epistemological questions about what the human mind can achieve in respect of knowledge (and indeed related questions about whether our knowledge is lost at death or whether the mind possesses a kind of immortality). Is there, or is there not, some divine mind that needs no body? And if there is, do we have one? And, assuming that the beasts lack it, how does this make our lives more rich than theirs? In current debates the question often focuses on issues concerning the possession of language.[1] In this chapter we shall take a sideways glance at these contemporary debates by way of an exploration of Aristotle's attempts to explain the continuity between animal capacities and the, supposedly distinctive, human capacity to think in conceptual terms. I shall suggest that Aristotle's attempt to trace continuity, rather than radical discontinuity, across the human–animal spectrum is a fruitful project that belongs with a humane and perceptive attitude to the non-linguistic members of our own species and other creatures. For our own achievements are surely not so very special, just because they are expressed in language. And the thoughts and hopes of other creatures need not seem so worthless and unimpressive, just because we fail to understand.

---

[1] The controversy centres on the work of Donald Davidson (e.g. his 'Thought and talk', in *Mind and Language*, ed. S. Guttenplan (Oxford: Oxford University Press, 1975), 7–23, and 'Rational animals', *Dialectica*, 36 (1982): 318–27; repr. in *Actions and Events: Perspectives on the Philosophy of Donald Davidson*, ed. E. Lepore and B. P. McLaughlin (Oxford: Oxford University Press, 1985), 473–80).

Owners of Concepts and Users of Language

Whereas in the period after Aristotle, the Stoics marked a clear distinction between rational and irrational animals, Aristotle was actually rather less explicit about whether humans were distinctive for being rational.[2] The famous definition of man as 'rational mortal animal' is not actually Aristotle's: Aristotle often identifies humans as mortal animals (i.e. possessing a soul—animal—but, unlike the gods, subject to death),[3] but to distinguish them from the many other similarly mortal animals, he generally appeals to the fact that humans are bipeds.[4] The Stoics, like Plato and Aristotle before them, spoke of those who possess reason as 'having speech' (*logon echein*); the terms for speech and rational thought are indistinguishable in Greek. *Logos* is both word and reason; it is the spoken utterance, the written treatise, and the inner thought. The Stoics added extra technical terms to distinguish the inner speech of reason from the outer speech of spoken or written utterances.[5] Thus rational animals were those animals that possessed internal language, not just a capacity for parrot talk, and (for the Stoics) only humans made the grade, together with the gods (who, so people traditionally assumed, spoke the same language and thought the same thoughts as ourselves, only more so).

But is language just a communication tool, for conveying existing information, using linguistic symbols to stand for external things or internal concepts, so as to serve a function for which other systems of symbols might do just as well?[6] Or is language a capacity that changes the whole nature of

---

[2] For the Stoics, see e.g. Diog. Laert. 7.61; M. Aur. *Med.* 7. 23. Aristotle does think that animals lack *nous*, or intellect, but it is not clear that we should identify this with 'reason' or rationality. It appears, rather, to be a capacity for thinking of a particular kind of abstract object, although the treatment of the intellectual capacity of the soul in *De an.* 3. 4–7 is, for the most part, deeply obscure. On the distinction made at *An. post.* 2. 19, 100²1–2, between animals that do and those that don't acquire a *logos* on the basis of enduring percepts, see further below p. 94.

[3] See e.g. *An. pri.* 1. 31, 46ᵇ2–11.

[4] See e.g. *Arist. Cat.* 1ᵇ19, 3²23, 25, 7²29, 36, and *An. post.* 2. 5, 92²1, etc. This habit goes back to Plato's divisions in the *Politicus*. On the other hand a division of *rational animals* into (a) gods, (b) men, and (c) people like Pythagoras is attributed by Iamblichus to Aristotle's lost *Life of Pythagoras*, but it does not seem to be authentic (the use of the term *logikos* to mean 'rational' appears not to be an Aristotelian usage): Iambli. *VP* 30–1 Deubner; Arist. fr. 156 Gigon (192 Rose).

[5] *Logos endiathetos* (internal speech) and *logos prophorikos* (uttered speech): 'They say that humanity differs from the speechless (*or* irrational) animals not by uttered speech but by internal speech; for crows and parrots and jays utter articulate sounds.' Sext. Emp. *Math* 8. 275.

[6] For instance, map symbols, pictures, number codes, and coloured counters can be used to stand for things, and models can be moved about to represent distant events and processes, all without syntax and without spoken or written language. Do these constitute a kind of linguistic communication (if to

the experience, requiring the user to classify things as bearers of names, as tokens of a type, and as examples illustrative of concepts? If language makes a real difference to the structure of our experience, then the information that we communicate by means of language, if it is about experiences structured in this way, would be information that could not figure in the lives of animals that lack language.[7] We (and the gods, angels, etc.) would inhabit a world that was just not there in the minds of dumb creatures; we would be talking about things of which they had no conception; we would report facts that had no counterpart in their minds. The syntactic structure of human language, its capacity to multiply symbols and meanings without limit, and its integral relationship with the institutions of human social life might make one think that there is a radical difference between the world experienced by a language user and that of any other creature.[8]

Similar conclusions emerge from the more traditional Cartesian under-standing of human and animal behaviour, if one assumes that the function of linguistic utterances is to convey information, to report facts structured in propositional form. Suppose that language construes the world as a set of facts in the following way: first it classifies objects under general terms or concepts, carving up the world of experience and using nouns as labels to group objects under general kinds; then it applies predicates to subjects, by constructing sentences in the mind in which some noun term is matched with some predicate term; these sentences in the mind are then uttered, in spoken or written signs, as sentences that are the images of private mental propositions. The inner propositions, on such a

count as language it is sufficient to make use of symbols to stand for objects), or do they constitute a kind of non-linguistic symbolism, because they do not employ syntax? But they could have syntax: for one could use a designated coloured counter for a particular syntactic relation. And if that is so, where does the sign language taught to apes fall in the spectrum of linguistic functions? For the ape 'talk' typically employs temporal juxtaposition of signs—largely concrete nouns and simple action verbs understood as imperatives—requiring the interpreter to infer the syntax, in place of the complex syntactical structures and grammatical forms of natural languages (see John Dupré, 'Conversations with apes: reflections on the scientific study of language' in *idem*, *Humans and Other Animals*, 241).

[7] I say 'animals that lack language' rather than 'non-human animals' deliberately, since besides the traditional caveat about angels and gods, we need to note that a language-trained ape would (presumably) fall into the language-using category. I think this observation derives from Dupré (*Humans and Other Animals*), but I have been unable to trace it there.

[8] 'Wenn eine Löwe sprechen könnte, wir könnten ihn nicht verstehen' ('If a lion could talk, we could not understand him'): Ludwig Wittgenstein, *Philosophische Untersuchungen*, trans. as *Philosophical Investigations*, by G. E. M. Anscombe (Oxford: Basil Blackwell, 1953), Part IIxi, p. 223; hereafter *PI*. For the significance of syntax, Noam Chomsky, *Language and Mind* (New York: Harcourt Brace and World, 1968).

theory, constitute the contents of the intelligent mind prior to linguistic utterances. The linguistic utterances then express them for public consumption. Someone who holds a view like that would, typically, deny that the animals have those inner mental sentences in which one attaches a predicate to a subject in thought, so that their failure to utter meaningful sentences aloud is due to an inner emptiness. Animals, it would be said, cannot produce these inner propositions, either because they don't have the words to label the concepts, or because they can't do syntax to put together complex structures in their minds. It follows that any articulate structures that emerged from their mouths would be mere parrot talk, or computer sounds. They would not be attached to any meanings in their consciousness. This seems to be what is meant when philosophers deny that animals are 'conscious'.[9]

So someone who pursued this kind of Cartesian line would conclude that if animals do not have subject–predicate structures in their thinking, then they are not intelligent, because intelligence is constituted by having beliefs—propositional beliefs—that intelligently (i.e. effectively) map on to how things really are and enable one to make correct judgements, and thereby achieve one's goals. And even those opposed to the Cartesian idea of an inner mental life will make similar moves, for the beloved Private Language Argument is supposed to show that language can only ever be an external, shared device, and one cannot have private thoughts to which one attaches only inner signs.[10] If that is so, then one should not attribute inner hidden propositional thoughts to creatures that do not happen to utter propositional expressions. Animals cannot have an inner, private mental life, structured by an inner private language-like thought pattern; and hence it follows that (aside from occasional artificially humanized apes) the animals' lack of any public mental life, expressed in syntactically structured language, seems to tell against their having any mental life at all. Or so the story goes. Thus, by rejecting a Cartesian notion of the private inner mind, and replacing it with public language—which serves not as evidence for the inner mind but as the direct expression of the individual's mental life—even the nominally anti-Cartesian philosopher seems to end

---

[9] That is, the animals might produce behaviour or language that appeared to us to be associated with meaning something, but they produce it for some other reason (say an innate habit of meaningless imitation, or just to get a banana). So it doesn't mean anything to them; they are not conscious that it has the meaning that we attach to it.   [10] *PI*, §§243, 244, 246, 261, etc.

up once again with the empty-headed Cartesian beast: a mere machine with no ghost.

To my mind, all these thoughts, on both sides of the Cartesian divide, seem to miss the mark, despite their respectable philosophical pedigree.[11] It seems to me that we need to resist the initial thought (perhaps inherited from the Scholastics via Descartes) that language and thought are essentially a set of propositions, whether in the mind or uttered aloud. We have only to think about the typical functions of language in human communication to see that the supposedly standard propositional form is not essential or even characteristic of many normal everyday human utterances. Of course, many of our formal and academic utterances are indeed designed to convey information, and those expressions are conventionally hammered into Ciceronian style. We also use sentences of classic subject–predicate form when we are not writing a paper or speaking on the radio, but expressing our inner feelings and interests, our social involvement, and our concern for others. We say 'I have a headache', 'I'm worried about my son', 'I don't know what to do'. But although these take a propositional form in the expression, it is not clear that these exchanges of ordinary social intercourse necessarily need words at all, let alone sentences, in order to say what we mean. Except when the intention is to share thoughts of an intellectual or deliberative nature, most could be done equally well with wordless forms of communication (facial expressions, bodily contact, inarticulate sounds, glances, and wordless signs).

My expression of regret for knocking over your glass ('I'm so sorry!') is formed as a proposition, with a subject 'I' and a predicate 'sorry'. Perhaps it looks like a description of my mental state, but it doesn't follow that my regret is a proposition in my mind, and you would get me wrong if you thought that what entered my thoughts at that point was a proposition to utter, rather than a feeling for which the expression 'I'm so sorry!' was a rather inadequate, inhibited, and socially constrained kind of substitute.[12] I didn't think 'I'm sorry' and then say it: I felt regret and then uttered a

---

[11] For more fruitful analyses of Wittgenstein's remark about the lion, see John Dupré, 'The mental lives of non-human animals', in *Humans and Other Animals*, 217–35, 232–5, and Beardsmore 'If a lion could talk'.

[12] It may be helpful to contrast my account of the feelings and emotions such as regret with the one recently offered by Nussbaum (in *Upheavals of Thought*). Although, if pressed to assent to the description 'cognitivist', I might agree that I take these emotions to involve a cognitive judgement of value, I do not share Nussbaum's view that this must involve attributing judgements with quasi-propositional

standard formula that I have learned to use on such occasions, a formula designed to convey (not describe) my contrition.[13]

Are such expressions as these crucially different (or expressive of a different kind of mental life) from the corresponding expressions of a domestic animal that lacks speech? Does the cat mean anything when she sits by the door and mews? Perhaps she means much the same as the toddler who says, 'Mummy, can I go out in the garden to play?', or the visitor who says, 'One minute: must just visit the bathroom.' We have our way of communicating our needs and desires; the cat has her way of communicating the same needs and desires. Our social utterances are polite formulae, obligatory or conventional for language-trained members of society. But they simply substitute for age-old methods of indicating emotions, desires, and intentions—age-old methods at which the cat is still, and will always be, an expert.

It is said that family dogs sometimes offer comfort to their owners when they are upset. The dog's comforting attention does not so much communicate information as offer support, perhaps. But how does it differ from the comfort offered by the human wife or mother? She comforts you with a gentle embrace and 'There there, have a good cry. We know it's

---

complexity to animals (see her Part I, ch. 2), because I do not think that it involves attributing quasi-propositions to our own emotional judgements. There is no complexity, no subject–predicate structure, required for having an impression of something delightful, horrid, nice, or appalling. One can judge value without distinguishing objects from their properties, and without forming complex structures that require abstracting goodness from the things that possess it. I am aware that there will be many readers who assert without hesitation that I am confused on this point. I would ask them only to reflect on whether this is because they have a dogmatic conviction that all judgements that we (observers or introspectors) can correctly describe as judgements 'that x is F' must have an internal mental form: viz. the thought 'x is F'. On my account, where a avoids x because it is F, x need not be an intentional object in a's judgement, but only an extensional object which a avoids. The intentional object, of which a is cognitively aware and which stimulates the avoidance, is F alone, which coincides extensionally with x. There may also be cases where some x figures as an intentional object in the animal's mind: Richard Sorabji has reminded me that I must deal with cases where the animal mistakenly anticipates that I have something—its leash, say—in my pocket, and its excited behaviour is aroused by the thought of that object, not of some property F of that object. Here the object of anticipation might not in fact coincide extensionally with anything at all (I might have nothing in my pocket), or it might coincide with something else (it was only my scarf, not a leash). But my point stands: that the thought is not propositional or complex. It is a simple thought of an object, the leash, which can be described by uttering a proposition ('He thinks you have the leash'), but is not itself a proposition.

[13] There are, of course, occasions on which one thinks, 'at this point I would be expected to say sorry', and then one says the same formula as one uses when one is sorry, but one says it insincerely. It is precisely this social habit of using language to inhibit communication that leads to the problem of other minds, and to the assumption that one cannot see the thoughts behind the words. But this does not mean that the truthful utterances, on which the deceptive ones are parasitic, are also accompanied by hidden thoughts: on the contrary, they reveal thoughts.

just awful for you.' Of course, there may be some things that your mother understands, things about why it's awful and what else might help besides a hug, of which the dog, we suspect, has no grasp; but that is much like the fact that a person who has never used a computer has rather little grasp of what it means to have the computer crash when you've just finished a paper, or what kind of a solution 'backing up' or 'rebooting' might be. Language that conveys information in propositional form can help us to extend our grasp of things beyond our immediate hands–on encounters; but that kind of informative language doesn't seem to be essential to meaningful communication, even of the most human kind.

So we need to be wary about assuming that the propositional structure of many of our utterances means that the point or content of the communication is essentially and universally propositional in form. We are inclined to describe the cat's meaning in sentences: 'she wants to go out', we say; 'look! she fancies chasing the birds.' The descriptions resemble the sentences that we would use to communicate the corresponding desires: I want to go for a walk; I fancy watching a video. We re–express, in our terms, what the cat has successfully conveyed in her terms. It looks propositional in our description, because our description is done in language: what else would we expect of a description in language? When we engage in such description, we are not pretending that the cat thinks or utters propositions, but we do mean that the cat has that thought in mind (namely, the one that *we* for our part would usually express in words, though not always). So, equally, we should not suppose, just because we describe our thoughts in propositions, that our thoughts themselves come in the form of propositions, private propositions in our head. Perhaps some do (I'm not sure).[14] But some are just the same kinds of thoughts as the cat's thoughts, which we also describe in propositions.

---

[14] There's a brand of Wittgenstein-inspired dogma that would have us say here that there is no inner proposition but only the uttered thought, and since that is propositional and is not a picture of the inner thought but an expression of it, then it makes no sense to ask about another thing, the inner thought. Thoughts, then, are propositions: namely, the uttered ones. But this will not do, partly because of the parallel case of pain behaviour, where we recognize that the propositional formula 'I've got a pain' is an expression of the same kind as crying, clutching, etc., and there is no reason to imagine that pain comes as a *proposition* for which the non-propositional crying is a less accurate expression (in a human or a dog or anything). It also will not do because of dissimulation. So, given that there can be a distinction between what we feel and how we express it, there is no reason to read back to the thought itself the propositional form of the honestly described thought. For some similar discussion to the same purpose in relation to Stoic *lekta* and animal thoughts, see Sorabji, *Animal Minds*, 22–3.

There seem, then, to be continuities between the experience of humans and the animals with which we are familiar. The clearest forms of cross-species communication occur between creatures that share the same home and some of the same lifestyle: we understand what our pets are telling us; trainers establish a rapport with their elephants; animal behaviourists get intimate with their chimpanzees; and aristocrats talk to their horses.[15] The fact that we are less able to read the minds of wild animals is no more significant than other cross-cultural failures of understanding, such as the fact that Wittgenstein's primitive tribe which is accustomed to demanding slabs and planks would be unable to engage in a conversation on medieval history, or that most of us on the east side of the Atlantic find Republican politicians not just hard to believe but impossible to understand.[16]

So what are we to think? Shall we say that the cat does not need the concept of a door in order to think that mewing by the door (that being our description of what she chooses to do) might well be a good way to get out? Or shall we say that, in so far as she is accustomed to use the door as a means of getting out of the house, she has, in fact, much the same concept of a door as we have, though she manages very well without a word for it?[17]

Do We Know What We See?

One marked danger with drawing a line between concept users and those who lack concepts is that it surreptitiously imports something like a Platonic two world view with a radical distinction between intelligible objects and sensible objects. Suppose you think that language-using animals have concepts, while the dumb animals have access only to the immediate input of their senses. If (as seems commonly to be assumed) concepts are something different from objects accessible to the senses, and non-human animals don't have access to concepts, then the human/non-human distinction

---

[15] See Gaita, *Philosopher's Dog*, 5–20.   [16] See Beardsmore, 'If a lion could talk', 41–2.

[17] On these issues (against Donald Davidson's claims about concepts and propositional attitudes) see esp. Dupré, 'Mental lives', 229–30. My view (that the notion of a 'concept' is not helpful here, and that propositions are not required or implied in animal thoughts) differs from that of Sorabji, who finds elementary propositional or predicational structures in the inner lives of animals by attributing a rich notion of perception (a propositional attitude) to Aristotle, and appealing to the notion of *empeiria* at *An. post.* 2. 19 (on which see further below). See most recently Richard Sorabji, *Aristotle on Memory*, 2nd edn. (London: Duckworth, 2004), pp. xx–xxi.

turns out to import an epistemological and metaphysical dualism, of the kind that is commonly attributed to Plato, not only distinguishing our conceptual knowledge from the perceptual knowledge of the beasts, but also dividing our perceptual objects from our mental ones. We risk finding that there is one world of the senses, a world in which animals live, where things are just as they look, and which contains the physical objects that are observed by the senses of animals and humans alike, and another world of concepts, to which we turn inside our minds, where we classify the things we see as falling under concepts, concepts which cannot be perceived, but only known. Such a world of Forms would be accessible only to humans (or humans and other rational beings).[18]

There are, of course, many things right about Platonism. It is especially important to ensure that we can separate our ideals from the grim reality of things around us here and now, and that we can keep our standards of truth unsullied by depraved values or distorted perceptions. But the idea that *all* our thoughts are about a different set of things from the objects that we perceive, *just because* they are thoughts and not sense perceptions, has rather less appeal. If I think of what I ate for breakfast, I think about the egg (that particular egg), the bacon (that particular rasher of bacon), and the slice of toast (with its butter and its marmalade): the very same ones I ate this morning. I don't think about the concept of egg, or the concept of bacon. My thoughts are directed at things out there, real eggs and real bacon. I saw them this morning, I ate them this morning, and I think of them now.

So we need an explanation of how thoughts can be of objects, present or absent objects, not concepts. An account of concept formation will not suffice (although it might also be needed, since we can sometimes have thoughts about abstract objects or conceptual constructs, such as the square root of 2 or the ideal husband, and even thoughts about concepts, e.g. when one thinks to oneself that the concept of a cooked breakfast is common to all civilized races). It needs to provide for the continuity of human and animal behaviour, to explain how we and other animals alike can pursue goals and undertake courses of action that presuppose thinking of, anticipating, hoping for, and grieving over things that are not available.

---

[18] When I call this view 'Platonic', I do not mean to imply that Plato necessarily held such a view. There are a few passages in the Middle Period works that seem to invite us to adopt some kind of dualism. Aristotle criticizes Plato for views of this sort, and Plato shows himself aware of the risks in the *Parmenides*.

So what philosophical outlook do we need to adopt to ensure that we can retain the common-sense idea that the content of our thoughts is the content of our world, the same world as we meet in our perceptual experience, and not a separate replica of it?[19]

In his discussion of human and animal behaviour, Aristotle sometimes invokes a mechanism that he calls *phantasia*, or (in the traditional translation) 'imagination'.[20] This phenomenon, to which I shall devote some attention later in this chapter, figures in Aristotle's discussions of the soul, and in some other works on the motion of animals and on the origins of conceptual thought. It seems that Aristotle invokes *phantasia* in order to develop a plausible account of animal behaviour that potentially avoids some of the traps we have just mentioned. Aristotle's solution is neither Cartesian nor Platonist. He doesn't endorse, or require, dualism—either epistemological or metaphysical. In fact, his account of animal behaviour, properly understood, seems to avoid such metaphysical gulfs, without turning animals into automata devoid of any understanding of their environment or their actions. We can find in Aristotle, I suggest, one way of construing the continuity between our experience and the cat's experience, and the continuity between our acts of meaningful communication and

[19] My thoughts about the breakfast I ate this morning are about actual individuals, the particular eggs and bacon that were on my plate. Some thoughts (such as my anticipation of the eggs and bacon that I hope to have tomorrow) are about an indefinite particular. I can also think of getting a plumber, as opposed to getting Mr Newman, whose plumbing services I have called on in the past. In these cases I am not thinking of the concept of egg or the concept of plumber, but rather envisaging that some particular might exist that fits the general description 'egg' or 'plumber'. We thus need to supply a mechanism to ensure that there are not only two kinds of object of attention, forms on the one hand and individuals on the other. We must also explain how we can think of particulars, whether indefinite or definite examples, as falling under specific kinds, where those kinds are forms or concepts. I am grateful to Richard Sorabji for drawing attention to the difference between hoping for an indefinite particular and remembering a definite one. One can, of course, also hope for a definite particular, and sometimes one may be disappointed in that hope.

[20] The translation 'imagination' is problematic. See the discussion in Malcolm Schofield, 'Aristotle on the imagination', in *Articles on Aristotle*, iv, ed. J. Barnes, M. Schofield, and R. Sorabji (London: Duckworth, 1979), 103–32, 103–7 (= Martha C. Nussbaum and Amélie O. Rorty (eds.), *Essays on Aristotle's De anima* (Oxford: Clarendon Press, 1992), 249–77, 249–53). Schofield finds the term not wholly objectionable, since he sees Aristotle as collecting a set of phenomena that include imagination among others. The term 'imagination' has been used more recently by Michael V. Wedin, *Mind and Imagination in Aristotle* (New Haven: Yale University Press, 1988), whose understanding of the range of phenomena to be included matches my own. I am not comfortable, however, with the pseudo-visual implications of 'image', since it implies that the mind is structured to think solely in terms of visual images, whereas *phantasia* must in fact serve to construe the materials of taste, smell, hearing, and even touch, even though Aristotle tends to give primacy to visual examples. Perhaps the idea of creating an impression (not physically but mentally) is better than the notion of forming an image. I should therefore prefer to translate *phantasia* as 'impressionability'.

hers, without invoking an unbridgeable divide at the language barrier. On this account, animals without intellect do not miss out on the objects of thought; nor do they live in an inadequate or ill-directed way; nor do the factors that explain their actions differ in any way from the factors that explain the corresponding behaviour in a human agent. Aristotle manages to preserve a distinction between intellect and the other faculties, without thereby breaking the evident continuity of human and animal behaviour or separating the objects of thought from the objects of perception. The notion of *phantasia* is one of the tools that Aristotle uses in order to deliver these results, in my view. Let me explain.

The question about the contents of animal minds (do they have concepts?) is related to questions about their purposive behaviour. *Phantasia* appears in Aristotle's psychological repertoire as a way of transferring content from the animal's perceptual experience to its purposive imagination, among other things. This, as I understand it, enables him to avoid the trap of supposing that concepts, of a linguistic or theoretical sort, are necessary for purposive action.[21] I think that we should understand Aristotle to be saying that all, or virtually all, animals act for a reason, and that humans act for a reason in exactly the same way, without appeal to any abstract concepts. What moves all animals, human and non-human alike, Aristotle argues in the *De anima*, is inclination,[22] and inclination is always purposive.[23] There are also intellectual capacities peculiar to humans, some of which can have a bearing on purposive action; but evidently they can only affect action if they can alter how attractive a given object of desire looks, since the object of desire is what arouses the inclination. That, according to Aristotle, is what initiates voluntary motion.[24]

---

[21] There are relevant discussions of Aristotle's understanding of how animals interpret the world in Richard Sorabji, 'Intentionality and physiological processes', in *Essays on Aristotle's* De anima, ed. Nussbaum and Rorty, 195–225, and *idem, Animal Minds*. As noted above, Sorabji traces the explanation to the richness of animals' perceptual content (which he takes to be quasi-propositional on Aristotle's view). He therefore takes imagination to be similarly complex. I disagree on both these points. Sorabji also seems to assume the dualism of perceptual versus conceptual objects that I am concerned to question.   [22] *orexis*, sometimes translated 'appetite'.

[23] *De an.* 3. 9, e.g. 432^{b}13; 3. 10, 433^{a}15.

[24] An example of how intellectual judgements may affect action might be if one reflected on the reasons for choosing a certain action and decided that it was not a good reason, or was morally corrupt. Then the reason might look less attractive, and the action would cease to be desirable and cease to move the will. (See *De an.* 3. 10, 433^{a}23, for the idea that the will is a form of inclination.) Cf. *De an.* 3. 11, 434^{a}9. Such a capacity for reflection, or beliefs about value, will not make the behaviour itself any more purposive than that of other animals, who similarly choose the action that is rendered most attractive in the circumstances, and choose it purposely and for a reason.

It has to be acknowledged that there are reflective possibilities provided by the intellect, such as the evaluation of reasons and choices as opposed to mere results, which will be available to human agents and not to other animals. These clearly open up additional kinds of explanation for why an agent acted thus and so. Why did she do that? To live up to her moral ideals; to avoid disgrace, etc. These explanations do not seem to make sense for an animal that cannot reflect or deliberate about the choices she is making. Nevertheless, the lack of such sophisticated evaluative responses in non-human animals seems irrelevant to their capacity to enjoy success or failure in their simple purposive actions.[25]

So it would surely be a mistake to confuse acting on purpose (intentional animal behaviour) with other, *intellectual* activities, such as reflecting on, or analysing, the reason for acting so (various kinds of reflective evaluation of one's own decisions and actions, or of the actions of others), or deliberating about the correct evaluation of competing options (various kinds of practical deliberation about one's own best course or the options open to others whom one is advising). It is not necessary to engage in such reflective analysis of choices and actions in order to engage in the simpler task of acting for a purpose, or acting as one intends. To exercise choice, to choose between conflicting desires, to exercise a preference, or to decide to act on one desire rather than another—for none of these things does one need to have a second-order opinion *about* one's choice or the goodness of that choice.[26] *Other people* might analyse one's choices and actions and conclude, correctly, that one had done something for a purpose, even where one was not passing judgement on that question oneself.

---

[25] The more sophisticated evaluations of motives and actions do open the way for a different kind of assessment of the source of success or failure, and for the possibility of a failure at a different level of ethical responsibility—a level at which the appropriate responses would include remorse, regret, and culpability, rather than frustration or disappointment. These kinds of failure and success seem to be exclusive to moral beings who can reflect on whether their goals are worthy ones.

[26] When Aristotle says that debating whether to do this or that is a function of *logismos*, and not an option for animals without the *logistikon* faculty (*De an.* 434ᵃ8), he need not mean that other animals cannot choose to do this rather than that when faced with alternatives. They will presumably (as we generally do) choose to do the one that seems immediately more attractive. Beings with intellect and a sense of time can, if they think of it, calculate the future outcome and thereby effect a different evaluation and hence different preference (*De an.* 433ᵇ5–7). Aristotle seems here to think principally of choices between immediate and long-term goals, rather than between two immediately attractive options, such as face Buridan's ass.

And suppose that it is a specially human thing to pass judgement on the choices one has made. This does not mean that is especially good or commendable (except in a human life). If it is specially human, it will certainly figure in judgements about how successful a *human* life is. But if we deny that it enters into the lives of other animals, we do not mean that something important for them is lacking from their lives. It is important in our lives, but it is surely not important in theirs.

So, noticing that some animals do not reflect on their reasons for acting is perfectly compatible with supposing that they do have reasons. They may be aware of their reasons. They can act on purpose and with a goal in mind. They can be successful or frustrated in achieving their goals. All this is possible without reflective judgement on the value of their goals and choices.[27]

Aristotle and Descartes: Animals and Machines

I have suggested that Aristotle's understanding of animal behaviour does not liken the animal to a machine, in the way that Descartes's does. But is this so? There looks to be a counter-example in a passage of *De motu animalium*, chapter 7. There Aristotle briefly compares the behaviour of animals to the movements of some kind of mechanical toy.[28] There is an uncanny resemblance between what Aristotle says there and what Descartes says in the *Discours de la méthode*, where he summarizes his views on the mechanical nature of animal motion, and in the related passages of his *Traité de l'homme*. The crucial (and notorious) passage is this:

Ce qui ne semblera nullement étrange à ceux qui, sachant combien de divers *automates*, ou machines mouvantes, l'industrie des hommes peut faire, sans y employer que fort peu de pièces, à comparaison de la grande multitude des os, des muscles, des nerfs, des artères, des veines, et de toutes les autres parties qui

---

[27] It is, however, nonsense for us to criticize animal behaviour by our own reflective criteria, by which we evaluate the reasons for action and the corresponding moral responses to it: it is nonsense to take the animal to court, to ask it to plead guilty, to instruct it about sin and redemption, or to invite it to vote on foreign policy.

[28] Arist. *De motu an.* (*On the Movement of Animals*), ch. 7, 701^{b}2–13. This passage (which is discussed in more detail below) is examined in Martha C. Nussbaum and Hilary Putnam, 'Changing Aristotle's mind', in *Essays on Aristotle's* De anima, ed. Nussbaum and Rorty, 27–56, 38–9.

sont dans le corps de chaque animal, considéreront ce corps comme une machine qui, ayant été faite des mains de Dieu, est incomparablement mieux ordonnée, et a en soi des mouvements plus admirables, qu'aucune de celles qui peuvent être inventées par les hommes.[29]

One thing to note is that Descartes is describing the bodies not merely of non-human animals, but those of human beings as well, in this passage. It is a quite general claim that animal bodies function like immensely complex and refined machines. Descartes will go on to suggest that non-human animals have nothing more than this (and for that reason one would be unable to tell the difference between a mechanical model of a monkey and a real monkey).[30] By contrast, in the case of humans it would be impossible to make an exact replica in the form of a machine, because there are additional mental functions that cannot be replicated in machines however complicated and clever. But it remains true that the normal bodily functions in human beings are mechanical, and could be replicated.

The same is true of Aristotle's passage, which is similarly designed to explain how animal behaviour quite generally is explicable (or partially explicable) by analogy with some devices he calls *automata*:

Just like the mechanical devices (αὐτόματα) move, once a small movement occurs, when the cords are slackened and they pluck each other ... and the little cart, where the child driving it pushes it straight and back it goes, in a circle again, as a result of having its wheels unequal.[31]

---

[29] Descartes, *Discours de la méthode*, in René Descartes, *Œuvres de Descartes*, ed. ch. Adam and P. Tannery (Paris: Univ. (hereafter AT) C.N.R.S., 1964–76), vol. VI, 1–78: Part 5, 55–6. 'This will not seem strange at all to those who, knowing how many kinds of 'automata', or moving machines, human ingenuity can construct (without employing more than a very few pieces, by comparison with the great multitude of bones, muscles, sinews, arteries, veins, and all the other parts there are in each animal's body), will regard this body as a machine—a machine that is incomparably better constructed, and one that has more admirable movements, than any of those that humans are capable of inventing, given that this one has been made by God's hands.'

[30] Ibid. 5, 56, 10–15 (AT). The claim that 'there would be no means by which one could tell that they weren't of exactly the same nature as these animals' (*nous n'aurions aucun moyen pour reconnaître qu'elles ne seraient pas en tout de même nature que ces animaux*) seems to imply that there is in fact a difference in nature between the puppet and the real animal, but that it is hidden from us. If so, it is not clear what the hidden inner life of the animal is. But the point may be just to do with the different origin: we would be unable to tell that the puppet was not a naturally occurring animal, a human artefact rather than one made by God.

[31] *Arist. De motu an.* 7, 701[b]2–3. The text is damaged (or possibly hard to construe because of the difficulty in envisaging what kind of device Aristotle has in mind). For details on the problems of this text, see Martha C. Nussbaum,(ed.), *Aristotle's* De motu animalium (Edition and Commentary) (Princeton: Princeton University Press, 1978) commentary *ad loc*.

Admittedly, the details of Aristotle's mechanical illustrations are hard to reconstruct. He refers, apparently, to two machines that do slightly unexpected things in response to small stimuli of a different kind. Neither device is identifiable precisely. However, his point is evidently that the physical structure of an organic body can be crucial to explaining how it will respond to stimulus. Take his second illustration, the little cart ($701^{b}3$). If the cart is so constructed as to have the left wheel larger than the right wheel, it will turn clockwise in a circle when pushed, whereas if it is constructed with wheels equal in diameter, it will go straight. In the same way, Aristotle is saying, not everything in an animal's behaviour is voluntary, in the strong sense, or chosen from various alternatives. An animal may respond in a characteristic way—say a bee buzzes—not because it chooses to buzz rather than sing, but because buzzing is the automatic effect of having one's body so constructed. Aristotle's other example ($701^{b}2-3$ and $8-10$), which is some kind of machine in which a small movement of rods and pulleys produces a much more pronounced movement at the other end of the mechanism, illustrates how quite extensive movements can be reflex responses to tiny stimuli from the environment. A third illustration introduced half a page later ($701^{b}25-8$), of a boat, in which minimal movement of the rudder at the stern effects a considerable swing at the bows, illustrates the same point. Aristotle's idea is that these reflexes are not purely determined by the environment: on the contrary, they would not occur as they do if the animal were not so constructed as to respond in that way, so that the explanatory force lies as much or more in an analysis of the organs in which the response occurs as in whatever external environmental stimulus initiates the movement. Nevertheless, although the responses are end-directed (just as the little cart seems to be made with uneven wheels so that it will turn in a circle), the animal itself is not choosing to act for that end at the moment when it acts on a reflex, any more than the cart chooses to move in a circle when pushed.

Given Descartes's reference to *automates* in the passage quoted above, it is hard to resist the idea that he had Aristotle's image in mind. *Automates* is clearly not his own word: it is a Greek word that he has borrowed in order to allude to the word *automata* used in the passage from Aristotle, and he then glosses it ('ou machines mouvantes') for the benefit of his French readers.[32] This is not the only terminology that he takes over from Aristotle.

---

[32] For Descartes's examples of the kind of machines he has in mind, see *Traité de l'homme*, AT IX, 130. 15–132. 1.

The whole paragraph to which this is the conclusion had been steeped in Aristotelian psychological theory, including the notion of the common sense,[33] imagination,[34] memory, and sensation. It is clear that Descartes has Aristotelian theory in mind, whether directly from Aristotle's own texts or by way of Scholastic philosophy. On the other hand, Descartes (either deliberately against Aristotle or as a result of a tendentious reading of Aristotle) drastically eliminates the conscious cognition that Aristotle had attributed to these forms of awareness.

However, we need to be careful not to read Descartes's deliberately materialist account of human and animal bodily functions back into Aristotle. This is tempting because of the striking verbal echoes. But the superficial resemblance is actually deceptive. It is true that, in so far as Aristotle uses the mechanical illustration to indicate how behaviour that is apparently goal-directed can sometimes be produced as a result of the mechanistic effects of bodily structures, his point is indeed the same as Descartes's. He shows that some of the apparently goal-directed behaviour of animals could be merely a reflex response in some kind of automaton, some device constructed to respond automatically to environmental stimuli. But Aristotle, unlike Descartes, immediately goes on to highlight a difference between the behaviour of his machines and that of living animals, which is that animals *adapt their behaviour* in response to the environment. In the case of the machines, the little cart either has equal wheels, in which case it goes straight, or it has unequal wheels, in which case it goes in a circle. If it could change the size of its wheels, it could determine for itself whether it goes straight or in a circle. Aristotle introduced these examples precisely in order to point out that animals, by contrast with machines, can—and do—change the shape and size of limbs and organs so as to adapt the resulting movements, and that they do so intentionally—'intentionally', that is, in a technical sense, in that the changes

---

[33] Descartes, *Discours de la méthode*, 5. 55. This is the internal organ to which sensations are referred from the various individual senses. Descartes deliberately parts company with Aristotle in locating this organ in the brain instead of the heart. See e.g. *Traité de l'homme*, 141.

[34] Descartes calls this 'corporeal imagination' and suggests that it performs mechanical tasks in altering the ideas received by the common sense and thereby distributes the animal spirits to the muscles to make things happen in the body. Thus the imagination has become part of the bodily machinery that generates the deceptively lifelike responses in animals, but without any intentional content. By contrast (as I shall suggest below), Aristotle seemed to use imagination to give animals access to intentional content which could allow them to have real purposes in mind, not just behaviour that looked as if it was purposeful.

are brought about by what we would call mental events in the animal's consciousness.[35]

So for Aristotle, but not for Descartes, the animal does, after all, elect to act in its own way in a certain sense, while the little cart does not. Even if reflex responses account for much of the animal's behaviour, this does not make it a mere automaton, on Aristotle's view, because it adapts to produce these goal-directed responses, and this adaptation is a response to the intentional objects of states of awareness.

Aristotle, like Descartes, is explaining the bodily behaviour of animals and humans as continuous. But, unlike Descartes, he thinks that all animals, both humans and beasts, are responding to intentional content. Both have a mental life, according to Aristotle, and it works in much the same way.

The Role of *phantasia* in the Mental Life of Animals

As I noted above, it is my contention that this continuity of mental content between beasts and mankind is provided by the mechanism known as *phantasia*, or 'imagination', in Aristotle's psychology.[36] This mechanism serves to explain how human beings and animals can respond appropriately to the remote prospect of things that matter to them, even in their absence, so as to enable them to engage in purposive behaviour. Because it uses perceptual content, not linguistic concepts, to define the objects of desire and attention, it allows for continuity between purposive animal behaviour and purposive human behaviour.

Aristotle appeals to *phantasia* in various contexts in his explanations of animal behaviour, but the most prominent discussion is in chapter 3 of *De anima*, book 3. This discussion is placed between the last part of his treatment of perception (finishing in *De an.* 3. 2) and the start of his treatment of intellect (the focus of *De an.* 3, 4−8). This fits with the idea that the phenomenon of imagination has a bridging function, accounting for the link between perceptual content and intellectual content in such animals as have both.[37]

---

[35] Mental events: φαντασίαι, αἰσθήσεις, and ἔννοιαι (*De motu an.* 701ᵇ17−18).

[36] I have argued this thesis more fully elsewhere: Osborne, 'Aristotle on the fantastic abilities'.

[37] For a clear analysis of the context and occasion of the discussion see Schofield, 'Aristotle on the imagination', 126−7 (= 271−2). Additional discussion is provided in Osborne, 'Aristotle on the fantastic abilities', 264−5. On the double construction of the chapter, see not only my own article, 'Aristotle on the fantastic abilities', 266, but also Jean Louis Labarrière, 'Des deux introductions de la *phantasia* dans le *de anima*, III, 3', *Kairos*, 9 (1997): 141−68.

But it appears that *phantasia* also plays a crucial role for those animals that do not have intellect. For them the deliverances of *phantasia* seem to provide an alternative source of intentional content. It is therefore not just a bridge between two faculties, but also a fund of intentional objects of a non-conceptual, non-propositional sort, which serve in place of concepts or objects of thought and enable an animal to perform a range of intelligent functions, functions that might look as though they depend on what we call propositional attitudes. It allows Aristotle to explain such apparently propositional attitudes, but without requiring propositional or conceptual content. Once we can do that for animals, we can then do the same for humans and thereby retain a continuity in the psychology of human and animal activity.

Thus, I suggest, *phantasia* makes sense, both within Aristotle's project and as an attempt to explain familiar phenomena concerning animal behaviour, if we suppose that it coincides with the ability that we and other animals have to pick out significant forms in our environment, and to use such forms when contemplating the objects to which they belong, whether present or absent. I take it that Aristotle thinks that the initial source of these forms is the world, not our soul.[38] The account would go something like this: we see the shapes before us now as *flowers* because some other flowers, out there, have *previously* prompted a 'flower' form to lodge itself as an interpretative model in the soul. We then use that 'flower' form as a model in interpreting the *present* visual field. So *phantasia* helps us to see the world as a set of discrete things, things of one kind or another.

Aristotle seems to think that we depend indirectly upon perception for all kinds of thought, including abstract conceptual thought,[39] although I think that we could take a different view on this and still find that *phantasia* is a useful explanatory tool. For instance, we could suppose (unlike Aristotle) that there are in-built Kantian constraints on what kind of experiences we pick out in perception, so that the interpretative forms are prior to perception rather than derived from it. In that case it would appear that the perceptual field is dependent upon thought, rather than the reverse. By contrast, Aristotle seems to suggest that we don't lodge a particular form in our repertoire of available things to think about until we have encountered the form perceptually at least once.[40] But wherever the conceptual tools

---

[38] i.e. there are no innate ideas. See further below.
[39] Arist. *De an.* 431^{a}13–17; 431^{b}2; 431^{b}20–432^{a}14.   [40] Ibid. 432^{a}7–10.

come from, the general structure of the animal's current experience of the world comes out much the same, if one thinks that the function of seeing things as examples of a certain type must be explained by some psychic resources of a quasi-conceptual sort. Providing these resources is what I take *phantasia* to be doing, at least some of the time, in Aristotle's psychology.

In describing the functions of *phantasia*, one can draw a distinction between presentational roles, on the one hand, and receptive roles, on the other. The soul that has the functionality associated with *phantasia* first *receives* information from the environment, and then subsequently it presents that information to the mind for attention.[41] It is *phantasia*, and *phantasia* alone, that plays a role in actually forming the objects of the mind's attention.

However, when I say that it presents objects for attention, I am not suggesting that *phantasia* is supposed to provide an alternative inner set of objects to perception or thought, as though one watched an internal slide show of fantastic images, a virtual world. Rather, I mean that in presenting a form, *phantasia* would be directing the mind's attention not to an internally created image but to the world that is so construed. We remain observers of the forms directly encountered in perception, not observers of our inner cognitive experiences. And that is partly because, for Aristotle, our inner cognitive experiences are nothing other than the actuality of their objects of attention. We experience a world that is made up of discrete, tidy objects; this means that our minds are constituted by actualized discrete, tidy objects. How do we explain our ability to construe a vague perceptual field as discrete, tidy objects, recognizable objects of attention, and then to recall the same objects for anticipation, in memory, for contemplative reflection and for judgement by the intellect? Aristotle puts these phenomena together and seeks a single explanation in terms of his notion of *phantasia*.

The *Physiology* of *phantasia*

Perhaps Aristotle needs something like *phantasia* if he is to succeed in explaining human and animal behaviour in a generally Aristotelian fashion.

---

[41] These roles will evidently be unique to *phantasia*. They do not apply to the cognate faculties for which it provides material, such as the various modes of cognition that figure in Aristotle's account, like supposing, interpreting, thinking, knowing, or perceiving. These are not faculties that *present* objects *to* the mind for attention; they *are* the mind's attention to such objects.

But can he make his proposal convincing as an account of what is actually going on in the mind? We might think that he ought to be able to identify a part of the animal's physiological structure to serve as the basis of the psychological capacity that he is introducing: ought there not to be some organ or process, present in all and only those animals that can use the functionality of *phantasia*, which would be the basis for thinking that this is a real faculty that we actually possess?

It is true that an account of the perceptual capacities of a creature normally presupposes that those capacities are to be located in organs that do the work. Even if we hold a rather anti-materialist account of the mind, we still expect that there are physical parts of the brain that correlate with the mental events, and a theory that posited a function for which there were no available organs would look strange. We do not expect great intellects to be lodged in empty heads, even if we think that the thoughts that such intellects have are immaterial.

Aristotle meets that expectation, for the majority of cognitive functions, with his account of the senses in book 2 of the *De anima* and the more detailed work in the *De sensu*.[42] He explains, for each of the senses, what kind of process, in what kind of organ, would be required, if his account of the nature of perception (and its phenomenology) were correct. He tries to tie these explanations to evident features of animal bodies, such as the observable structures of the organs traditionally associated with a particular sense. For instance, his account of the phenomenon of hearing appeals to features of the ear and to the behaviour of air in a closed channel.[43]

---

[42] Whether the physiology of Aristotle's account can be adapted to modern physiology (being replaceable by some alternative physiology according to functionalist thinking about compositional plasticity) or is ineluctably bound up with an implausibly outmoded physics is the subject of the notorious debate between Burnyeat ('Is an Aristotelian philosophy of mind still credible? A draft', in *Essays on Aristotle's De anima*, ed. Nussbaum and Rorty, 15–26), Sorabji ('Body and soul in Aristotle', *Philosophy*, 49 (1974): 63–89; repr. in *Articles on Aristotle*, iv, ed. Barnes et al. 42–64, idem, 'Intentionality'), Nussbaum and Putnam: (Hilary Putnam, 'Philosophy and our mental life', in idem, *Mind, Language and Reality: Philosophical Papers*, ii (Cambridge: Cambridge University Press, 1975), 291–303; Nussbaum (ed), *Aristotles De motu*; Nussbaum and Putnam, 'Changing Aristotle's mind'). Regardless of whether the eye jelly becomes red as apples become red—Burnyeat is surely right that the sense registers a circular shape, rather than becoming circular—it seems clear that Aristotle thinks physiological underpinning of some sort is required (some bodily organs must have suitable matter) for perception, but not for thought, and this suggests that he is aiming to meet this expectation. On the other hand, the material process clearly needs to be distinguished from the kind of alteration that is reddening, turning circular, or becoming smelly, given that there is a crucial difference between the air picking up a smell and the nose picking up a smell (*De an.* 424^{b}16–18).

[43] *De an.* 2. 8, 420^{a}3. For most of the senses, further physiological speculation is provided in the *De sensu*, though, curiously, hearing is scarcely treated there.

In his account of *phantasia* he does not do that. But we need not take this lack of a specific organ of *phantasia* to discredit the explanatory force of the idea. Aristotle is right that we take the five senses to be very closely tied to particular physiological organs: you can't see if you don't have working eyes; you can't hear if you don't have working ears. But this does not apply to other functions of the soul: our spatial awareness, awareness of ourselves, sense of shape, size, and weight of objects, and our grasp of the unity of an object that manifests features accessible to different senses: all these are functions of our soul that are not obviously particular to any clearly defined organ.[44] Aristotle speaks of the single central sense as something unified, receptive of input from all the separate organs, and this is where perception is ultimately located, but this function does not manifest itself as occupying a distinct organ.[45] We deduce that such a function is required, and our inability to locate a specific organ for it does not count against the need to presuppose that the functionality is there. The evidence is in what we do, not in what we are made of.

The same clearly applies to the functionality of *phantasia*. If we find it useful to identify such a function, because it is an economical way to explain a range of phenomena with a related kind of phenomenology, then we do not need to wait for neuroscience to identify a physical seat (or seats) for supplying the functionality. Aristotle raises some sophisticated questions about what it means to talk of a 'part' of the soul, which we should do well to take on board. He says, at *De anima*, 432[a]22:

But there is an immediate problem about how we ought to say that the soul has parts and how many. For in one way they seem to be infinite and not just the ones that some people say there are, distinguishing the reasoning, emotional and appetitive parts, or (for others) what has reason and the irrational. For using the differences that they employ to mark off these ones, other parts that have even greater differences than these will also appear—parts about which we have just been speaking: the nutritive, which belongs both to plants and to all animals, and the sensitive, which one would not easily place under either the category of irrational or that of what has reason. And again the fantastic ability, which is distinct from all of them in its being.

---

[44] Current neuroscience has had some success at identifying local areas of the brain dedicated to some of these functions. Others may be attributed to the combined use of a variety of resources. But the functions can still be usefully distinguished and defined, independently of whether an organ has been identified.

[45] Aristotle thought the relevant organ was the heart (e.g. *Juv.* 469[a]5–20), but his error in this respect is precisely occasioned by the fact that there is no obvious organ dedicated precisely to this function.

Yet it's a real puzzle whether it is the same thing as one of these, or something else, if one is to establish separate parts of the soul. (*De an.* 3. 9, 432ᵃ22–ᵇ3.)

It is clear from this that Aristotle does not exactly mean us to understand the fantastic part of the soul as a separable function, except in so far as we can distinguish a range of tasks that it is to perform, and we can generally identify which creatures display those functions to a recognizable degree. Since the functions of *phantasia* largely go along with the functions of perception, one might take it to be a sophisticated function of perception;[46] but that is not necessarily a helpful way of proceeding, especially if it appears that the events that we call sensation can be performed by primitive creatures who show no sign of employing fantastic abilities.[47] For this reason it is helpful to identify the range of abilities that belong under this heading as the work of a 'part' of the soul, called the fantastic part, where this does not mean a physically separable part, or that there is an identifiable part of the body that is its organ. The classification is phenomenological, not physical.[48]

So what is distinctive about Aristotle's work is not that he has 'discovered' some part of the soul that we have forgotten, but rather that he develops this more gradual classification of psychological functions that challenges the division between rational and irrational souls. He does so because he observes that many of our activities are based not on reason and calculation, but on the same kind of motivations as animals have. His outlook stresses the continuity between human and animal behaviour, and then seeks the explanation, convinced that there must be, in fact, a way in which animals can act intelligently without intellect. He posits *phantasia* to make sense of that conviction. *Phantasia* is a useful device for the purpose: for it gives us a name under which to subsume the capacities that bridge the gap between

---

[46] This is the tempting thought that is explored and problematized in *De an.* 3. 3; the close association between fantastic functions and perception is also taken as read in *Mem.* 450ᵃ10–25. But the systematic coincidence of imaginative functions with perceptual functions does not necessarily indicate that it is helpful to assimilate the two capacities.

[47] Aristotle wonders whether even the most primitive creatures should be said to have *phantasia* of some indeterminate sort at *De an.* 433ᵇ31–434ᵃ5. His answer to the question is unclear. Cf. also 428ᵃ10–11; Philoponus, *In DA*, 500.13.

[48] Aristotle speculates about the physiology of receiving and storing fantastic forms at *De an.* 428ᵇ10–17, 429ᵃ1–2, and *Mem.* 450ᵃ25–ᵇ11; but his account is something very like the wax tablet image in Plato's *Theaetetus*. The idea that there must be some change that accompanies perception, and that it works a bit like making stamps in some plastic material, is only deduced by inference from the effects for which the facility has to account. There is no suggestion about where the equipment is located or what it is made of.

the output of rational thought and the input of the undigested senses. Giving these capacities a name is crucial to recognizing how they govern our lives.

More on Animal Behaviour

Besides his main chapter on *phantasia* at *De an.* 3. 3, which is primarily devoted to showing why this capacity is not to be identified with either sensation or thought, Aristotle occasionally appeals to the functions of *phantasia* in order to account for some of the typical activities of animals. It is worth looking at one or two of these passages in order to get a better sense of the difference that it can make to understanding the cognitive aspects of animal behaviour.

One crucial passage is in *De anima* 3. 9, just after the passage quoted above (about parts of the soul). Aristotle is considering what makes animals move. 'Animals' here means humans and other animals alike. First, he observes that the movements involved in growing and withering away are not confined to animals but occur in plants too, so he attributes these factors to what he calls the reproductive and nutritive soul (a feature common to plant and animal souls).[49] Growth in plants is not due to anything different from growth in human children: we have exactly the same basic soul. Second, he considers (but postpones discussing) the automatic functions such as respiration, and sleep, which he thinks are problematic.[50] The key case, however, is locomotion: what is it that makes an animal get up and walk somewhere? Here is what Aristotle says:

But concerning locomotion, we need to enquire what it is that moves an animal to the travelling sort of motion.

(a) It's plain that it's not the nutritive soul. For this motion is always for the sake of something and is accompanied by *phantasia* or inclination. For nothing moves if it is not inclined or avoiding, except under compulsion. Also plants would then be subject to motion, and would have some organic part for such motion.

(b) Similarly it's not the sensitive soul. For there are many animals that have sensation, but are stationary and immobile to the end. So if nature does nothing pointless and doesn't omit anything that is necessary, except in things that are

---

[49] Arist. *De an.* 432^{b}9–11.

[50] Ibid. 432^{b}11–13. These topics are covered in the *parva naturalia* (*De somno* and *De respiratione*) which are a kind of supplement to *De anima*.

maimed or unfinished, and such animals are finished and not maimed (as indicated by the fact that they are reproductive and have an acme and a decline)—so that they would have the organic parts for travelling [if they were designed to travel].

(c) But also it's not the rational soul and what is called *nous* that moves them. For the contemplative mind does not contemplate anything practical, nor does it say anything about what is to be avoided or pursued. But movement is always of a creature that is avoiding or pursuing something. And it's not when one contemplates something like this that one already commands pursuit or avoidance—e.g. one often thinks of something frightening or pleasant, but one does not command that it be feared; rather the heart is moved (or if it's pleasant, some other bit!). (*De an.* 432^{b}13–433^{a}1)

Aristotle considers three options, designated (a), (b), and (c) here, and concludes that the cause of motion cannot be any of these three basic attributes of the soul: nutrition, sensation, or thought. If it were thought, then thought would have to tell us to be afraid or to want the thing. But it doesn't have to do that. Fearing something or fancying it is not a rational conclusion, drawn by the intellect and conveyed to the animal as an instruction from reason. Yet sensation alone does not seem to account for the motive power of the perceived object. The proposal that Aristotle offers is that locomotion is the result of the phenomena that arise from *phantasia*.

But it appears that these two things cause the motion: either inclination or intellect, if one were to locate *phantasia* as a kind of thinking. For many people follow appearances contrary to what they know. And in other animals there isn't thinking or reasoning, but *phantasia*. ... So that it's not surprising that these two things seem to cause motion, inclination and practical thinking: for the object of inclination moves us, and for this reason thinking moves us, because the object of inclination is its starting point. And when *phantasia* moves us, it doesn't move us without inclination. So in fact there's just one thing that moves us, the object of inclination. (*De an.* 433^{a}9–21.)

In this passage Aristotle concludes that *phantasia* is not the immediate or only source of the desire to move. We actually get up and walk because something looks attractive (the object of inclination).[51] This is not generated by practical thinking. Rather, practical thinking takes the attractive object as its starting-point and works out how to get it. Thinking does not make

---

[51] The object of inclination stands here for an object of pursuit or avoidance. Aristotle focuses on the attractive, but the story will be the same in reverse for objects of avoidance.

the object look good (though presumably it could make certain methods of obtaining it look good). But even without thinking at all, we can still pursue goals that look good, because *phantasia* presents things looking good and thereby generates objects of desire or inclination for animals to pursue. These will be the starting-points for our practical thinking, just as they are the starting-points for animals' end-directed activities:

So it is always the object of inclination that moves us, but this is either what is good or what *appears* good. But not anything good—rather the good thing that can be done. What can be done is what is contingent and could have been otherwise. (*De an.* 433ª27–30)

Here the reference to what 'appears' good is widely recognized to be a reference to *phantasia*, the capacity that makes things appear to us to be such-and-such. *Phantasia* explains how we are sometimes mistaken in pursuing things that are only apparently desirable, which could not happen if the faculty that identified things as good was an infallible one (such as perfectly functioning intellect, or perception that just sees what is there).[52] We have to explain motivation towards undesirable ends, in humans as well as animals. Here we see that this is due to presentations of otherwise undesirable things, under a description that appeals ('looks good to me') and draws us to pursue them as objects of inclination.[53]

The Continuity between Fantastic Presentations and Conceptual Thought

If this interpretation is right, Aristotle invokes the fantastic functions of soul to provide for intentional motivation without conceptual thinking, for all animals with or without the intellectual functions of the soul. Nevertheless, we might still think that the presence of intellect in some animals makes a

---

[52] On the idea that *phantasia* provides for the possibility of error, see esp. *De an.* 428ᵇ17–29 and Victor Caston, 'Aristotle and the problem of intentionality', *Philosophy and Phenomenological Research*, 58 (1998) 249–98.

[53] Sorabji discusses these and other passages in support of his claim that Aristotle consistently denies reasoning and belief to animals: Sorabji, *Animal Minds*, 12–6. My point is slightly different: viz. that motivation by the object of desire, generated by perception and *phantasia*, is not peculiar to the irrational animals. It is common to humans as well, so there is no discontinuity here, but rather an attempt to secure continuous and consistent explanations of animal and plant behaviour.

substantial division between human mental capacities and those of animals, because it brings with it the option of rational calculation of practical goals. Surely, someone might say, even if at times we behave like animals and have nothing more in mind than pursuit of what takes our fancy, yet at other times it seems that we think about reasons and causes, moral value and utilitarian benefits, honour, virtue, and shame. These seem to be thoughts that animals cannot have: they seem to be about another set of objects, not the concrete objects of desire out there in the world represented to us under some description by *phantasia*, but something else—some kind of reflective notions, the product of quite different intellectual capacities. So it would seem that we still have a division between conceptual thinking and objects of perception; it's just that Aristotle has used *phantasia* to extend what we can do without concepts, so as to cover a rather richer range of deliberate goal-oriented planning that now becomes common to both animals and humans.

But this is not the end of the story. Aristotle also appears to use *phantasia* to account for the content of theoretical thought,[54] so that theoretical thought too is about the ordinary things of the world, that same world which *phantasia* constructs for our perception. Mind, he says on several occasions, never thinks without a fantastic presentation (a *phantasma*).[55] It thinks the forms in the fantastic presentations.[56] And he even goes so far as to worry, *De anima* at 432^{a}12–14, whether the basic thoughts are anything other than the fantastic presentations. These claims might seem strange if we thought that fantastic presentations (*phantasmata*) were a kind of image, as though every time we think of anything (God, the square root of 2, truth, the propositional calculus, the evil of war, or the Form of Equality), a visual image floats before the mind's eye. But that is plainly a travesty of the idea, since *phantasia* can receive and present the forms from any kind of sensation, so that even if something like images are at issue, they would need to be images from heard or smelled or tactile experiences that came to mind, just as much as images of visual experiences.[57] So we should not think

---

[54] He does this by means of what I have elsewhere called sticky forms (in Osborne, Aristotle on the 'fantastic abilities'): i.e. the forms acquired through *phantasia*, which stay around in the mind to be available for attention, memory, dreams, hopes, and fantasies (*De an.* 429^{a}4–6).

[55] *De an.* 431^{a}14–17; 432^{a}8, 12–14.   [56] Ibid. 431^{b}2–3.

[57] Some passages do imply that the fantastic image comes with a good deal of its original circumstantial paraphernalia, and that forming a concept of the form in the abstract is a further task, to be done on the basis of the image but not identical with it (e.g. when we imagine a triangle that has a finite size, but treat it like a diagram of a triangle in which the size is irrelevant). See *Mem.* 449^{b}30–450^{a}7. But this does not affect the point that visual images are only a sample of the kind of input one might get

of two-dimensional, flat versions of what we see, and we therefore should not think of a play of cinema images floating before the mind's eye. But in any case, the whole notion of an image is surely too crude, for the point is that the form is retained (as it is in perception too) as an abstract structure with which to construe the world; it can be thought of, so to speak, without its matter. This probably means that the form is detached from any particular instantiation in matter: we don't have the tree itself, wood, leaves, and bark, in our head when we think of the tree.[58] I think it remains controversial how far other non-essential features are also excluded.[59]

In this way *phantasia* turns out to be a gift for abstracting, for gathering an understanding of what makes a thing the thing it is, from one example. It is a gift for being able to identify a second example as something of the same sort, even though the second example is not very like the first. Aristotle is quite right that most animals have an uncanny knack for getting through the world in this way, picking out what counts as food, identifying what is prey and what is predator, spotting and avoiding dangers that they have never met before.[60] It is plausible to suppose that a knack of this sort would also assist in the otherwise extraordinary facility with which children acquire language (including vocabulary for items that cannot be picked out as medium-sized stable objects of the sort that we typically suppose can be readily handled and named).[61]

It seems to me that Aristotle must be right about the continuity between the facility that animals show for identifying salient features of their environment (and reacting in a similar way to them, and others like them, on subsequent occasions) and the facility that we show for acquiring and using

from the senses, and the work of *phantasia* is much less easy to replicate in crude physical terms for the other senses, or for the memories of conceptual thought, etc.   [58] *De an.* 431[b]28–9.

[59] I suspect that I disagree with Sorabji here. He has prompted me to look at the example of the triangle in *Mem.* 1, but this does not seem to me to be decisive, since one might hold that thinking of a triangle on the basis of a *phantasma* would have to involve a *phantasma* of a triangle with a certain size; because having a size is part of what it is to be a triangle. But the fantastic presentation might already have excluded other non-essential features of the original triangle from which it came, including, e.g. any three-dimensional depth it might have had, any roughness or texture in the lines, and so on. So I would argue that the fantastic presentation is already schematic and presents only the form of what it is of, instantiated with precise illustrations of those features that are essential to any item of that kind, as in a diagram, but excluding all characteristics that do not essentially belong to that specific form.

[60] We secrete saliva at the sight of food, no matter what the food looks like. Simone Weil, *Lectures on Philosophy*, trans. Hugh Price (Cambridge: Cambridge University Press, 1978), 30.

[61] It is often assumed that children learn nouns for familiar people and things first and most easily, and that they learn by ostensive definition. My experience conflicts with this; my younger daughter's first four words were unmistakable: 'up', 'down', 'empty', and 'more'.

universals, as they figure in thought, language, and consistent behaviour.[62] It is more obvious to us that we are generalizing because we can reflect on our general terms and represent them to ourselves as general terms, and think that there is some special logical status about terms that are general terms. But in essence the simple use of general terms (as opposed to the reflective analysis or meta-representation of them as individuals in the class of general terms) is nothing more than the consistent practice of uttering the same response in relation to the same kind of thing, or in order to repeat the same kind of result: a practice that is not confined to humans. We might add that for us, such repeated language tends to acquire semantic content: the vocabulary becomes a symbol which we interpret as signifying something; it is not just a pattern of consistent behaviour elicited as a reaction to a repeated stimulus. But it is clear that many other animals (not only the language-trained apes, but horses, dogs, and other sociable animals) can also be taught to invest such symbols with meaning.[63]

Suppose we acquire the notion of a tree and the notion of the notion of a tree. Is one of these harder to explain than the other? Aristotle does not actually need to invoke any more complicated mechanisms for either, for *phantasia* will supply the basic materials for both, I think. It is true that Aristotle emphasizes the idea that *phantasia* is generated by perceptual experiences: a motion that accompanies the perceptual experience generates the stored *phantasma* that will serve as a model in future experiences, and this does not occur without what he calls *aesthesis*, which we translate as perception.[64] The simplest cases appear to be ordinary experiences of external things in the environment. Trees generate notions of trees. But there seems to be no obvious reason why the experiences that generate phantasmata should not be mental ones, so that one can acquire and store forms of forms, representations of kinds of representation. Notions of trees and so on generate notions of notions. Assuming that there is such a thing as the experience of perceiving, and that experience too is the work of perception, there is no reason why the same mechanism that produces representation should not explain meta-representation.[65] The mechanism is very much like that picturesquely

---

[62] Cf. Descartes, *Principles of Philosophy*, I 59, 27–8 (AT).

[63] See Dupré, 'Conversations with apes', 238–9. On the difference between disciplining a dog (or a child) and modifying its behaviour according to behaviourist models, see Gaita, *Philosopher's Dog*, 175–8.   [64] Arist. *De an.* 428ª10–17.

[65] On the idea that one can perceive whether one is seeing or hearing, *De an.* 3. 2, 425ᵇ12–16. The capacity for this discrimination is attributed to an activity of the unitary sense-organ, and hence counts

illustrated in Plato's image of the wax tablet at *Theaetetus* 191d. Plato is explicit there that we hold the wax under not only our perceptions but also our thoughts or concepts, so that we can have an imprint of the things that happen in our minds as well as of the external objects. Just as we can recall such mental contents in memory, so we can recall them as samples of a kind (the class of concepts, true beliefs, imaginary fears, and so on) and thereby generate second-order concepts, the notions of certain kinds of notions. Aristotle omits what Plato supplied in that crucial allusion to remembering thoughts. He does not explicitly assign such second-order meta-representational content to *phantasia*, but since he thinks that all thought uses concepts acquired in the form of fantastic representations, he would clearly need to do so, if he were asked to explain that kind of thinking.[66]

What Aristotle does provide is an attempt to account for concept acquisition in general by way of generalization from experience.[67] He does this in *Posterior Analytics* B19. Aristotle does not there name *phantasia* as the capacity that provides the transfer of content from sense perception to abstract universals, but it seems clear that the process he describes is closely related to the ones I have ascribed to *phantasia* here. We need not be fussy about terminology: the idea is not affected. Here is what Aristotle says (he is addressing the difficulty that we need to be able to acquire knowledge of the starting-points of demonstrative knowledge, without deriving them from prior knowledge that we don't have):

So we must have a capacity, but not such that it will be more honourable in terms of its accuracy than these [sc. the primitive immediate principles that are to be explained]. But indeed this does appear to be something that belongs to all animals. For they have an inbuilt discriminatory capacity, which they call sensation. And given the presence of sensation, in some animals there occurs a settling-in of the sensed content, and in others that does not occur. In those in which it does not

as a kind of perception (and hence an experience that would be subject to the second-order work of *phantasia*). My own interpretation of *De an.* 3. 2 is defended in Catherine Osborne, 'Aristotle *De anima* 3. 2: How do we perceive that we see and hear?', *Classical Quarterly*, 33 (1983): 401–11.

[66] For the idea that the intentionality of one's thought content is invariably supplied by the presence of a *phantasma*, see *De an.* 431ª16. Because of this, the idea that I am explaining here, whereby meta-representation of one's thought processes involves *phantasia*, is not an alternative to saying that one 'thinks' of one's thinking, but rather an explanation of what that would be (in the case of human thought). The answer may be different in the case of gods.

[67] I think that Modrak is right to stress, in relation to these issues, the idea that Aristotle is explaining concept acquisition (which *is* what he means by first principles). See Deborah Modrak, *Aristotle: The Power of Perception* (Chicago: University of Chicago Press, 1987), 158–71, and further below, n. 72.

occur, for them there is no knowledge beyond the case of sensing—either no knowledge quite generally or no knowledge in the cases where settling does not occur. But in those in which it does settle in, while they are sensing, there it already exists in the soul.[68]

The passage reminds us of the sticky forms produced by *phantasia* in the course of perception in *De anima* 3.3.[69] Here in the *Posterior Analytics* Aristotle appears to say that some animals do and some don't retain their sensed experiences, but where they do, we have already something that counts as knowledge. But this is not the end of his inquiry, for he wants more than just a knowledge of the single sensation: this will not do as the starting-point of demonstration. His first principles are (he imagines) universals of some sort, and it is these that we need to be able to acquire by some means other than demonstration. How do we get from single perceptions to possessing universals in the soul? Aristotle goes on:

But when lots of these occur, then a further difference comes about, so that some animals acquire *logos* from the settling-in of these things, while others don't. (*An. post.* 100ᵃ1−3)

This is not entirely perspicuous, partly due to the use of the word *logos*, which might mean something like language or reason or theory or formula. But Aristotle clearly feels the need to summarize and repeat the point of what he has just said, and this makes clear that he means that there are three stages: perception, memory, and generalization:

So from sensation comes memory, as we said, and from the frequent repetition of the same memory, experience. For the repeated memories constitute a single experience. And from expertise (or from the entire universal coming to rest in the soul, the one alongside the many, which would be the same in all of them) the starting point of art and of science (art if it's about becoming, science if it's about being). (*An. post.* 100ᵃ3−9)[70]

---

[68] Arist. *An. post.* B 19, 99ᵇ32−100ᵃ1. The text of the last sentence has been in doubt, because there seem to be only a limited range of things that Aristotle might be saying, none of them easily extracted from the MS wording. I believe this to be a possible rendering of the readings in the MSS.

[69] Arist. *De an.* 429a4. See above, n. 54.

[70] This passage, and the larger context, is helpfully discussed by David Charles, *Aristotle on Meaning and Essence* (Oxford: Clarendon Press, 2000), 149−61, although it is not clear to me that the route to 'thought' is a correct description of what is going on here. It is natural to read the word 'or' in 'or from the entire universal coming to rest in the soul' as meaning 'in other words'. See also Sorabji, *Animal Minds*, 33−4, and *idem*, *The Philosophy of the Commentators: A Source Book, Psychology* (London: Duckworth, 2004), ch. 5b.

Generalization arises from taking the repeated memories to constitute a single experience of the same kind and observing what is common to them all. This seems to equate with the idea in the previous passage, at 100ª3, that some animals get a rationale or *logos* when they get repeated memories. So it seems that it is sufficient to see one's repeated experiences as tokens of a type. As soon as one can do this one has the universal grasp that is *logos*. Aristotle is not explicit here as to whether it is restricted to humans, but he is explicit that it is a simple function of repeated perceptions, of the same kind as those that animals with at least some capacity for memory are typically enjoying.

Still, we might feel that this does not adequately explain, any more than *phantasia* does, how we can pick out the salient forms from non-identical experiences and generalize to an essence or form that constitutes the rationale, or *logos*. But if, as we saw above, *phantasia* enables intelligent responses to a very small sample of tokens of a type, because it picks out and interprets relevant formal features even in a single sample, this would help to explain how stacking up experiences of the same type could yield a grasp of similarities that constitute a universal.

Aristotle is not explicit about where we are to draw the line between those animals in which the experience becomes one and implicitly universalized and those which just have particular memories of particular encounters. I do not think that we have to suppose that only humans have the capacity to become experienced in handling their repeated encounters with things of the same type.[71] Of course, Aristotle is trying to explain the source of the knowledge *we* need to get deductive sciences going; he needs to show that *humans* could indeed have access to knowledge of the right sort.[72] This does not require that he show that *only* humans have knowledge of the right sort. Rather, it will be more plausible that we do have it if it is a capacity that extends some way down the order of nature below us, being based on standard capacities common to a range of such animals.[73] The fact that the other animals do not actually produce deductive science may be to do with

---

[71] At the opening of the *Met.* 980ᵇ26–7 (quoted below in Ch. 5) Aristotle suggests that the non-human animals have a minimal share of experience (ἐμπειρίας δὲ μετέχει μικρόν).

[72] The principles in question appear to be equated with universal concepts, or perhaps more likely, grasp of the essences of things which generate and ground sound definitions from which deductive proofs can start. See Modrak, *Aristotle*, 164.

[73] I use the notion of an order of nature 'below' us by convention and for convenience, but note the arguments against the traditional notion of an evaluative *scala naturae* in Aristotle below, in Ch. 5.

other limitations, and not in any way with a failure to understand the world as made up of sets of things of the same kind, in the very way that we do.

Aristotle and Plato

It is often supposed that Aristotle is trying to provide a purely empiricist account of the grasp of concepts, which would contrast with Plato's idea that conceptual knowledge is a knowledge of the Forms, which (according to the theory of recollection) are encountered only in another life. It is worth noticing however, that the relation between Plato's version and Aristotle's version is not as simple as that summary might make it seem; nor are the two theories really at odds in their conclusions.

Let us start with Plato. According to the theory defended by Socrates in the *Phaedo*, at least as I understand it, we arrive in this world equipped with a capacity for recalling concepts of which we have had no direct experience in this world. Some things in this world are sufficiently like those Forms that they are capable of jogging our memory, reminding us of what we once saw in the disembodied state, even though at the same time they also strike us as inadequate likenesses of the originals. This capacity for seeing things in relation to Forms accounts for our shared conceptual map of the world, because we identify things in this world as tokens of a type, or as striving to instantiate a type. That is done on the basis of concepts that can only be explained (Socrates suggests) if all humans have experienced the Forms directly, and what appears to be concept acquisition in this life is merely a process of being dimly reminded of something buried in the forgotten regions of the soul. The myth in the *Phaedrus* seems to reflect the same thought, in its suggestion that all human beings must have obtained some glimpse of the Forms before birth, however fleeting and partial, since that is what enables us to see things as instances of a kind.[74]

---

[74] Pl. *Phdr.* 249b c. In my view this mechanism is supposed to explain conceptual capacities in all humans and not a small elite of philosophers, and it is supposed to be used in all ordinary discourse, since it explains the human capacity to see items in terms of the tricky concepts that are classically invoked as Forms, such as Equal, Beautiful, Large, and so on. In reading not just the *Phaedrus* in this way, but the *Phaedo* too, I disagree with Dominic Scott, *Recollection and Experience* (Cambridge: Cambridge University Press, 1995), but I think this is not the place to engage in a full debate on that issue. See Catherine Osborne, 'Perceiving particulars and recollecting the Forms in the Phaedo', *Proceedings of the Aristotelian Society*, 95 (1995): 211–33.

This means that, according to the recollection theory, the soul acquires concepts in a period of exposure to direct contact with the Forms, and it is in terms of those concepts that we interpret the input of the senses during the embodied life. The soul comes ready equipped with a capacity to see the current field of experience in terms of those Forms—sticky Forms which are stored deep in the soul from before birth.

It seems to me that Aristotle's version, which uses *phantasia* as a means of acquiring and deploying the concepts, has exactly the same structure as Plato's recollection motif. The same is true of the version in the wax tablet section of Plato's *Theaetetus*. But in both these latter cases the concepts (Forms) with which we currently interpret our environment are initially encountered in this life (with matter), not before birth (without matter), as in the *Phaedo* and the *Phaedrus*. Aristotle tries to answer the objection raised by Socrates in the *Phaedo*, to the effect that we could not have acquired the Form 'Equal' earlier in this life, since the first time we noticed that something was not quite equal, we already saw it in terms of equality.[75] Aristotle's response is only partly adequate: perception, he suggests, grasps the form without the matter, so we can get the pure form stashed into the soul as a result of perception.[76] We don't need to encounter bodiless forms in a bodiless life, he thinks, for the body is what gives us perception, and that is a mechanism structured to give us forms. Then *phantasia* (or, in the *Theaetetus*'s version, the wax tablet) will allow us to retain the form given in perception and use it again for identifying further types of the same sort, and thus for extracting and applying the universal, and hence engaging in deductive science.[77]

The response is only partly adequate, for it misses the point of Plato's demand that we must once have stocked our soul not from dirty material

---

[75] Pl. *Phd.* 75b.

[76] The idea of perception grasping the form without the matter is developed in *De an.* book 2. At *An. post.* 100^a17 Aristotle explains that perception is of the universal ($\kappa\alpha\theta\delta\lambda o\nu$), because although we see a particular man (Callias), what the perception grasps is man, the universal.

[77] Burnyeat's suggestion that Aristotle's use of the wax example at *De an.* 424^a17-24 is polemical against Plato seems to me to be mistaken (Burnyeat, 'Is an Aristotelian philosophy of mind still credible?', 21). For both thinkers do exactly the same thing with the wax: viz. take an imprint from uninterpreted forms in the world. Both use the imprint to convey the idea that the soul is receptive of forms; both use previously imprinted forms as the tool to recognize subsequent imprints of the same form (though Aristotle names this process *phantasia* and restricts it to some animals). Burnyeat is incorrect in suggesting that the *Theaetetus* uses the process of stamping the wax block for judgement. Imprints in the block are perceptions or the records of perceptions: judgement comes from assimilating one already imprinted and not yet obliterated perceptual print to something external, newly encountered outside the block.

objects but from a direct exposure to the splendid Forms. That is, our problem with acquiring the form from earthly experience was not that the objects of experience are dirtied by matter, and are particular. If that were the problem, then Aristotle's method of abstracting the form from the matter in perception and generating general ideas by way of multiple encounters with particulars would do. But Plato's point was rather that we can invoke a perfect form, one that we have not encountered since our birth, to identify an imperfect particular as failing to live up to an ideal. We can recognize the inequality, or shortfall in equality, of some object even without ever having encountered a case of genuine, or even approximate, equality. Indeed, Plato would say, most of the Forms we think with are never encountered neat enough in the objects round about us to give us the concepts that we use to classify things.[78]

Aristotle has no answer to this challenge. He assumes that our concepts are derived by abstraction from multiple particular examples, and that we can extract from the particulars a general account of what form they all share, on the assumption that they do all share it, and that the form we thus acquire is nothing over or above what we encounter in objects of that kind. He cannot, therefore, satisfy Plato's quest for an explanation of how we can see the objects as aspiring to something better, something that we have never encountered in this life.

But despite that difference, Plato's method of establishing concepts in our mind is fundamentally the same mechanism as we have attributed to Aristotle on the basis of the passages in the *De anima* and the *Posterior Analytics*: namely, some mode of direct awareness of an archetype, combined with memory. Plato thinks that one exposure to the archetype or Form is sufficient to lodge the form in our mind, but then so too does Aristotle if I am right about how *phantasia* enables us to construe perception in the light of just one example previously encountered. Aristotle's reference to multiple memories seems to be for the purpose of explaining our ability to generalize rather than the ability to identify salient forms in objects around us.

So, effectively, Aristotle tries to provide, via *phantasia*, a substitute for Plato's direct encounter with the Forms, so that he can use the same model of concept acquisition, but derive it from sensory experience in this life alone. Yet it seems as if we still need to borrow from Plato the thought that our soul comes already equipped with a predisposition to slot the forms it encounters

---

[78] I take this to be a crucial claim for the recollection argument in the *Phaedo*. See Osborne, 'Perceiving particulars'.

here into pre-cut conceptual spaces, so that, for instance, we come out with a concept of exact equality (which we see typical examples coming close to, but failing to achieve), rather than a concept of *less than equal* and a concept of *more than equal* (which *exactly equal sets* fail to achieve); and so that we emerge with a concept of *beauty* which the mediocre fails to achieve, not a concept of *mediocrity* as the ideal to which beautiful things fail to live up. To get such a structure into our thinking without innate ideas, and retain an objective realist structure to conceptual knowledge, was Plato's great achievement.

For both Plato and Aristotle these conceptual capacities are continuous between humans and other animals. In Plato, at least occasionally, the difference between human and animal mental capacities can be explained by reference to how well one got to view the Forms before birth.[79] For Aristotle it depends on how well your memory can retain and store forms from experience. Neither thinker builds in a strong divide between those animals which can bring concepts to bear on their understanding of the world and those that cannot.

---

[79] See the myth of the charioteer in the *Phaedrus* for a picturesque re-creation of the reasons why we have differing abilities in this respect, esp. 248d, etc.

5

On the Disadvantages of Being a Complex Organism: Aristotle and the *scala naturae*

In the last chapter we saw that neither Plato nor Aristotle needs to insert an unbridgeable gulf between the mental capacities of humans and those of other animals. The source of conceptual and linguistic content is, for both thinkers, a simple imprinting process that is continuous with the process by which simpler animals acquire habitual understanding of the world around them.[1] Our focus in this chapter will, once again, be Aristotle, and our question will be whether Aristotle does in fact think that human life, and its complex range of psychological and intellectual functions, is superior to the simpler life of more basic organisms. Does Aristotle have a *scala naturae* as he is usually taken to have? And if so, are we at the top? My answer will be 'No' to both questions: and in particular 'No' to the second because where there is no ladder, there is no top rung to be on.

The Inferiority Complex

It is by nature that living creatures are born having perception, but some of them have no innate capacity for forming memories from perception, while others do. And for this reason the latter animals are more intelligent and more capable of learning than those who are unable to remember—some are intelligent but not

---

[1] This summary oversimplifies the situation in Plato, since animal souls are ones that have achieved even less vision of the Forms than the least well-managed human souls (like, actually none at all), and in this sense there is one fundamental difference. Human souls can at least vaguely recall at least one poor-quality glimpse of a Form from a relatively recent occasion, whereas animal souls might not have had their vision recharged for many generations (*Phdr.* 249b). But still, there is nothing fundamentally different about the soul's capacity. The difference is in its currently accessible conceptual content.

able to learn, if they are unable to hear sound (e.g. bees and any other animals of that kind) while those that learn are the ones that have hearing in addition to memory. Thus the other animals live for the most part by appearances[2] and memories, but also minimally acquire experience, while the human race also lives by skill and calculations. (*Met.* A 980[a]27–[b]28)

Aristotle, writing the opening sentences of the *Metaphysics*, seeks to explain why human beings pursue knowledge in a way that animals do not—although he immediately goes on to comment on the difference between experience, skill, and knowledge, implying that *for human beings* it is worthwhile to achieve wisdom and scientific understanding, and it would not be sufficient to stop at the level of mere perception or experience, as it would be for other animals. But he does not seem to rate the abilities of humans higher as a result. The passage does not have any practical or evaluative motive. Aristotle's concern here is simply to characterize the desire for abstract knowledge that appears to be peculiarly human, and to stress the *continuity* of this ability with capacities exhibited not only by the more intelligent animals, but to some degree by every living creature that has perception, even of the most elementary kind.

Although this passage comes from the *Metaphysics*, the thinking it expresses is familiar from Aristotle's biological inquiries, and more particularly from his works on psychology. It also relates to the passage of the *Posterior Analytics* that we examined in the previous chapter.[3] The notion that what we call 'soul' is found in all animals and plants, varying only in how extensive is the range of capacities exhibited by each species, is central to the *De anima*. Thus it is classic Aristotelian theory to claim that perception, delivered through at least one of the five senses, is common to all animals however simple, and that, as we saw in the last chapter, the same basic perceptual faculty is ultimately the foundation of human capacities for abstract knowledge, which presuppose the same elementary abilities together with various additional facilities for storing and handling the data.

It might seem odd that, in this passage at the opening of the *Metaphysics*, bees are said to be incapable of learning because they cannot hear sounds. Apparently an otherwise intelligent animal is constrained by lacking some

---

[2] *phantasiai*, 'fantastic presentations'. See above Ch. 4, where I argue that *phantasia* is what Aristotle invokes to account for the animals' ability to configure their experience and thereby envisage objects as items of interest. [3] Arist. *An. post.* B 19. See above pp. 93–6.

sense-organs (assuming that the bee's lack of hearing is due to the absence of the necessary organs of hearing, ears or whatever).[4]

But the passage is not isolated or out of line with what Aristotle says elsewhere. Bees figure in the *Parts of Animals* too as creatures of unusual intelligence, and there we are told that their cold thin non-blood fluid is particularly good for perception. This accounts for their intelligence.[5] Because of this, the bee is said to be more intelligent than many blooded animals.[6] But presumably this acute perception does not include hearing, and on the issue of learning and deafness, Aristotle explains in *De sensu* that the sense of hearing is crucially important for learning (*mathēsis*), because in order to learn, one needs to hear spoken sounds with linguistic content.[7] He seems to think that hearing is more important than sight for intellectual development, whereas sight is more directly useful for survival. Perhaps this talk of hearing and learning among animals is linked to the fact that some animals recognize and respond to audible commands, in the manner of trained dogs and horses.[8] Aristotle's claims about the bee in the *Parts of Animals* seem to imply that, in this case at least, we encounter an animal that is unusually intelligent, perhaps more intelligent than dogs and horses, even if the latter, in virtue of their possession of both memory and hearing together, are in some sense more capable of what he calls 'learning'.[9] Indeed, the sequence of thought in the passage from the *Metaphysics* quoted at the beginning of this section does imply that the bee has memory,[10] as well as a peculiarly fine perceptual faculty, and it seems to follow that it would certainly be capable of learning, were it able to hear.

---

[4] Not all animals that hear have ears in the sense of outward flaps, but they would need either ears or some organ of hearing with the necessary auditory canals to the brain or heart, which however may not be visible (*Hist. an.* 492^{a}24; *Part. an.* 656^{a}34–^{b}17; 657^{a}18). Since Aristotle is prepared to grant that fish and dolphins hear, although he cannot trace their organs for this, on the basis of their responses to sound (*Hist. an.* 533^{a}31–4^{a}12), his claim that the bee does not hear is presumably founded on observation of its responses.   [5] *Part. an.* 648^{a}2–9.

[6] Ibid. 648^{a}6, 650^{b}26.   [7] *Sens.* 437^{a}10–17.

[8] cf. *Hist. an.* 608^{a}17–20. Here Aristotle observes that learning in such animals as can understand human utterances requires not just hearing the noises, but also 'discerning the distinctions in the signs'.

[9] For the references see above, n. 4.

[10] The possession of memory ought to mean that bees do employ *phantasia* (on which see above Ch. 4 and Osborne, 'Aristotle an the fantastic abilities').

The Ladder of Life

Aristotle examines the functions of the soul in living things starting from the bottom up, as it were, in his treatise on the soul (*De anima*). Some functions, he reckons, are common to plants and animals alike, and these we might think of as the most basic functions of life: nutrition, growth, reproduction. Then there is perception, which belongs to animals, not plants, and which comes in various forms, of which you can't have the more advanced kinds without the more basic kinds. The most basic kind is touch, and some animals get by with just that. Beyond perception there is one further critical faculty: namely, intellect. A different kind of function is locomotion, again for animals, though not all. This presupposes appetite or inclination (*orexis*), which is dependent on certain aspects of the critical faculties (i.e. perception and *phantasia*).

It is tempting to talk as though these functions were ordered in a hierarchy. I used the phrase 'from the bottom up' of Aristotle's treatment of functions of the soul, and I talked of 'more advanced kinds' in the case of the sequence of sense faculties. But although there clearly is an order of some sort here, in that the later members of the sequence presuppose the existence of the ones treated earlier, we need to be careful not to think of it as an order of increasing value. It is true that the functions that are more generally shared are basic, in that you need them even if you have nothing else. That makes Aristotle's order of treatment, starting with nutrition and reproduction, a sensible one for explaining the functions of the soul. But the idea that the more exclusive or specialized functions are 'more advanced' is not warranted. It is a way of thinking that we easily slip into because we cannot help thinking of simple creatures with few functions as primitive, lacking in the developed features that belong to species that have moved further along the path of evolution. That model is not Aristotle's model, and we need to be careful not to import it into his biology. For Aristotle there is no such thing as evolution: the species are fixed, and each fully formed member of a species has all the functions that it is good for such a thing to have, so as to live a full life being what it is. There is no sense that the members of that species are worse off, or less well adapted, for not yet having become something else (as there is in evolutionary theory).[11]

In what follows I shall attempt to explain why Aristotle's view of nature as an order of increasing complexity does not imply that humans are better, more advanced, higher, or in any other way superior in the order of nature than less complex creatures. For it is only modern biology (or a popular understanding of modern biology) that takes greater complexity to be a mark of superiority.[12]

The Non-Hierarchical Hierarchy

For Aristotle, human beings have the full range of functions of the soul, including intellect, along with the full range of perceptual organs, and all the available processing mechanisms for the data given in perception, appetite, desire, and goal-oriented locomotion.[13] This fact accounts for humanity's distinctive manner of life and the ways in which it differs from the manner of life of creatures with a more restricted range of capacities. It is correspondingly reflected in human ethical priorities, because human life has a distinctive purpose and end, which cannot be fulfilled without the exercise of the more complex human manner of life. So the more complex life is essential for a human life to be a full and happy one, achieving what humans are capable of achieving.

---

[11] There are a number of temptations to hierarchical thinking implicit in evolutionary thinking. One is the temptation to think that a more basic or simple creature is primitive or lacking in some features that others have already achieved by more successful adaptation. Another is thinking that evolution is always for the better, so that those who have survived are in some sense better equipped or more able. A third is the temptation to think that complexity is superior to simplicity, because complex organisms arrive on the scene later than simple ones. None of these are proper tenets of evolutionary theory (though they seem to be widespread in popular thinking about biology). On the contrary, simple organisms are often very well fitted for survival; evolution produces mutations that are less fitted for survival as well as improvements; highly evolved creatures often die out because they are specialized; there is nothing inherently valuable about complexity; and in any case there is no reason to think that survival is a measure of value.

[12] On the danger of implicitly endorsing the evaluative motifs in popular evolutionary thinking, and the pervasive idea that man is always at the top of something, see Mary Midgley, *Beast and Man* (London: Methuen, 1978), 145–64.

[13] This claim is implicit in the *De anima*, though Aristotle nowhere actually says so. He does attempt to show that there are no further perceptual faculties that we do not possess (*De an.* 3. 1). The nearest to an explicit claim is that at *Hist. an.* 608^{b}6–7: 'for humanity has a nature that is complete', though this relates more to the possession of the full range of moral character traits, than to mental abilities.

In theory Aristotle should, if he is to be consistent, identify a corresponding connection between the strengths and capacities of each other animal species and the distinctively fulfilling lifestyle for that species. The fulfilling life for a pig would not and should not include many of the things that are essential to the fulfilling life for a human being, because pigs don't have those capacities and goals, and were never meant to do so. In each case both the goals themselves and the corresponding characteristic lifestyle of the animal ought to be species-specific, and nothing will be deduced directly from these species-specific functions about how the quality or value of the life of one species relates to the quality or value of life of members of another species. Nor ought we to be able to discover any rules about how we should treat other animals or how they should behave towards us, since there is no way to measure the goals of one species against those of another in a case of conflict. The cumulative structure of plant and animal souls, which Aristotle describes in the *De anima*, does not in itself have any ethical implications.

In the sequence of soul functions in the *De anima*, there are some capacities which all animals share. In respect of those capacities, all animals, humans included, share the corresponding goals and values. Humans, no less than plants, seek nourishment and reproduction; other animals besides humans explore their environment and use their capacities for locomotion and perception to acquire information. The human quest for abstract knowledge, with which Aristotle opens the *Metaphysics*, is, there, simply identified as an extension of that habit of seeking information about the environment that is common in all animals. In that respect there is nothing particularly special or distinctive about human inquiry: nothing makes our manner of seeking information and carrying out our plans more important, especially good, or superior to those of others. Our investigations are not better ones, or directed at better goals: they are just our inquiries: they belong to our life plans, based on our values and aspirations. Our values and aspirations reflect our capacities and goals. The more capacities we have, the more distinct goals we have to pursue to achieve success. So we may have more things to do, but it does not follow that they are better things to do. There is no reason—not so far—to suppose that the goals of other species are inferior to our own.

That, at least, is how it should be. There are some apparent counter-examples in Aristotle's political works which might suggest otherwise, when it comes to the relation between humans and other animals. For instance at *Politics* 1. 5 Aristotle says that for domestic animals (as for slaves) it is better, safer, and natural to be under the control of a human master. But here too we need to see that the point is species-specific. What justifies the mutually beneficial arrangement whereby a beast is in symbiotic relationship with a human master is that it enables the animal to live well and to fulfil its own best nature.[14] It is not that the purpose is solely for the fulfilment of the human side of the partnership, although it is also for that: the animal owner is better able to achieve his potential in partnership with the ploughing ox, and the ox is better able to achieve his potential in partnership with the crop-growing farmer. Furthermore, the arrangement is beneficial to the farmer in giving him the opportunity to exercise the human capacity for ruling. This would be a further reason for Aristotle to recommend the practice without compromising his grasp of the idea that practices are good just in so far as they realize a creature's potential in accordance with what is best in the nature of each participant.[15]

There is another famous passage in the last book of the *Nicomachean Ethics* which is more problematic. It suggests that there is no such thing as happiness for the non-human animals. Aristotle is arguing that the activity that above all constitutes happiness for human beings is contemplation (*theōria*), because this is the activity that we share with the gods. The conclusion is supported by two arguments: one to show that the gods do engage in contemplation (and nothing else)[16] and the other to show that the closest approximation to that activity in humans is the happiest life for humans. The latter argument is based on the premiss that animals do not enjoy any kind of happiness. Since they do not enjoy happiness, and the one activity that they do not share with men is contemplation, this indicates that the activity that is missing, the one which the beasts do not share with human beings, is the crucial one for happiness.[17]

And the activity that is most closely akin to this one [sc. contemplation] is the happiest among human activities. Another sign of this is the fact that the other animals do not partake of happiness, being completely devoid of this kind of activity. For gods, their entire life is blessed; for humans [their life is blessed] just to the extent that some semblance of this kind of activity exists; but of other

---

[14] *Arist. Pol.* 1254^b 10–14.   [15] See further below, appendix to this chapter.
[16] Arist. *Eth. Nic.* 1178^b 8–22.   [17] Ibid. 1178^b 24–32.

animals, none is happy, since it does not engage in contemplation in any way. As far as contemplation extends, that far happiness extends too, and those to whom contemplation belongs more, to them also being happy (belongs more): not accidentally but in respect of the contemplation. (*Eth. Nic.* X. 8, 1178^{b}22–8)

It is worth taking care to understand exactly how this argument works. It is not designed to show that the beasts cannot be happy, because they do not engage in contemplation. Rather, the fact that they are not happy is used as a premiss, in order to show that the missing activity is the contemplative life. The suggestion is that we can observe an exact coincidence between the occurrence of happiness and the occurrence of contemplation, and between the degree of contemplation and the degree of happiness, and this suggests that the connection is not accidental, but that the happiness accrues just in virtue of the contemplation.

If follows, then, that Aristotle takes the animals' lack of happiness to be a self-evident fact, not deduced from their lack of contemplation but interestingly coincident with it, from which we can discover that their lack of happiness is indeed due to their lack of contemplation. First, then, we must be aware that no animals are happy: this cannot be a matter of dispute, since then we could not infer that contemplation was the only route to happiness. Only then, when we have conceded that they are clearly not happy, can we ask why they are not happy.

This line of thought must surely strike us as odd. How can we take it for granted that the beasts are not, and never would be 'happy', so securely that this could serve as an uncontroversial premiss in an argument about the nature of human happiness and that of the divine? It seems clear that the notion of *eudaimonia* that Aristotle has in mind cannot be the one that is typically implied by the word 'happiness' in English. Nothing in our concept of happiness makes it inconceivable that irrational animals might enjoy happiness. Clearly there is something in the connection between *eudaimonia* and the notions of divinity (as implied by the *daimon* element of the word) and of 'blessedness' (evidenced by the interchangeability of *eudaimonia* and *makariotes* in the chapter in which this passage occurs) which makes it conceptually obvious that it is not part of the flourishing life of a beast (however much it does what beasts are best at doing) to achieve *eudaimonia*. In other words, it seems that we should not use the word '*eudaimonia*' or 'happiness' to equate to *success*, for any creature, regardless of species (and then infer that failure to achieve *eudaimonia* is failure to achieve a good life). Rather, we should read *eudaimonia* or blessedness as specific terms, referring to the specific kind of success that counts as a good life in those creatures for whom *eudaimonia* is happiness (if you like). In other animals it will not be *eudaimonia* that counts as happiness, but whatever is the fulfilment of that creature's best capacities. It does not seem, then, that we should deny them the right to the term 'happiness' *as we use that term*; nor should we suppose, in denying them the term *eudaimonia*, that we are depriving them of a life that would have been good for them. A human life that is lacking in *eudaimonia* may be a disaster, to be remedied by engaging more fully in some approximation to divine contemplation and exercising the *nous* a bit more, but it is no disaster for a snail who has no *nous* to exercise and no divine aspirations to boot.[18]

For these reasons I do not think that the passage in the *Nicomachean Ethics* counts against the view that all creatures are capable of success in their enterprises. Nor does it count against the view that other animals thereby achieve what we should call 'happiness', although that happiness does not coincide with *eudaimonia* as it does in humans and in the gods. Nor does it count against the view that the successful life for each creature is species-specific, reflecting the best goals and aspirations of that species, not those of any other species—except, apparently, in the case of humans, for whom it seems that happiness lies in the achievement of goals that transcend the species, by the exercise of a capacity that is divine, not merely human.

Thus what we might initially think of as a hierarchy of psychological capacities in plants and animals, as described in the *De anima*, is not accompanied by any privileging of the functions at the further end of the sequence, or of the characteristically human functions, except as they fulfil or complete capacities found in the other species. The series of capacities does not in itself indicate anything about how we ought to behave towards other species, about whether we should use them for our own ends, about the worthiness of their pursuits, or about the worthiness of our own pursuits.

---

[18] The systematic connection in Aristotle's ethical work between human well-being and activities that approximate to *theōria* has been convincingly explored in Gabriel Richardson Lear, *Happy Lives and the Highest Good: An Essay on Aristotle's* Nicomachean Ethics (Princeton: Princeton University Press, 2004). Her treatment of this passage is on pp. 194–5: she invokes it in explaining the link between approximation to contemplation and human happiness, and that is fine as far as it goes; but since animal happiness is not her topic, she does not address the issue of whether the contemplative goals are meaningful as goals for animals at all.

Indeed, if what we mean by a 'hierarchy' is a series in which some living things are thought of as *higher* on the scale or superior, and thereby dominant and more worthy of respect, then it must be a mistake to think of Aristotle's sequence of psychological capacities as a hierarchy at all.[19] Perhaps this seems a bold claim, since we have become so accustomed to categories such as 'higher animals' and 'lower species' that we scarcely think twice when they are used even by supposedly value-free modern biological and psychological scientists. Perhaps we might have supposed that this entrenched picture of a *scala naturae*, humans at the top and animals of decreasing complexity at lower and lower rungs on the ladder, might ultimately derive from Aristotle. But in fact this is evidently not the case. If we look at Aristotle's own account of the range of psychological capacities, we find that he never once uses terms such as 'higher' or 'lower', or 'superior' and 'inferior'. Characteristically, he observes that 'some animals' have a certain capacity, while 'other living things' do not, but he never claims that the capacity that they lack is a higher or superior capacity—except perhaps in the case of *nous* which, as we have already noticed, is peculiar and the source of the peculiar theoretical 'happiness' of humans and gods. But that is not strictly a natural human capacity, but rather a divine one; I'll return to it in due course.

So comparative evaluations of the capacities found in plants and in human or non-human animals seem entirely absent from Aristotle's discussion, at least so long as we exclude the faculty of *nous*. On the contrary, when he discusses the sequence of psychological capacities, Aristotle's interest is in the *cumulative* nature of the sequence: he compares it to that of the geometrical shapes, in so far as later members of the sequence presuppose, and build upon, earlier members:

The circumstances in connection with the soul are just like those of shapes: for it is invariably the case that the previous one exists potentially in the subsequent one, both in the case of shapes and in the case of creatures with soul. For example the triangle in the quadrilateral and the nutritive soul in the perceptive soul. Hence in each case we have to enquire what soul each has, for example what is the soul of a plant, what is the soul of a human being, what is the soul of a beast, but we must also investigate what explains why they are in a sequence in this way; for

[19] *Pace* David W. Hamlyn, *Aristotle's* De anima *Books II and III*, ed. J. L. Ackrill, Clarendon Aristotle Series (Oxford: Clarendon Press, 1968), pp. xi, 88, 93–4; K. V. Wilkes, '*Psuchê* versus mind' in *Essays on Aristotle's* De Anima, (ed. Nussbaum and Rorty) 109–28, 110.

the perceptive does not exist without the nutritive, but the nutritive is detached from the perceptive in plants. And again without the sense of touch, none of the other perceptual faculties exists, but touch exists without the rest; for many of the animals have neither hearing nor a sense of smell at all. And of those that are perceptive, some have a locomotive ability and some do not. And finally, and fewest of all, reasoning and thought. For among mortal creatures those that have reasoning also have all the rest, but those that have each of the other capacities do not all have reasoning, but some do not even have *phantasia*,[20] while others live by this alone. (*De an.* 2. 3, 414ᵇ28–415ᵃ11)

Thus, just as a more complex geometrical shape incorporates the simpler ones, but not vice versa, so the capacities are not randomly distributed, such that some animals have some and others have others, but they form a series in which each member presupposes all the previous ones. For modern commentators and translators it now seems virtually impossible to write about this series without slipping into terminology that implies that later members in the series are higher, superior, more advanced, or more complex.[21] But of these only the last term would correlate in any way with Aristotle's image of the 'nested sequence'[22] of geometrical figures, in that the later figures are indeed more complex, and, in virtue of that complexity, contain and incorporate the earlier ones in the sequence.

Complexity, however, is not by itself a term of value. On the contrary, for Aristotle, as for his contemporaries, it is normal to think that what is pure, simple, non-composite, and primary is of superior value compared to what is composed out of multitudinous facets. Just as, in the sphere of knowledge, Aristotle thinks of the primary simple concepts, or elementary propositions, from which proofs can be derived as the *archai* (principles: the

---

[20] On this capacity see Ch. 4 above.

[21] 'The higher functions': Sorabji, *Animal Minds*, 9; 'The higher functions are dependent on the lower'; 'sight is presumably at the top': Hamlyn, Aristotle De anima 88. 'The lowest', 'next above it', 'the highest faculty', 'man and any higher beings', 'lower forms of life': W. K. C. Guthrie, *A History of Greek Philosophy*, vi: *Aristotle: An Encounter* (Cambridge: Cambridge University Press, 1981), 285–7. '*Psuchai* can be thought of as pyramidal in structure, hierarchically organized in such a way that all the higher reaches of the pyramid presuppose the lower. At the simplest and lowest level we find the plants…'; 'the higher, the animal the more diversity and range are found in its… capacities'; 'lower capacities subserve the higher ones'; 'the more complex the organism, the more intricate the interlocking'; 'the more basic ("lower") levels of the *psuche* make the exercise of the higher ones possible': Wilkes, '*Psuchê* versus mind', 110–11. Notably this language is absent from Gareth B. Matthews, 'De anima 2. 2–4 and the meaning of *life*' in *Essays on Aristotle's De anima*, (ed. Nussbaum and O Rorty) 185–94.

[22] Matthews' term: Matthews, 'De anima 2. 2–4 and the meaning of *life*', 191.

term connotes both origin and supremacy) and as more intelligible than the conclusions derived from them, so also in geometry—as in the example he gives here—the elementary simple shapes form the starting-point from which complexes can be derived. Derivation is a downward process from simplicity and intelligibility to dependence and composition.

In the same way, then, the functions of sensation and thought, being dependent on the elementary life faculty of nutrition and reproduction, and presupposing both it and the prior members of their own sequence, are derivative and complex. Animals that have these functions are more dependent on a greater range of derivative mechanisms. Aristotle would not, and does not, find their position in the life sequence a position of pre-eminence.

Nous and the Divine

Indeed, this observation might cast some light on Aristotle's apparent ambivalence about the nature of the intellectual capacity that he calls *nous* (intellect or insight). This faculty is attributed not only to human beings, in which case it does indeed presuppose all the life faculties that come earlier in Aristotle's nested sequence, but also, apparently, to divine beings too, including perhaps the first thinking thing that moves the world. Yet the divine is not an ensouled body, *empsuchon*, though it can be classed as a living thing, *zōon*. It is not a thing with a soul, because it lacks (it has no need of) the nutritive and perceptual faculties of mortal souls. Such functions are the actualities of organic bodies in their potentially functioning state. The divine does not have any organs, and it therefore does not have any of the functionality of those organs. This means that, for the divine alone, *nous* will actually occur *without* the prior members of the nested sequence.

Aristotle says little or nothing about how this anomaly can be reconciled with his notion that the life functions are a cumulative set. Indeed, it is only occasionally that he even hints at the existence of something beyond the human in the sequence.[23] But in the third book of the *De anima* he struggles to preserve some kind of *nous* that is pure, simple, and unmixed (*De an.* 3. 5), and separable—again rather to the surprise of recent commentators, given the general trend of his psychological thinking in which functions

[23] Arist. *De an.* 414[b]19, 402[b]7.

of the soul are supervenient upon the physical processes in some suitable bodily equipment. Even if various possible kinds of matter can be equally efficacious as the material for such equipment, it still seems that there must be some matter, some bodily equipment. This makes it odd to claim that there could be a certain kind of mental function that is realized in *no matter whatsoever*, at least for gods and perhaps even for humans too, in so far as they manage to attain some semblance of divine capacities.

Many problems remain in interpreting these aspects of Aristotle's work, and I do not intend to explore the details here. But I think that it might be enlightening to observe the parallel between gods and plants. The more complex activities of the soul, with their complicated organs and multiple functions, are derivative and dependent, in so far as they presuppose animals with a host of other functions that are earlier in the nested sequence. You can't have a body with vision unless it also has touch, and it won't have touch unless it also has growth and nutrition. Such a complexity of functions brings with it a complexity of needs and a life highly dependent upon the provision of a large range of opportunities and supplies. The more complex you are, the more improbable that you will achieve the kind of bliss that is total fulfilment of your goals. Plants, by contrast, have just one simple function, nutrition (taken to include growth and reproduction), and their needs are easily satisfied. Gods, however, are just as simple as plants, only their one function is thinking, and is simply achieved in a life of pure thought.

For this reason we have to suppose that intellect is not dependent upon the other faculties that were described as having the structure of a nested sequence. Intellect can and does exist without the others. But, unlike nutrition, intellect is supposed to need no organs. It evidently does not fall under the generalization that functions of soul are actualities of an organic body that has life potentially, and in this sense the gods are not at all like plants, and the intellect is not a part of the soul. This, I think, explains why *nous* comes to need special treatment in Aristotle's account. But this rationale is badly obscured if we understand Aristotle to be defining a hierarchy in which the later faculties are *superior* or higher or more honourable than the simpler ones, or in which the more intelligent animals are *superior* or higher up a scale than the plants and sponges.

In fact, the sequence is a *cumulative* sequence, but not a hierarchy. Humans live as good a life as sponges do—only that, unlike sponges, humans also depend upon an incredible array of additional complex perceptual, locomotive, and intellectual faculties, which they need to exercise if they are to achieve their best in life. This makes it much harder to be a successful member of the species if one is human than if one is a sponge. Hence, to ensure that gods can be permanently successful, the gods must have goals that are as easy to achieve as the goals of a sponge.

Worthy and Unworthy Subjects

Does Aristotle *never* use evaluative terms? Although he does not say, or ever imply, that the series of living things is a hierarchy, or that some animals are higher up a scale than others, he does, on a few occasions, speak of animals as more or less worthy (*timios*).[24] In chapter 5 of *De partibus animalium* 1, Aristotle's famous hymn in praise of biology exhorts us to study the whole range of animal species:

It remains to speak of animal nature, and as far as possible to leave out neither what is more unworthy nor what is more worthy. For even in those which are aesthetically unpleasing, nevertheless nature's creative work provides unrivalled delights in research for those who are naturally philosophical and able to discover the explanations. ... Hence we must not make a fuss, like children, at the study of the unworthier animals, for there is something wonderful in all natural things. (*Part. an.* 1. 5, 645ᵃ5–10, 15–18)

In this passage it seems that the 'unworthier' beasts are those that are revolting in appearance, those that we, or children in particular, might find distasteful to handle and investigate. Aristotle is surely not making any theoretical classification of beasts as worthy or unworthy, at any rate not in terms of their mental capacities. Evidently his reference to the 'more worthy' and 'less worthy' simply alludes to a popular prejudice based on the physical features of the specimens. Perhaps he is dissociating himself from that prejudice. Instead, Aristotle would say that dissecting the hornet or the jelly fish is just as rewarding as testing auditory responses in new-born lambs. We like handling lambs. We recoil from hornets and jelly fish. But

[24] The word *timios* is clearly an evaluative term, and one probably in popular use for ranking animal species by how impressive or admirable they are. Compare Aristotle's report of Anaxagoras's theory of 'mind'. Anaxagoras, says Aristotle, has mind belong to all the animals 'both great and small, both worthy and more unworthy'. (*De an.* 404ᵇ4).

our preferences are irrational and not conducive to good scientific results. From the point of view of research, the supposedly 'less worthy' animals are just as worthy subjects of inquiry.

Yet this may not be all that there is to it. Aristotle certainly does have some prejudices. The passage just quoted follows immediately upon a passage distinguishing two branches of nature study and endorsing some grounds for preferring the branch that relates to unchanging eternal entities:

Among things established by nature one lot are ingenerate and imperishable and exist for all time, while the other lot partake of development and decay. The result is that less research is open to us concerning the former which are worthy and divine; for indeed precious few of the things one might investigate about them, and about which we long to know, is evident by way of perception. But we get on rather better as regards knowing about perishable plants and animals, because of our shared home; anyone who wanted to put in sufficient effort might gather many things concerning each family of things that exist.

But either kind has its charm. Regarding the first lot, even if we have only slight contact with them, nevertheless because of the worth of the knowledge it is more pleasing than all the things in our realm, just as getting a chance glimpse of our loved ones, and just a small part, is more delightful than full and accurate vision of a whole lot of other vast things. But in the second case knowing more of them and better gives us the highest grade of science, and their nearness to us and the greater familiarity of their nature is some compensation vis à vis the philosophy concerning the divine things. But since we have already covered the first class of entities and stated what is apparent to us, it remains to speak of animal nature. (*Part. an.* I. 5, 644^{b}23–45^{a}5)

Although Aristotle is not saying that the study of perishable nature, on which he is currently engaged, has no value, he does grant that its subject-matter is less splendid than the subject-matter of the alternative kind of natural science: namely, the permanent imperishable natural entities, the subject-matter of astronomy. Aristotle's current biological investigation has advantages only in the relative accessibility of its evidence, and hence in the quality of the scientific knowledge that is achieved, but not in the status of its subject-matter.

Here, then, Aristotle explicitly grades the items in the natural world and evaluates one group as more honourable than another. But notice that this is a simple two-class system, in which the *whole* of the first group, the imperishable entities of astronomy, are the worthier ones, and the *whole*

of the second group, plants and animals including humankind, are the
unworthy ones, the study of which is a rather humdrum affair. Thus there
is a distinction between more and less worthy beings, but mankind falls
into the lower class, with the rest of earthly nature, and there is no grading
within those mortal things, which are all alike, united by their coming into
being and passing away.

Given this simple dichotomy, we can now understand Aristotle's vague
allusion at *De an.* 414^{b}18−19 to the possibility that *nous* might belong not
only to humans but to some others:

But some animals have, in addition to these [sc. various kinds of perception and
phantasia] the faculty for moving from place to place as well, and others also have
the thinking faculty and *nous*, as for example human beings and if there is anything
else of this kind, or more worthy. (*De an.* 414^{b}16−19)

'If there is anything else of this kind, or more worthy', should not be taken
to imply that Aristotle already rates *humans* as worthy or honourable, or
that he rates them worthy on account of possessing *nous*. Mentioning that
something else is 'more worthy' does not imply that it is more worthy
than something that is already 'worthy'. On the contrary, I am suggesting,
humans, being animals, are not the sort of thing to qualify for the term
'worthy'. Humans and worms alike fall into the class of the less worthy,
regardless of whether they too possess some kind of *nous*. Perhaps some
of the worthiness would rub off on to humans from the fact that they
have *nous* and *nous* is associated with the divine and unchanging world of
the gods and the stars. But if so, such worthiness as accrues to the human
race does not come from its possession of the great array of more complex
psychological functions that are characteristic of its position at the far end
of the sequence of plants and animals. It comes from something that is not
strictly a psychological function at all.

The Dim and the Dumb

We might be tempted to look for value judgements about the inferiority
of other species within the animal kingdom in *De partibus animalium* 4. 10.
There Aristotle observes that the human race is the only species to stand
upright, and that the upright posture is due to the fact that humanity's
nature and essence is divine (*Part. an.* 686^{a}28). This means that in order

to fulfil their function properly, human beings need to have upper parts lightweight (so as not to hinder the processes of thinking and of the common sense, as a result of having too much weight at the top pressing down on the central parts, where the heart and inner sense-organ are located).[25] Aristotle goes on to classify all other creatures, apart from *Homo sapiens*, as 'dwarfish' (*nanōdēs*).[26]

One might imagine that Aristotle meant that the other creatures were stunted or deformed, and not as nature meant them to be, as though man was the only creature that was made properly. The term *nanōdēs* functions as a technical term in Aristotle's biological vocabulary. It is used to refer to the arrangement whereby one has disproportionate weight and stature in the upper part of the trunk, and inadequate parts below, so that an upright posture is not realistic. In such creatures, Aristotle says, their bodies inevitably fall forward towards the ground, and hence for the sake of health and safety, nature provides them with front feet, rather than the arms and hands with which we are equipped at that point. So the horizontal posture in quadrupeds is not designed for a purpose, but rather is the foreseeable consequence of the dwarfish proportions of the body; and the four-footed structure is then a solution, designed to ensure that creatures with these 'dwarf-like' proportions can function safely.

This line of thought seems to be rather surprising in Aristotle. It would fit better with Plato's story in the *Timaeus*, in which quadrupeds and other many-footed beasts are the result of deformed generations born after the first race of humans had ceased to practise philosophy.[27] But for Aristotle, at least as we normally think of his biological theories, there is no such evolution of species, and quadrupeds are not failed human beings. The heavy chest and horizontal posture cannot be a deformity, since deformities occur when nature's design is accidentally unfinished or fails. If these creatures regularly have the horizontal posture, that must be how nature intends them to be.[28] Nor does it prevent them from functioning effectively, since clearly the

---

[25] For the location of the sense-organ in the heart, see *Part. an.* 647^{a}25 and *De motu an.* 702^{b}20. Unlike Plato's *Timaeus*, which located the intellect in the head and the emotions in the heart (69c–e), Aristotle holds that the brain contains only a useful cooling organ with no mental functions.

[26] *Part. an.* 686^{b}3.

[27] See further below (and cf. the treatment of Plato above in Ch. 3, pp. 56–9).

[28] The only case of deformity would then be 'dwarfish' proportions in a member of the human species, where the provision of arms and hands is designed for an upright posture, but the weighty upper torso is inadequately supported on just two delicate legs.

things that they can do well are the things that they are best fitted to do, and those are not things that require an upright posture.

Or so Aristotle should have said. For if it is only humans who have an intellectual part to the soul, then only humans are designed with an intellectual function, and the lack of such a function is not a mistake in the other beasts. However, Aristotle does not always adhere to the principle of explaining nature teleologically, rather than in terms of material causation. For a little later on in the same chapter he suddenly appeals to the dwarfish construction of their bodies as the reason why such animals are less intelligent:

This [sc. their dwarfish construction] is why all the animals are also more stupid than human beings. For even in humans—for instance children as compared with men and those who are natural dwarfs among the adult population, even if they have some other strength to an unusual degree, yet as regards possession of intellect they are lacking. The explanation, as was said before, is that the source of the soul is excessively hard to move and encumbered with body. (*Part. an.* 4. 10, 686b23–9)

This text makes it look as though the reason why animals are less intelligent than humans is not because of any psychological deficiency, or the lack of a capacity for reason and intellectual thought, but simply due to pressure from their badly designed bodies, which makes it hard to operate the higher functions of the soul. It is simply a physical disability, like disabilities in dwarfs: animal souls would be as intelligent as ours if they were put in suitably slender, upright bodies that would permit them to operate their higher faculties.

This claim looks very like the suggestion that apes fail to use language because they don't have the voice-box equipment to articulate the sounds of a human language. It is solved in the case of apes by teaching them sign language, so as to bypass the physical disadvantage. That leaves us, in the case of apes, with the task of discovering whether the animals also lack any mental equipment which could prevent them from operating at the same level as human adults. But Aristotle's example is more problematic: the claim is that the physical structure inhibits the mental functions, not just the means of uttering them. So there seems to be no way we could discover whether, when the cow seems a little dim as regards reading, writing, and arithmetic, it is merely because her chest and back are lying too heavy on her heart, or more radically because she doesn't have a soul equipped for such functions—not unless we could test for a relative quick-wittedness in younger and less fleshy members of the species who have not yet acquired the full and corpulent torso of the adult.[29]

But surely Aristotle should never have tried to explain the cow's lack of intellect as a sad consequence of her poor figure. For on his understanding of nature, nature which makes nothing in vain and equips us all with the best tools available for the complete and effective realization of our specific nature, the cow's figure is just fine for a cow, and has nothing whatever to do with her slow thought processes. Indeed, it is precisely because she was never going to be a great thinker that it is fine for her to have that very splendidly heavy frame, which makes her a superb puller of ploughs. Such a frame would not be ideal for a being equipped for divine thinking. But she is not such a being.

It seems, then, that the appeal to a frustrated intellect confined in a deformed body makes some sense in the case of deformed members of the human species: disabilities can be explained as the accidental consequences of bodies that did not turn out right. If Aristotle wants to say that what appears to be mental deficiency in some human cases of dwarfism may not be genuine mental deficiency but rather an unfortunate consequence of the physical deformities that accompany it, that is fine.[30] But, for Aristotle, normal cows, dogs, and horses are not deformed or disabled in having four feet. It is crucial to his whole outlook that he disagrees with Plato's *Timaeus* on this matter. The *Timaeus* had entertainingly supposed that quadrupeds are degenerate humans who have lost the ability to use their brains:

And then again the beastly kind of land animals emerged from the people who never employed philosophy, and didn't think about the nature of the universe at all, because they didn't any longer use the circuits in the head but followed the lead of the parts of the soul in the region of the chest. As a result of these preoccupations they leant on their front limbs, which dragged their heads too towards the ground (by affinity); they got heads that were long and all kinds of shapes, in whatever way each one's circles were jammed in as a result of idleness. (Pl. *Tim.* 91e2–92a2)

---

[29] Aristotle thinks that young quadrupeds are better proportioned, and get worse, whereas young humans start out more like quadrupeds and get better (*Part. an.* 686b6–17).

[30] The thought is a development of Plato's account of psychological disorders in *Tim.* 87c. It is less clear that Aristotle can get away with saying that human infants are held back from adult mental acuity merely by their top-heavy physical proportions. But compare Pl. *Tim.* 44a b, where the confused state of the human infant is due to the physical constraints consequent upon entering a body.

Aristotle's project in his discussion of the graded souls of plants and animals was to deny that model and replace it with one in which each kind of living thing has exactly the range of functions that it requires to be that thing, not because it has lost some that it should have had, or because it is leaving some idle and non-functional, but because that is all it ever had, and all it ever needed, to be the sort of thing that it is, and to be a fully functioning thing of that kind.

So unless the *Parts of Animals* is an early work, that has failed as yet to grow out of the Platonic model of transmigrating souls with temporarily non-functioning intellects,[31] and to replace it with an Aristotelian account of the distinctive features of animal behaviour that go with genuine animal souls, we should do best to dismiss as a simple error the idea that animals are disfigured dwarfs, held back by their cramped intellects. Aristotle has been tempted by the thought that physical constraints could account for weaker intellects in malformed humans, and he then foolishly toys with the idea that physical factors might similarly explain the lack of intellectual functions in animal souls. But that is not his considered doctrine. For animals just don't have the divine intellect that humans have. Their capacities stop short at perception and *phantasia*—which are, after all, the only things an animal needs to do very well at animal life.

The Struggling Stars

We should return therefore to the earlier conclusion, that all animals, humans included, fall indiscriminately on the unworthy and disadvantaged side of the divide. This conclusion is born out by a passage in the *De caelo* 2. 12 in which Aristotle reflects on the complexity of the motions of the heavens.

Why, Aristotle asks, are the heavenly bodies arranged in such a curious order? The puzzle is this:[32] on the supposition that motion originates from a perfect principle on the outer edge of the cosmos, which itself needs no motion to achieve perfection, one might suppose that the things nearest to it would need the least complex motions to achieve their perfection, and the further a thing was from the outer edge, the greater the number of motions it would need to go through. But this does not appear to be

---

[31] See above, Ch. 3.   [32] Arist. *Cael.* 291^{b}29–292^{a}10.

the case. For although the outermost circle of the fixed stars predictably has a pure and simple circular motion, we find that the order of the planets, sun, moon, and earth is the reverse of what we should expect: the earth is effectively stationary, as though it achieved perfection in the simplest way of all; the sun and moon are relatively simple in their motions; and the planets are far more complex, despite the fact that astronomical observation confirms that the planets must be further out than the moon and sun. Yet complex motion is inferior and suggests a being that struggles in manifold ways to achieve the best, something far removed from the easy accomplishment of the good that we would expect in a being that starts out close to perfection.

The thinking behind this difficulty confirms what we already detected in connection with animal souls and the simplicity of the divine life[33]: namely, that Aristotle regards the complexity of one's activities as an indicator of one's *inferiority* and *distance* from perfection. Indeed, he proceeds explicitly to compare the multitudinous and complex motions of the planets with the similar complexity of human action, the most complex and varied of the animals. Given that the complexity of human behaviour indicates its extreme distance from that easy achievement of perfect ends effected by the divine, so, surely, the complexity of the planetary motions must similarly suggest a particularly lowly position in the solar system, he supposes.[34]

This ought to be sufficient to assure us that, in the case of humanity, Aristotle sees the complexity of the soul's functions as a mark of degradation and impoverishment. There is nothing very good about greater complexity. There is nothing very good about the planets: their complex motion indicates the struggle that marks their achievement of success. There is nothing very good about human beings: our lives are a whirl of wandering motions, a frenzied attempt to achieve a simple perfection by way of a crazy mess of epicycles and retrogressions, all too reminiscent of the wandering planets.

However, things are not so simple. Modern readers imbued with the idea that man must be supposed to be at the head of the animal kingdom—not Aristotle's word, of course—have sought to find in this passage about the complexity of planetary motion some way in which mankind still emerges

<hr />

[33] See above, pp. 109–13.   [34] *Cael.* 292[b]1–10.

as top animal, and the remainder of the plant and animal kingdom as deficient.[35] The issue turns on this passage:

For it appears that well-being belongs without any action at all to what has the very best conditions; and for what has conditions as near as possible to the best, well-being is achieved through minimal action of one kind only, whereas for things whose conditions are furthest from the best, well-being is achieved through a greater range of actions—just as for the body, one is in good condition with no exercise at all, another by taking short walks, another requires jogging, wrestling and aerobics, while for yet another this particular good is no longer achievable whatever effort is applied, but only something else. (*Cael.* 292ᵃ22−8)

It is the very last clause of this sequence that raises the difficulty. Up to that point Aristotle had been emphasizing that the further from perfection one is, the more complicated the manœuvres required to reach it. Each thing can achieve the good, but the efforts, and the number of different kinds of effort, required to achieve it increase, the poorer one's initial condition. In the last clause, however, Aristotle grants that well-being, as such, might simply be not achievable for some whose initial condition is far removed from the good; instead, some other goal will be attained, something that presumably falls short of well-being, but is a good nevertheless.

The issue that now faces us is what items, if any, fall into the class of beings of this less fortunate sort, whose best attainable condition falls short, in practice, of real well-being? Aristotle's explanandum was the striking simplicity of the motions of the stars, moon, and earth by comparison with the complexity of planetary motion, and it seems sensible to take his point here to be that, after all, the relative simplicity of the more central bodies (earth, moon, and sun) does not, this time, indicate *proximity* to their best goal, but instead their relative incapacity. Thus we can explain why the first heaven has the simplest motion, because being nearest to perfection it does achieve well-being in the simplest possible way. The earth, by contrast, although it is stationary, as though no complex activity were required for it to achieve its goal, is in fact merely aiming at a lesser goal, some kind

---

[35] Guthrie's summary of the chapter (pp. 200−3) in the Loeb edition of the *De caelo* (Aristotle, *On The Heavens*, ed. W. K. C. Guthrie, Loeb 6 (London: Heinemann, 1971) takes this line, and it also appears to be assumed by Robert Sharples, 'Responsibility and the possibility of more than one course of action: a note on Aristotle De caelo II.12', *Bulletin of the Institute of Classical Studies*, 23 (1976): 69−72, and Cynthia Freeland, 'Aristotle on perception, appetition and self-motion', in *Self Motion from Aristotle to Newton*, ed. in Mary Louise Gill and James G. Lennox (Princeton: Princeton University Press, 1994), 35−63, 55.

of reduced level of achievement. For the earth to achieve true well-being would involve activities far more complex than those of the planets, and such complex activities are not practical. The earth, he suggests, is like someone who is not fit enough to engage in vigorous exercise, which would be the way to a really healthy lifestyle, but can at least prolong some minimal quality of life by taking things gently. So far, then, we can deduce that sun, moon, and earth must evidently be items of this unambitious sort, with earth being the least ambitious of the three.

What about animals? Aristotle likens the complex activity of the planets to the complex activity of animals and plants, to show that both engage in various activities precisely because they are at a considerable remove from their goal and must work hard to achieve it.

Hence we must think of the activity of the stars as being of the same sort as the activity of animals and plants. For here also the activities of humankind are the most numerous. For the human being is capable of achieving several kinds of well-being, and hence carries out several activities, and for the sake of different ends. But there is no necessity for action on the part of one who is in the best state. For it is itself the end, whereas action always involves two things, when there is both the end and what is for the sake of the end. The other animals have fewer activities and plants perhaps only one minimal one. For either there is one end which it would attain—as humans do—or the several ends are also stages on the way to the best. (*Cael.* 292^{b}1–10.)

What Aristotle does *not* say here is that plants and non-human animals fail to aspire to the best, the way earth and moon do. Clearly the human activities, being most complex, resemble the planets' activities and thereby indicate (i) that humans are at a considerable remove from the ultimate goal, and (ii) that their goals are complex because they are focused on various kinds of good, not their ultimate and best goal. Hence the complexity of human behaviour reveals the relatively imperfect condition of the human species by contrast with simpler beings who can achieve their goal with one simple activity.

But other animals have a smaller range of behaviour, while plants have only one simple activity, as Aristotle observes in the penultimate sentence. Is this because they are closer to perfection (like the fixed stars)? Or is it because they are so far from it that (like the earth) they are not aiming at real perfection, and have to settle for a rather simple way of life instead? We need to look again at the last sentence to see which way we should take Aristotle to be going: 'For either there is one end which it would attain—as humans do—or the several ends are also stages on the way to the best.' This can be taken in two ways. Either Aristotle is saying that (a) plants have just one immediate end, which they successfully attain (just as humans successfully attain their various ends), and thus plants achieve equal success, though with much less struggle than animals do, while (b) animals have a series of ordered ends to which they are directed and by means of which they achieve success in a way more complicated than that of plants, though their series of ends will be shorter and more easily pursued than the complicated series to which humans are oriented. Or alternatively, Aristotle is saying that we don't know in the case of plants whether (a) there is just one immediate end, which is thus readily attained, *or* (b) the only end to which they are oriented is merely a preliminary end, a stage on the way to the best, and not what is really best. Thus we cannot tell whether Aristotle thinks that animals and plants that engage in a smaller range of activities and have less complicated life functions are the sort of things that do immediately and easily achieve perfection, and hence can be compared to the outer stars, whose goal is so easily attained with simple circular motion, or are the sort of things that seek only one or two of a range of preliminary goals that are merely steps en route to their real end. This latter interpretation would make them like the unambitious sun and moon, bodies that never could aspire to perfect activity. There would be a built-in failure in nature, most of whose creatures would never attain their true goals.

The assumption that Aristotle *has to mean the latter* clearly depends upon the idea that he *must* believe other animals to be less able to achieve perfection than human beings are. But this was the thesis that the passage was supposed to be used to prove. It is only if we first assume that humans must be living more perfect lives than simpler animals that we can then take Aristotle to mean that the less complex animals simply do not aspire to perfection, and could not achieve it if they did. But the alternative is to suppose that they have a simple perfection to which they aspire and which they can achieve by relatively simple means, that there is no unattainable good that is their true goal. If this is so, as I think more likely, given Aristotle's general view that nature leaves nothing imperfect except by accident, then plants are not only more simple but also more blessed in their simplicity; the complexity of the human soul shows how hard we have to strive to attain perfection. And this is because it is a perfection from which we are far removed.[36]

What remains incontrovertible on any account is that for Aristotle the complexity of human functions reveals that humans are not close to the best, but very far removed from it, and that the complexity of the human psychological functions is for him the clearest evidence not that humans are at the top of some scale of being, but that they are far down the ladder and struggling with a whole lot of relatively ineffective tasks.

Nature's Shape

Complicated psychological capacities will not, then, demonstrate that humans are especially valuable or honourable in Aristotle's world structure. Rather, the reverse. But if not the soul, perhaps the human body will do the job? Is it not the case that Aristotle thinks that humans have a better arrangement of their parts than other animals?

Our first question should be about what is at the top and what is at the bottom. Is it any disadvantage to be the wrong way up?

The natural dimensions in which animals are marked out are six: upper and lower, front and back, right and left. All the living things have an upper and lower part. For it is not only among animals that there is upper and lower, but in plants as well. The distinction is one of function and not just of position relative to the earth and the sky; for the source of the intake of nourishment and growth for each thing, that is the top; whereas the last place to which it travels, that is the bottom. The former is the starting point, the latter the end, but the starting point is the top.

However it would seem that for plants it is rather what is at the bottom that is their proper thing. For top and bottom are not positioned the same way for plants as they are for animals. At least they are not positioned the same with regard to the universe as a whole, but similarly as regards their function. For the roots are the top for plants; that's where their nourishment is taken in for growing plants, and they absorb the nourishment through them, as animals do through their mouths. (IA 4, 705^{a}26–^{b}7)

---

[36] An alternative view, likely to be attractive to those who emphasize the global teleology of Aristotle's account of nature, is that animals achieve a step on the way to a final goal, and then achieve the genuine goal vicariously in so far as their preliminary goal is to be of service to human life, in which their ends are realized. For the pros and cons of this view (which I am attempting to resist here), see David N. Sedley, 'Is Aristotle's teleology anthropocentric?', *Phronesis*, 36 (1991): 176–96 (a good account of the pros), and Robert Wardy, 'Aristotelian rainfall or the lore of averages', *Phronesis*, 38 (1993): 18–30, for some not wholly adequate attempts at the con. More on this below, n. 44.

On one account of this passage from *De incessu animalium*, Aristotle presupposes that the mouth should be at the top and that plants are upside down, whereas animals get it right, and humans more so than anything else. But notice that he does not exactly say that. He says not that there is an absolute top and bottom, but that top and bottom are different for plants. They do indeed have their roots at the top, what is the top for them, i.e. the starting-point of the procedure of ingesting, absorbing, and excreting. They ingest via their roots, and they excrete at the opposite end. We ingest via our mouths, and excrete somewhere below. So in relation to the whole universe our top is towards the top of the universe, whereas their top is towards the bottom. But who cares where the top or bottom of the universe is, as long as you have your mouth where your food is? Certainly plants have got it right there. It wouldn't help them at all to be growing the other way up just because the world is the other way up. So again we find Aristotle saying that there is not just one right way up: which way is right for you depends on what sort of creature you are. After all, four-legged creatures tend to have their mouths at the front and their bottoms at the back; this isn't quite the way we would want to be, but it has one or two advantages, such as the fact that their heads are at a different angle, so their ears stick up on top of their heads and catch sounds from all round, and that they don't get tired of standing as we do.[37]

Top and bottom are not the only dimensions that carry implicit evaluations to modern ears: right and left do too. Aristotle is quite confident that the distinction between right and left that is normal in right-handed humans is the natural way for things to be and explains not only the fact that we tend to carry our bags on our left shoulders, to hop on the left foot, to step out with left foot forward, to defend ourselves with the right hand, and so on, but also why, for instance, shellfish with spiral shells have the shell on the right side. Everything in nature pushes off, so to speak, with the right foot. But again, as with top and bottom, Aristotle does not say that this orientation is absolute. Rather, like top and bottom, it is defined by function rather than by absolute position:

Those animals that can of their own accord initiate motion from place to place (in addition to participating in sensation) have an additional distinction besides those already mentioned, namely left and right; as with the distinctions treated earlier,

---

[37] *Part. an.* 657ᵃ12–17; 689ᵇ17–21.

these are determined by a certain function and not by position: for whatever is the body's natural source from which its locomotion starts, that is the right for that thing, whereas what is opposite and naturally inclined to follow after it is the left. (*IA* 705^{b}14–21)

Thus Aristotle is not saying that you have to have your right side on the right and your left on the left or you aren't well formed. On the contrary, left-handers will simply be people who have their right on the left, and vice versa. There's nothing absolute about where the right has to be located.

Nevertheless, Aristotle does think that it is more natural to have your right side on the right, and that because the distinction is more pronounced in humans than in some other creatures, humans are, in some sense, more natural too, because it is natural to have such a distinction.[38]

The left parts are neglected in humans most of all the animals because they most of all the animals have what is natural. And the right is naturally better than the left and separate. Hence the right parts in humans are most dextrous. And with the right parts being distinctive, it follows that the left are more immobile and particularly neglected in these animals. (*IA* 706^{a}17–23)

What does 'natural' mean here? Is it a term of evaluation? Does anything follow from the claim that our bodies are constructed in nature's way? Perhaps the point will become clearer if we ask about right and left in the universe as a whole.

Why does Aristotle think that it is natural to have motion initiated from the right, rather than having your right side at the back or on the left? The answer has something to do with the fact that the universe as a whole is constructed with motion originating from what Aristotle thinks of as the right. Of course he is thinking of the earth as stationary and the heavens as revolving from east to west in the manner in which we see the sun

---

[38] At *Part. an.* 2. 10 (656^{a}7) Aristotle decides to talk about humans first, and he justifies this with three considerations: (1) humans alone of all creatures have a share in the divine; (2) we know more about human parts of the body; and (3) human parts are in the natural places for such parts (right on the right, top at the top, etc.). It is tempting to think that these are justifications based on the idea that humans are the best of creatures, and hence should be studied first. But a glance at the second point should make us realize that the justification has to do not with considerations of the intrinsic value of the object, but with the best pedagogical order of proceeding. We start from what we know best, and what has the least exceptions to the general rule that parts have their natural places. Why start with what has a share in the divine? Either because that should be dealt with first or last, if it is a feature not shared with others; or because the heavens are divine, and they are the model we have to start from in understanding what it is to have parts disposed in natural places. We do not need to read any order of merit into the idea that humans are studied first.

traverse the sky from morning to evening. Which side is right and which left depends on whether you are facing north or south; indeed, Aristotle himself, at least in the *De caelo*, notices that it hardly makes sense to speak of right and left sides of something which is a sphere and whose motion is rotation.[39] On the other hand, because Aristotle thinks that the heavens are alive, and that their motion is the locomotion of a living creature, he continues to suppose that it too must be initiated from what would be the right side of that creature. So, he supposes, there must be some extended way in which we can talk of the rotation of the heavens being 'from the right'.[40]

Obviously we could criticize Aristotle for the various confusions he has failed to iron out. If, as elsewhere, he took seriously his model of the universe as having 'up' as the outside and 'down' as the middle, there could be no right and left, and neither north nor south would be the top.[41] And why suppose that human right and left is matched to that of the universe, since that is only true if we stand with our backs to the south? Still, this is all beside the point, for my claim is simply this: to say that human differentiation of the body is 'more natural' is simply to say that it matches the structure and motions of the outer heavens. That may be nature's way for humans. But this is not to say that for something else, having your right side somewhere else would be any kind of hindrance to getting along well as whatever kind of creature you happened to be. Snakes, for example, do fine with no legs:

The reason for the leglessness of snakes is (a) that nature makes nothing in vain but always looking to what is best out of the options available for each thing, keeping the characteristic identity of each thing and its essence; and (b) what we said before, that none of the creatures that have blood can move with more than four points. Hence it is clear that blooded animals that are disproportionately long in relation to the rest of their bodily nature, like snakes, cannot have any feet; for they cannot have more than four feet (for then they would be bloodless creatures) but with two or four feet they would be virtually completely immobile, so slow and ineffective would be their movement of necessity. (*IA* 708^{a}9−20)

---

[39] *Cael.* 285^{a}28−^{b}8.

[40] On the right and left material, see Geoffrey E. R. Lloyd, 'Right and left in Greek philosophy,' in *idem, Methods and Problems in Greek Philosophy* (Cambridge: Cambridge University Press, 1991), 27−48.

[41] Aristotle's account of why the South Pole must be the top, and our hemisphere the bottom one, even though the east is the right, is completely opaque, and much discussed as a result. But the precise claims are unimportant, given that the whole notion of top and bottom is confused in the first place.

Given the shape of its body and what is essential to being a snake as a snake ought to be, the best way to be is legless. Those considerations are nature's main concern: namely, what it is to be a creature of that sort, and what is the best way for it to be constructed given that essence. It follows that the only reason why humans turn out to have right and left legs differentiated, in the way that is natural, is that this is the proper and preferable way for humans to be, and fits with what it is to be human. But nothing whatever follows about whether the resulting human lifestyle is better for humans than the resulting legless lifestyle is for snakes.

Conclusion

It is time, however, to get to the real point. If, as I hope I have shown, psychological complexity is not a mark of human superiority, the traditionalist who assumes that Aristotle thought that humans were naturally superior to other animals has to resort to what he says about animal bodies, and to his claims about the more natural or complete arrangement of the physical parts in our bodies. But even supposing, counterfactually as it happens, that Aristotle had tried to infer from the shape of our *bodies* that our life was superior to that of things that live upside down or have their right side on the left, would that really be what the traditionalist wanted to find? Surely the question of whether we can hop on the foot nearest to where the sun goes down has absolutely nothing to do with what was really at issue, whether humans are at the top of a hierarchy of animal kinds. This issue was not a physical issue, about who has the best-equipped body, but a moral issue, about whose life is most admirable and who has been given the opportunities for achieving a fine life. It would hardly be answered by finding that Aristotle thought that we had bodies better fitted to walking with our heads in the air. That claim would have to be tied to some further claims to show that having such a body was not just proper and natural, but also noble or honourable; or that it gave humans some special claim to greatness.

In fact, that inference is not present in the Aristotelian texts. Nor would it be justified if it were there, since Aristotle has never offered any suggestions to support such a claim. On the contrary, he has emphasized, in the human case no less than in that of the snake, that nature simply aims to achieve whatever success is suited to the individual creature's nature. Nothing implies that the measure of success attained by humans, with their natural bodies, is either qualitatively or quantitatively different from that attained by other species, with their natural bodies.[42]

It is certainly true that the huge extent to which we fall short of perfection means that we, more than anything else, need an extraordinary complexity of psychological functions if we are to come close to a fulfilled human life. But once achieved, that proper human life would apparently be no different in value from the equally appropriate life achieved so much more simply by a contented cow. Success in each life is measured against a standard set by the aspirations of a species.[43] There is no single purpose to which we all aspire, and no hierarchy of contributions towards each others' ends.[44]

The only sequence of ends that we know is within our own concerns, where one of our many complex goals will often be subordinate to another, within the set of our own life functions. In this respect we are not only disadvantaged by comparison with our fellow mortals, but we clearly fall far short of the divine, since for Aristotle's god just thinking is sufficient to reach perfection, and there is no need for any hierarchy of ends, or any calculation of means towards the ultimate goal. Regretfully, nothing is ever so simple in our crazy mixed-up human lives.

[42] Aristotle resists the idea that humans are badly made and ill equipped, hence worse off than the other animals (*Part. an.* 687^{a}23). The point is perhaps addressed to Protagoras. See above, Ch. 2, pp. 30–4, for this material. But the claim that humans are not worse equipped should not be taken to mean that they are better equipped. The passage goes on to show the advantages of some of the factors taken by Protagoras to be disadvantages, but things that are advantages for humans might not be advantages for other animals.

[43] This remains true even on the alternative view whereby some rather basic animals have their aspirations set very low, to match their capacities, like the stationary earth (see above, p. 122). This may make their aspirations simple to achieve, but relatively unimpressive. It might be such a thought that makes the global teleology view attractive, since it would give such animals both the contentment of achieving their aspirations and the merit of contributing to greater aspirations by virtue of their contribution to the goals of others.

[44] For the rival view, that nature is teleologically focused with man as the beneficiary of all the other species' achievements, see Sedley, 'Is Aristotle's teleology anthropocentric?'. That view is the more traditional one (although Sedley was addressing a recent fashion for species-specific goals, which is standardly traced to the influence of Nussbaum (ed.), *Aristotle's* De motu and Allan Gotthelf, 'Aristotle's conception of final causality' in *Philosophical Issues in Aristotle's Biology*, ed. Allan Gotthelf and James G. Lennox (Cambridge: Cambridge University Press, 1987), 204–42, originally published in 1976), and there have been other defenders of the traditional kind of global teleology, in particular with respect to the explanation of rainfall. But see further below (appendix to this chapter) regarding the passage from the *Politics* that gives the clearest support for that view.

Appendix: Slaves and Women

In the *Politics* Aristotle famously considers whether slavery is a satisfactory institution, and concludes that it would be satisfactory if (and only if) all those enslaved had a certain sort of soul that lacked the full autonomy of the normal human soul: that is, if all slaves had the sort of soul that needed to be under another person's authority because it could not take decisions for itself. Such people do exist, Aristotle thinks.[45] And when they do exist, they are naturally designed for the life of a slave, and are better off in such a condition, just as people with normal souls who are capable of autonomy are better off exercising their autonomy as free agents.[46]

Aristotle's account of how the various assistants that a man has with his household (women, slaves, domestic animals) relate to each other is not crystal clear. On the one hand, Aristotle appears to say that the person who is fit to be slave is the one who differs from the free person as the body differs from the soul (which seems to suggest that the slave is a merely physical tool with no psychology at all).[47] In the same breath he compares the freeman and his slave to man and wild beast, which implies that the slave is not even fit to be tamed but has an uncontrollable nature. In the previous sentence he had indicated that in every species the male is fit to command and the female to be commanded, which implied that the free-born wife is in the same condition as the male or female slave, and that the male slave was in a position to command at least with respect to females of the species. Yet a few lines later Aristotle distinguishes between human slaves and animals, domestic or otherwise, on the grounds that natural slaves can at least appreciate reason while animals aren't aware of reason at all but just live by appearances (1. 5. 9).[48]

---

[45] *Arist. Pol.* 1. 5.

[46] *Pol.* 1255a1–3. The dispute about whether slavery is just arises in part, Aristotle observes (*Pol.* 1. 6. 1), because one can be made a slave by convention, and the question whether one is a slave in terms of one's legal position is distinct from the question whether one is a slave in one's nature. Nevertheless, Aristotle seems surprisingly complacent about the ease with which one can supposedly identify someone who is better off under a master's direction, and in general about the practice of enslaving foreigners.

[47] *Pol.* 1. 5. 8. But see further below for a more sympathetic analysis of all these comments.

[48] The point here is presumably that if you explain to a slave why a certain task is necessary, the slave will understand even if he could not have decided to pursue that activity off his own bat. With an animal you just have to give the orders accompanied by rewards and punishments, because it will not be moved by any sense of the reason why.

Given these wildly fluctuating estimates of how much of a soul the slavish slave is supposed to have, it is hard to say exactly where on the spectrum of rationality women come. But chapter 12 of the first book of the *Politics* provides a much more positive estimate of the relative status of men and women, since there we find that the manner in which a man has authority over his wife is the same as the way he might take his turn at holding office in the city, as one among equals, the one who happens to be in charge because it is his turn. For some reason, which Aristotle cannot explain, it is never the woman's turn in the household. But all the same, the man seems to be asked to rule on that basis, and not as a dictator or monarch, and in a quite different way from the manner in which he governs the lives of his children or slaves.

None of this gives a very secure sense of whether Aristotle thinks that women, slaves, children, or animals are inferior kinds of beings (as opposed to just beings that have rather different strengths and weaknesses, of soul or body). Children are, of course, immature ones, and hence the guidance of the father is a temporary way of completing their incomplete souls. But in the case of animals, slaves, and women, it is not clear whether the souls should be viewed as deformed, missing a part that is essential to their well-being as a member of the species (which therefore has to be supplied by the man), or whether they are perfect in their own way (but that way is constituted by being dependent—which is a perfectly fine way to be, in its own fashion, though the way they then need to live is peculiar to them: it would not be a good way to live if one were by nature independent and fit to rule).

My suspicion is that Aristotle should have taken, and perhaps does take, the latter view. He explicitly says that the natural slave—a person who is good at physical tasks and capable of following simple instructions, but not good at running a household or organizing his own life—is better off living under the care and instruction of a master who has the capacities of soul that fit him for such a position. Aristotle claims that both parties benefit from the arrangement, because it allows the master to exercise his capacity for authority and the slave to live a rationally ordered life and fulfil his or her potential.[49] The slave does not have the capacity to live well independently, but living well (and achieving success in all the areas for

[49] *Pol.* 1254^{a}22–33.

which the person is best fitted) is a possibility if someone else is in charge
and oversees the domestic arrangements.[50]

It seems clear that Aristotle thinks that for all these dependants—women,
slaves, children, and domestic animals—life is better in a household run by
a rational being than it would be without. This seems to be what he means
by saying that they naturally belong to someone else, because they are like
a kind of external extension of his own body: he looks after and provides
for them as he provides for his own body; he tells them what to do as he
orders his own body according to his own decisions.[51] The thinking is only
half convincing once we get to animals. For sure, some domestic animals
live in a symbiotic partnership with their human householders. We see the
evidence of that kind of give and take every time the domestic cat proudly
presents its owner with the corpse of a mouse. But the mouse, by contrast,
is clearly a good deal better off if it retains its independence, takes its own
decisions about what to do and where to go, and does not take orders
from the rational owner of the household. At this point it becomes clear
that the interests of the householder and the interests of the animal can
diverge, in a way that the interests of the soul and the interests of the body
do not typically diverge (though that too is problematic).[52] So it seems
that Aristotle is over-optimistic in blithely supposing that the less rational
creature is better resigning his autonomy and trusting to guidance from the
rational human patron.

All this may be very well, but it still does not answer our question as
to whether Aristotle looks down on the less rational creatures as inferior

[50] Described sympathetically, Aristotle's account of natural slavery can be made to look like an
enlightened kind of 'care in the community', enabling adults with limited intellectual capacities to have
a meaningful and useful life in a supportive family home. It then becomes clear that Aristotle's offence is
primarily his endorsement of the assumption that the relationship must be one of possession: that slaves
can be bought and sold as property, and that the slave is a living tool for achieving one's own ends.

[51] I have deliberately looked for a sympathetic way of reading the otherwise rather offensive section
at *Pol.* I. 5. 7–9, which appears to say that the slave relates to the freeman as body to soul or animal
to human, and that the slave is naturally someone else's property. One might suppose that Aristotle has
just retained the idea that slaves are property uncritically from his milieu (much as we take for granted
the idea of buying a horse). In fact, however, it may be that he thinks that such language of possession is
justified in virtue of this idea that the master operates, as it were, as the thinking part of the household,
with the rest of the household as his extended body responding to the guidance of their ruling part.
The appropriate challenge would then be to ask why one should be supposed to buy (or to own) parts
of one's own body—but some people today seem to think that it makes sense to speak of rights of
ownership over one's own body, and for them Aristotle's claims here should be unproblematic.

[52] It would be off the point to explore this issue here, but it does seem that in cases of substance
abuse, etc., the desires and habits of the soul can be contrary to the interests of the body, in an analogous
way to abuse, cruelty, and maltreatment of slaves, women, children, and animals.

in the hierarchy of nature. The thinking in the *Politics* does suggest that for life in a political community one needs to be in a household, and that household should be governed by a man of reason. This is part of what it is to be a man, according to that work. For the human species is naturally political, naturally fitted for the kind of give and take of governing and being governed that belongs to a species all of whom have the reasoning part fitted for taking a position of authority in the community. If some parts of the human community do not display that kind of authoritative rationality, then we can either give up on them as imperfect, or we can incorporate them into an overall design of the community that allows them to be political animals in a derivative sense. Aristotle makes this second move, by treating women, children, and slaves as derivatively involved in the free society of equals, in virtue of their belonging to the head of the household.[53] In a sense we can see this as an attempt to retain the idea that they are fully human and capable of achieving the human good, because they participate in the same crucially human goals and activities via the active rationality of their master/husband/father figure. By treating the human community as the natural mode of living for humans, Aristotle avoids making the less rational humans less fully human.

Nevertheless, it would be foolish to deny that when we are considering degrees of rationality, Aristotle ranks humans and animals in an order of decreasing rationality. Gods are, of course, at the top. But then there are free male human beings, who give reasons. There are free-born women, where it is not entirely clear why they are never given a turn at ruling and giving reasons. There are slaves, who listen to reasons. And there are beasts, who don't even listen, but can nevertheless act in accordance with reason when trained to do so. So there is a hierarchy of understanding and of reason.

---

[53] At *Pol.* 1280ª31–5 Aristotle observes that a community of slaves or other animals (*sic*) would not be a *polis*. This is obviously right, since a *polis* is a community of rational beings; but it does not count against the idea that Aristotle's motive in making the slave naturally part of the freeman's household is to make slaves naturally part of the human *polis*, by virtue of being attached to a thinking mind who is like an external soul for them. This means that the requirement for *eudaimonia*, viz. a life in accordance with rational choice (*proairesis*), can be met for slaves within rationally ordered households (but not for a community composed of slaves only). Notice that the common mistranslation 'a collection of slaves or of lower animals' at 1280ª31 (Peter Garnsey, *Ideas of Slavery from Aristotle to Augustine* (Cambridge: Cambridge University Press, 1996), 113) illicitly imports Darwinian hierarchical terminology.

But, this will not amount to a hierarchy of value, but only of reason.[54] For animals such as human beings, for whom rational life is important, by Aristotle's standards, it would be important that one should have reason—either have it oneself or be in a position to hear it from one's master. So for human life, a deficiency in reason is potentially damaging and may result in a dysfunctional household or a less successful life. But it does not follow that a lack of reason would make a lion dysfunctional. Nor does it follow that practical reason, of the sort shown by the head of the household, is a feature that has value in itself, in the order of nature as a whole. It has value for human life. But it does not follow that what has value for human life is in general valuable, in some order of nature. That would only follow if the best available human life were the paradigm of the best life *tout court*, what nature intended to be best in the entire order of things. But that is not so in Aristotle's world, as we have seen. No. The life of the outer sphere of the fixed stars, majestically rotating on its axis and planning neither political strategies nor household economics but just thinking pure thoughts: that is the closest we know to the perfectly simple ideal way of being. But then it is not (in practice) the best way for us. Nor is it the best way for mice.

---

[54] A text from the *Nicomachean Ethics* ($1149^b 30-5$) is often used as a proof that the lack of reason in animals makes them ethically inferior and unnaturally deformed, but this is based on a misinterpretation and widespread mistranslation of the text. The phrase ἐξέστηκε τῆς φύσεως, ὥσπερ οἱ μαινόμενοι τῶν ἀνθρώπων cannot be translated 'they are a falling away from nature, as are the madmen among human beings', but clearly has to mean 'they are out of their wits'—or alternatively, 'they have taken leave of their natural disposition'—'as are madmen among human beings'. The previous parenthesis should be closed before this sentence, at $1149^b 34$. The point is that we cannot call animals who show bouts of rage 'intemperate' or, *mutatis mutandis*, 'self-controlled' because their bad temper (or resilience) is not under rational control (since they do not have reason or choice). So when they get angry, they are not to blame for intemperate aggression. They are not responsible: they do not decide whether to retaliate in anger in the way that a sane human being decides (but a madman does not). The same meaning (of a faulty but accidental departure from the natural disposition) can be consistently applied in *Gen. an.* 4.3 (768^a), where Aristotle is diagnosing faulty cases of genetic mapping, when reproduction fails to produce an exact copy of the male parent: but in each case the application is to a single case of stepping outside the normal behaviour for a creature of that type (or departing from the normal pattern for a process of that type), not the degeneracy of a whole portion of the animal kingdom (*pace* Garnsey, *Ideas of Slavery*, 110).

PART III
Being Realistic

6

On the Vice of Sentimentality: Androcles and the Lion and Some Extraordinary Adventures in the Desert Fathers

Androcles and the Lion

Here is Aelian's version of the famous story of Androcles and the lion:[1]

The next pieces of evidence also demonstrate that memory is found even in animals, and that it is a capacity of their own even without any of the techniques and sciences designed to develop it—such as some wonder-workers profess to have discovered. A certain man by the name of Androcles who chanced to be a household slave, ran away from his master, who was a member of the Roman Senate. He'd committed some offence, I've no idea what. Well, he escaped to Libya and leaving the cities behind he headed off into the desert "where they mark the places only by the stars" as the saying goes. When he was utterly parched by

---

[1] The story was made famous in the English-speaking world by George Bernard Shaw's 1912 play *Androcles and the Lion* (published in 1916), which makes Androcles a Christian fleeing persecution, not just a runaway slave as in Aelian, and develops the story into a comedy reflecting on religion and the motives for martyrdom. The ancient versions of the story are not linked to Christianity, or to any form of religious sanctity, however. Similar stories to the one linked with the name of Androcles are found in Pliny, *Natural History* 8. 56 and 57 (the former is a story about Mentor of Syracuse and is set in Syria; the latter is the story of Elpis of Samos, to which Aelian alludes at the end of his Androcles story. Elpis's lion has a bone stuck in its teeth, not a thorn in its paw. Neither of Pliny's stories includes the motif of friends reunited in the circus). Another version, close to Aelian's and including with the 'friends reunited' motif is included (under the title 'The lion and the shepherd', no. 563)—along with Gellius's Androclus story (no. 563a)—by Perry, among Latin fables that are considered Aesopic (Ben Edwin Perry *Aesopica* (Urbana, Ill.: University of Illinois Press), 1952, 609, no. 563). But the tale is clearly not by Aesop: it lacks the classic 'lessons from ordinary life' structure: it belongs rather to the genre of pseudo-historical marvels. The circumstances (including circuses at which malefactors are thrown to the beasts and emperors grant pardons) are also entirely Roman.

the extreme heat of the sun he gladly took refuge by retreating into a cave to rest. But actually this rock was a lion's lair.

By and by the lion came back from its hunting, wounded and in pain from a harsh thorn. It came upon the young man and looked at him meekly, and began to fawn upon him, and it held out its paw, and pleaded for him to try to remove the thorn. Androcles cowered back at first; but when he realized that the beast was tame, and when he noticed the problem it had with its foot, he pulled out the thing that was causing the trouble and relieved the lion of its pain.

So the lion was pleased with the treatment and by way of paying its medical fees it treated Androcles as a friend and visitor, and it shared what it brought back from its hunting. It ate the meat raw, as is the way with lions, while Androcles cooked just for himself, and they enjoyed their common table each in accordance with his own nature.

Three years Androcles went on living in this manner. But by and by, being in desperate need of a visit to the barber, and afflicted with a terrible itching, he left the lion and entrusted himself to luck. In due course, as he wandered about, he got caught and they asked him where he was from. They sent him bound back to Rome, to his master. The master punished the slave for the wrongs he'd done and Androcles was condemned to be thrown to the wild beasts, as food.

Well, that Libyan lion too had somehow got caught. And it was let out into the theatre, and so too was the young man who'd once lived under the same roof and shared his dwelling with that very lion but was now destined to die. The man didn't recognize the beast, but the beast immediately recognized the man, and fawned upon him, and folding up its entire body threw itself at his feet.

At last, rather late in the day, Androcles recognized his host and threw his arms round the lion and embraced him like a friend returning from a time abroad. (Ael. *NA* 7. 48)

According to Aelian's version of this classic fable, when Androcles shared the lion's table, he took care to cook his portion of meat, while the lion ate his portion raw.[2] In Aulus Gellius's version of the same story, the hero, there called Androclus, has no source of fire, so he is unable to cook his meat, but he dries it in the sun instead.[3] Thus both Aelian and Aulus Gellius insist that the lion adhered to its leonine ways—it remained an eater of raw flesh—and the man stuck with his human table manners—he remained an eater of cooked flesh.

---

[2] Ael. *NA* 7. 48 (second to third century AD). On the genre of this work see below, pp. 151–2.
[3] Gell. (second century AD) *NA* 5. 14.

In befriending and taming the lion, Androcles does not teach it to eat human food, nor does he alter its lion-like lifestyle. And Aelian never implies that the lion would have been improved had it become more like Androcles in its habits. Far from it. The lion's preference for omophagy seems to be of no moral significance. It is just the way lions choose to live, and it shows that it is genuinely still a lion. As regards the things that matter morally, however, Aelian makes the lion rather superior to the man, in a range of characteristics that prove to be far more significant, in moral terms, than either its habit of eating raw meat or its lack of human speech. There is no doubt that Aelian—or his source—was reflecting upon conventional criteria for gauging human superiority: the idea that cooked food is a mark of civilized life and the idea that articulate speech indicates that human beings are better or more intelligent than the dumb animals. The story of Androcles questions or rejects those evaluations. For, as we shall see, those supposed criteria are not, after all, the crucial things that mark out a creature as morally superior.

In due course, when Androcles and his lion meet again in the arena, the man fails to recognize his old friend, whose hospitality he had enjoyed for three years. The lion, on the other hand, identifies Androcles at once. In Aelian's view, expressed in the opening words of the quotation above, the moral of this story is that memory is a faculty possessed by animals. Aelian does indeed portray the beast as having a good memory for faces—a better memory, in fact, than Androcles has. But it is not only his memory that is superior. Aelian's story is constructed a round two occasions on which the lion tries to communicate with the man, despite lacking the power of speech: first, on their first encounter in the desert, when the lion needs to get Androcles to help with his swollen paw, and second in the arena in Rome when he needs to re-establish mutual recognition. On both occasions he eventually succeeds in communicating with Androcles, but his initial difficulty is caused by the man's failure to comprehend, not by the animal's lack of wit or by any lack of the means to show what he intends to say. The man, by contrast, though he does have speech, does not even attempt to communicate until it is long overdue, when he eventually becomes aware that the lion has something to say. Androcles wakes up to this rather belatedly both times. Thus Aelian's story portrays a lion who is equal to, or better than, the man, in intelligence, in memory, and in the power of communication.

So Aelian has constructed—or relayed—a story that turns on the idea that the beasts (or at least lions) may be cleverer than you thought, and, indeed, a good deal cleverer than human beings. Yet we might well feel that he has not, as he claims, proved that animals have memory. In fact, the evidence cited is singularly useless as a proof of that claim, since it is obviously a fairy story and proves nothing about the empirical facts of animal intelligence. Whether animals have good memories seems to be a simple matter of fact, and as such it could perhaps be established by scientists working in animal behaviour laboratories, but not by the telling of stories and fables. The story is actually rather better as a proof that the things that count in moral evaluation are not, as it happens, matters of that sort at all: they do not have to do with intelligence, memory, consciousness, or linguistic abilities, but rather deeds and motives of a more practical nature—good will, loyalty, friendship, kindness, gratitude, generosity, and hospitality.

Are these deeds and motives exclusive to humans, or could they be more widespread in the animals that are close to us in complexity and lifestyle? Of course, we might need a leap of imagination to see something comparable, something describable in those terms, in animals that are not typically part of our social scene. But a story is exactly the right way to invite us to make that leap of imagination. To prove that these attitudes—of loyalty and devotion, kindness and good will—could indeed extend beyond the scope of human society, and could even provide us with a role model for the improvement of our own moral sensibilities, we have to engage in a thought experiment—or at least, we have to engage in a thought experiment if, like most of us who live in a city, we have lost touch with the earthy practicalities of living alongside animals and eking out our living with their assistance, from a landscape that is not just ours but theirs too, as was mankind's more primitive lot. We have to try to imagine an animal following the same moral codes as human beings and for the same reasons, and doing so without the corrupt motives or social pressures that so readily sully human kindness and affection in its more specious forms. Could a beast show genuine loyalty, generosity, hospitality, and so on, as we know those virtues? Aelian's lion clearly does, and the story, though fabulous, is not unimaginable. So it does indeed show that moral responses are not dependent upon human mental faculties.[4]

---

[4] Notice that in this context it may be important that we are to imagine a lion with considerable powers of memory and recognition: it would be hard to demonstrate that loyalty was the motive for its response if the lion's memory was too short to enable him to identify his old friend in the arena. But again, there is nothing implausible in the idea that a lion might have superior powers of memory and recognition, compared with human ones, and the suggestion that an animal might seek to communicate

Aelian's story is no more than a legend, despite Aelian's attempt to suggest that it proves that animals have memory. But it is a legend that makes us rethink the facile inferences from use of speech to moral and intellectual superiority. It asks us to *imagine* a situation in which a beast who has no language still responds with genuine sympathy to a human companion and remains loyal to that companion in a situation of extreme trauma. In this way it shows us that the lack of language is of no significance to the virtue itself. In the tale, the lack of language figures as a difficulty only in so far as the human imagination is reluctant and slow to see virtue unless it is expressed in words. In other words, we come to recognize that seeing virtue in others requires imagination and empathy: it requires us to see the animal as a creature capable of kindly feelings and meaningful responses to its fellow creature. The story engineers a change in our take on the world: we come to see the lion as not just an alien and ferocious beast, but as a soul: as one of our kind.

Imagination is one of the characteristic marks of the humane person, as also are empathy, compassion, love, sympathy, and the ability to see and respond to the needs of others despite superficial barriers of race, class, or (in this case) species. It is not clear that the kind of science that would condemn the use of imagination and story-telling in constructing its proofs can ever lead to the humane responses that are the hallmark of human moral understanding.[5]

A Leap Too Far?

Compassion and fellow feeling are one thing: arguably, they are among the most important foundations of a moral response.[6] They allow us to identify

---

information to a language user is also made concrete in the idea of a creature needing assistance with a painful thorn. So here too we may see the story as a thought experiment designed to prove that these notions (or projections) are coherent and conceivable—or about as coherent and conceivable as they are for members of radically untranslatable human societies—rather than an empirical proof that animals do act in this way.

[5] On these lines see Gaita, *Philosopher's Dog*, esp. 76, and (an example already classic in the field) the Tanner Lectures given at Princeton by J. M. Coetzee, and published as J. M. Coetzee, *The Lives of Animals*, ed. Amy Gutmann (Princeton: Princeton University Press, 1999) together with the essays of the respondents in the volume, several of whom recognize that a story is what is required in response to Coetzee's novel. An expanded version of the novel was published as J. M. Coetzee, *Elizabeth Costello* (London: Random House, 2003).

[6] I don't mean 'foundations' in any technical theoretical sense. I simply mean to observe that actions done from other motives, without compassion or whatever, are not the moral actions that they appear

with others, to engage with them, to feel for them, to empathize. Yet there is a vice that we know as sentimentality, which seems to involve leaping too far in imagination—feeling for what has no such feelings, empathizing (or thinking that we are empathizing) with what has no such pathos, seeing love, loyalty, and compassion where there is only instinct and conditioned reflex, 'sympathizing' where the *sym-* is merely in our imagination.

Sentimentality is a vice of which every thinker accuses his opponents—and from which he is at pains to excuse himself—in the debate about the humane treatment of animals. Utilitarian thinkers, for instance, who stake their position on the presence or absence of pain need to calculate when and how one might be entitled to inflict pain on another sentient creature, for the sake of maximizing the overall benefit to other sentient things. So they need to know whether the animals in laboratories are, in fact, suffering as we imagine them to be suffering. It is no good just imagining that they are suffering, and it is certainly no virtue to engage in imaginative extensions of our sympathies. Thus for one who defends humane treatment of animals by appeal to a hedonic calculus, it is crucial to avoid being accused of sentimental anthropomorphism, of naïvely assuming that what would be painful to a human subject would be painful—and painful in the same way, to the same degree—to creatures with different lifestyles and expectations. Does pain behaviour in an animal betray pain comparable to ours? The utilitarian is soon called upon to quantify different types of pain, and to weight them for their short- or long-term significance to the sufferer.

It is for reasons such as these that what start out as moral inquiries quickly turn into investigations of animal psychology. Showing that animals should not be tortured in laboratories turns out to involve torturing animals in laboratories. It is a question of fact, and answering it requires not a philosopher, or a saint, but a detached, amoral scientist, with a controlled experiment, designed to discover whether this or that animal—the fish or the earthworm—has the relevant sort of nervous system or produces the morphine-type pain-relief chemicals, as we do, when hurt.[7]

---

to be. So, to express the thought in technical language, one might say that compassion and fellow feeling are the *sine qua non* for being a decent person. On the centrality of genuine love and compassion, not a sense of duty or obligation, nor rational strategic calculation of economic goals, one can learn much from Arthur Schopenhauer, *On the Basis of Morality*, trans. E. F. J. Payne, with an introduction by Richard Taylor (Indianapolis: Bobbs-Merrill, 1965), ch. 3.

[7] See Rollin, *Animal Rights*, 31–2. Rollin notes the irony of needing to kill the rabbits in the experiment that showed that rabbits do not suffer from cholesterol-induced aortic lesions if they are

On the other hand, for thinkers with a Kantian or Cartesian agenda, or those who take moral conduct to be based on a social contract, the issue will be whether a creature is rational in the relevant way: is it an implicit member of the moral community? Treating non-human animals, who are never destined to grow up to be rational moral agents, as though they were the infant (or imbecile) offspring of our own tribe, whose moral deficiencies are a matter of neither depravity nor stupidity but merely temporary (or pathological) immaturity, invites the charge of sentimentality. To defend the humane treatment of animals, one has to devise coherent ways to extend the moral sphere beyond those who are already fully rational or are an integral part of the rational human community, so that animals too can be accorded some partial protection, but without sentimentally pretending that the beasts are—if we only knew it—silently practising to perfect their predicate logic, or wickedly reciting the categorical imperative to themselves, even as they maul the innocent gazelles with their bloody claws.

So the defender of humane treatment is constantly looking over his shoulder at the spectre of sentimentality. The fears are made more plausible by a debased Aristotelianism that creeps into most contemporary accounts of the so-called virtues, and encourages the hasty retreat to scientistic investigations of the objective facts: as though if we could establish exactly where pain behaviour manifests 'real' pain, or where apparently rational behaviour manifests 'real' deliberation, we could accurately draw the line between those creatures for which we rightly feel sympathy and those with which we feel a purely sentimental bond, due to our tendency to childish anthropomorphic fantasies. Yes, we imagine that there is such a thing as too much, as well as too little, kindness, and we call that sentimental. For every virtue, Aristotle declares, there are two corresponding vices: too little and too much. We think we know what it is to feel too little pity or appreciation for small fluffy things. That is callousness or cruelty. Sentimentality is feeling for them *too much*.

But this is odd, for the quasi-Aristotelian notion of the virtuous mean between too little and too much does not match up with our real-life judgements of profound moral goodness. The saint whom we admire for her depth of heartfelt commitment is not someone who judges when to stop

loved and cuddled, but not the irony of having to inflict pain on laboratory animals in order to discover whether one is inflicting pain on laboratory animals.

feeling kindness and withdraws her affection at the point of mediocrity, to avoid being overzealous.[8] Perfect Christian love is an ideal of total giving: an extreme, not a mean. This truth is not undermined by the fact that most of us do not live up to the ideal. If a feeling is admirable, it is admirable to feel it deeply and to develop such sensitivities in ourselves and in others. Moderation, if it is tolerable at all, is always at best an expedient for practical living, and at worst a failure of nerve. It is never the standard of excellence.

So what is sentimentality? It seems to be a concept that we need, and it seems to capture something that is indeed morally corrupt and reprehensible.[9] We can find some attitudes objectionable because they are over-sentimental, even if we endorse the idea that true virtue is unbounded commitment, not a moderate mean, and that unbounded commitment will flow from an ability to feel with and for another, from the heart and not merely from a sense of duty. Even if the place of morality is in the sentiments, responding to the right things and in the right degree is essential. Some sentiments may be inappropriate. And we can find unduly sentimental responses not only with regard to the non-human animals, but in our relations to other human beings, and, indeed, to plants, artefacts, and natural objects.

The idea that sentimental responses are based on some kind of factual mistake—one that can be corrected by physiology or psychological inquiry—has superficial plausibility, because it seems that our sentiments need to be appropriately matched to the thing for which we are feeling.[10]

---

[8] This is not to say that one would never judge the right point to stop providing support or practical charity, say. But this would be because one judged that to continue the assistance was no longer a kindness: the motive would be love, and there is no limit on that.

[9] See here Robert C. Solomon, *In Defense of Sentimentality: The Passionate Life* (Oxford: Oxford University Press, 2004). But despite his provocative title, Solomon is only defending appropriate emotional responses against the perceived negativity of Western philosophy *vis-à-vis* the feelings in general. He is not defending the vice of excessive sentimentality: rather, he is suggesting that all normal emotional responses have got unfairly tarred with the brush that makes us recoil against depraved emotional indulgence. My concern here is to explore the distinction between sound humane feelings (good) and the excessive indulgent emotions that we call 'sentimentality' (bad).

[10] For some previous attempts to answer something like the question 'What is sentimentality?', see Mark Jefferson, 'What is wrong with sentimentality?', *Mind*, 92 (1983): 519–29; Michael Tanner, 'Sentimentality', *Proceedings of the Aristotelian Society*, 77 (1976–7): 127–47; Roger Scruton, *Animal Rights and Wrongs* (London: Demos, 1996), 99–103; and Mary Midgley, 'Brutality and Sentimentality', *Philosophy*, 54, no. 1979 (1979): 385–9. Jefferson canvasses the idea that some fiction is involved, whereas Tanner concentrates on the shallowness of the feeling expressed in a sentimental work of art. Scruton refers both to fantasy or illusion about the object of affection and the self-directedness of the attention; Midgley offers the risk of anthropomorphism as one aspect of her definition of sentimentality (which she defines as 'misrepresenting the world in order to indulge one's feelings'). I do not see the need to confine the sentimental to the self-indulgent (although I would include this). A whole society

This leads to the idea of 'desert': is the object *deserving* of moral considera-tion? Is it *worthy*? Does it *merit* moral treatment? Is it 'morally considerable' (in the philosophical jargon)? These thoughts make us try to draw limits around which kind of animals and objects are sufficiently important to count as objects of moral concern. The project is not just essentialist in its treatment of species, but also implicitly evaluative and anthropocentric, in that it typically takes human life as the paradigm of supreme merit and judges other kinds by how far they fall short of the qualities that are taken to count as deserving.

In this way an essentialist metaphysics springs up to support the naturalist focus of the moral evaluations, so that classification of natural kinds becomes the focus of the moral exercise, and the characteristics that an item must have, to count as a fit object of moral sentiments, are listed as necessary and sufficient conditions. Because morality is conceived, first of all, as a system of intra-human relationships, with an open question as to whether, secondarily, it should be extended to include relations with what is not human, 'desert' is conceived as equivalent to being quasi-human: to qualify as an object of moral concern, one must resemble a human being in whatever is the relevant respect that makes human beings objects of moral concern. So the philosopher's move to protect herself against the charge of anthropomorphic sentimentality is to try to establish just how far anthropomorphism is true and justified: to determine which things *are* indeed relevantly human-like. Then, she will maintain, it will be sentimental to have kindly feelings for others that do *not* fall into the deserving category. But to treat as quasi-human the ones that fall into the precious anthropomorphic class—that is not sentimental.

In this way, morality becomes a matter of biological taxonomy, typically based on evolutionary theory. Using biological classifications, moral theory tries to draw a line, either fuzzy or clear, between what is, and what is not, sufficiently close to *Homo sapiens* to count as a pseudo-person. Practical debate in bio-ethics then centres on where that line should be and how the results can be squared with our moral intuitions.[11]

(e.g. the British people) might become sentimental just because they habitually read too much into their pets' lives and responses, not through any desire to increase their emotional thrills.

[11] It is correct, as Rollin shows (*Animal Rights*, 57–8), that it is no objection to the theory that the line is fuzzy—in Rollin's case the line between those that do and those that don't have 'interests' in the way that humans do; but the same goes for any criterion of relevant similarity that yields unclear

But it is surely instructive to discover that there are considerable difficulties in squaring our moral intuitions with the metaphysical results achieved this way: the children's adorable pets may be members of the very same species as the terrifying vermin in the sewers that we seek to wipe out with traps and poison; in one circumstance we find them lovable and cuddly, and in another, vile and repulsive. If they have the same capacities, must one of those responses be callous? (Or if not, then is the other sentimental?) Does a member of a species deserve moral consideration in virtue of its membership of that species? Do humans deserve moral consideration in virtue of membership of the human species? Surely not. The whole notion of deserving seems to get the moral picture wrong. Indeed, the idea that one is an object of moral concern because of one's biological species, or because one is human-like, seems to be a confusion. The classifications of biology are not of any moral significance unless there is some value attached to being in a particular biological class. But that is precisely what is at issue.

So the appropriate match between sentiments and their objects does not seem to be a matter for biologists to decide. Being 'too sentimental' is surely not a matter of confusing one species with another. Take sentimental attachment to objects and places, for instance. Here the sentimental attitude is not typically or exclusively due to anthropomorphism, or to attributing the capacities of one species to a species that does not share those capacities. My attachment to my childhood home is a case in point. Suppose it grieves me to find that the new owners have built an extension on the yard where I used to play, so that where I used to bounce my ball against the wall, one can no longer play those games. Am I sorry for the yard, that it has been covered over, or for the wall, that it was knocked down? No: I have sentimental feelings about the place and about the games I used to play against the wall, and I feel protective towards them. I would like them still to be there, still to make other children happy as I was happy. But those feelings do not depend upon my supposing that the yard or the wall is sad about it, or feels regret like me. Rather, it is that I feel an attachment to places and things that have meant a lot to me: they occupy my affections. So it appears that

cases on the borderline—for there may be clear cases at the extremes which are uncontroversial. My objection is to the idea of looking for anthropomorphism as a criterion at all, not to its unclarity at the divide.

the sentimental feeling for something is not necessarily dependent upon imagining that the object of affection has anthropomorphic sensibilities.

Excessive Attachment

Of course there is nothing offensive in sentimental attachment as such, and fondness for places and things, animals, people, and plants. Such attachments are normal. The vice of sentimentality is excessive attachment, when such attachments become too strong or too self-centred, to the detriment of other demands upon one's moral attention. But it is tricky to discern what is the proper level of commitment. I think that this is probably because there is more than one error of judgement that can lead to over-sentimental responses, so that the mistake may be not merely in the level of commitment but also, sometimes, in the attitude towards the object of affection. The latter kind of error, for example, might take the form of self-obsession, where one is more fond of oneself than one is of the other (so that the affection bestowed upon the beloved object is really an expression not of love for the object but of one's attachment to oneself).[12] The former kind of error might take the form of obsession with something else, where one attaches such vast importance to one object of affection that one fails to recognize the need to attend to others.[13] Both are forms of what Augustine would have called 'disordered love'.[14]

In the first case, for instance, one might be unduly attached to one's pet animal, because it appears to return unconditional affection. Mistaking the animal's loyalty and uncomplicated devotion for a discerning estimate of one's own admirable qualities, one might come to prefer the pet as company over the more critical and difficult human relations—or one might seek to replace a lost or fragile human relationship with the apparently secure

---

[12] This is the self-indulgence noticed by Scruton and Midgley (see above, n. 10).

[13] It is this latter case that invites reflection on what kind of object merits what level of commitment, but there need not be a context-free answer to that question, for it depends upon what other objects of love are competing for attention. If one is alone on a desert island with a dog, talking to the dog all the time is fair enough. If one's dying granny is in the house, one should share one's affections between the dog and the granny.

[14] For reflections on these things, see Catherine Osborne, *Eros Unveiled: Plato and the God of Love* (Oxford: Oxford University Press, 1994), ch. 1.

affections of a loving pet. These attempts to substitute the affection of an animal for human relationships seem to be disordered. Yet this is not to say that it is wrong to enjoy a happy and affectionate relationship with a pet animal; nor am I denying that such companionship can provide a source of comfort in grief.[15] Sentimentality seems to arise when one reads more into the animal's affection than is really there: when one supposes that the dog is a better companion than a human friend because, unlike the human friend, it never doubts one's perfection or disagrees with one's views. Such sentiment might be described as anthropomorphic, in that it includes an unrealistic attribution of human capacities—for intellectual and moral discrimination—to a beast whose affection is really based on a simpler range of social instincts; but perhaps we see it as a moral fault more because of the human self-obsession that is expressed that way than because of the mistake about what the animal can do.

In the second case, excessive attachment to some animals diverts attention from the needs of one's human neighbours. For instance, someone might feel deep indignation at the cruel treatment of small and vulnerable animals in laboratories, chickens in battery cages, and terrified creatures herded to slaughter houses, while ignoring the sufferings of human children, or of the unappealing and outcast adult or elderly members of her community, or indeed (in extreme cases) even her own family. Sympathy for innocent animals subjected to torture is fine, but if it is founded on unfulfilled maternal instincts—imagining that the animals feel what a small human child would feel in those circumstances, or regarding them like a cuddly toy—rather than on lucid recognition of the moral claims of vulnerable creatures in our power, then the sympathy may turn into a kind of obsession that detracts attention from more pressing objects of concern, including justice and care for friends and family.

Again, as before, the obsession might be diagnosed as a form of anthropomorphism: perhaps it involves mistaking an animal's implicit trust for the immature dependency of a human baby. If a baby were in need of care, it might be reasonable to privilege attention to its needs over attention to the needs of adult members of the community: the baby is dependent on constant care as a sane and competent adult is not. An animal, by contrast,

---

[15] For a touching account of such a relationship between a child and a dog, and between an adult and a bird, see Gaita, *Philosopher's Dog*, ch. 1 (but for the problematic divide between due care and excessive sentimentality, see ch. 2 of that book).

even a domestic animal, is not dependent on human care in the way that a baby is dependent on adult care. For sure, a baby animal is often dependent upon its mother, and in the absence of its parent we may try to act as we would for an orphaned human infant. But an adult animal is not normally dependent on us, except just in so far as we have denied it its normal independent life. It is not, in its natural habitat, something for which we are obliged to make personal sacrifices, let alone sacrifices on behalf of other humans—taking bread from the children to feed it to the dogs—unless it belongs to our own family or flock, such as those we have reared and tamed for living in human society or in farms, or in captivity. So we might indeed try to identify the tendency to act in an overly patronizing way towards creatures with independent lives, and whose lives have not been disrupted by human interference, as a form of anthropomorphism, if we suspect that it stems from misdirected maternal affections.

Yet even here, there seems some strain in the supposition that sentimental attitudes are always based on mistaking animals for people. Perhaps we *should* see the animals more as we see other people. Then we might see more clearly how patronizing, degrading, or obsessive such responses sometimes are. If that is right, we should not be so quick to assume that we can explain sentimentality as due to a kind of anthropomorphic thinking.

For the moral philosopher, the accusation of sentimentality looms because of a tension between our normal moral sensitivities—on the one hand—which are outraged by cruelty even to the humbler orders of creation ('plucking the wings off flies'), and—on the other hand—our sophisticated moral theories, which try to pretend that morality is primarily an attitude to other adult human beings. If the natural objects of moral concern are human beings (so the thinking goes), then extending moral concern to the beasts must involve seeing the beasts as people too. So if, on closer inspection, we find no evidence of the relevant humanoid characteristics, we accuse ourselves of foolish anthropomorphic sentimentality, or even squeamishness when we are outraged by the maltreatment of worms or slugs or flies (as we are).

But why should we ever have supposed that moral outrage is properly concerned only with other adult human beings? Why not suppose that Farmer Giles's cows, and the boy next door, are, and always have been, as good an object of our tenderness as the bank manager's uncle? Why not suppose that when we take children to be the paradigm of objects of moral care, that is not a peculiar inconsistency that needs careful justification, but central and important to our understanding of morality? We care for children because they are what they are: vulnerable, needy, and miracles of precious life. And if that is so, it is unclear why we should ever have doubted that the same goes for those animals that fall into our potentially brutal hands, or under our brutal and insensitive wheels, and hence depend wholly upon our gentleness for their survival.

In fact, if we think about it, we shall see that we do not base our moral judgements on estimating any kind of perceptual response in the recipient of care or of cruelty. The condemnation of cruelty requires no mutuality. It is not necessary that the victim of cruelty feel outraged—or feel anything at all—either about itself or about anyone else, but only that the onlooker should do so. It requires no proven capacity for suffering on the part of the victim: for us to feel compassion, or indeed anger, at the unjust treatment of another, it is not necessary that the victim feel pain.[16] For cruelty is committed wherever the *perpetrator* of abuse feels neither awe nor terror at inflicting wanton insults upon a living creature; there is callousness wherever humanity's foolish arrogance does not hesitate before the magnificent fragility of a life that is not its own. But the callousness is on the part of the perpetrator: we do not need to check whether the victim was troubled, for we can see a callous deed in the attitude of the agent.

Androcles Again

So is the story of Androcles and the lion a sentimental fantasy? Is it a leap too far, into unrealistic wishful thinking and childish anthropomorphism? I think not, so long as one takes it to be part of an exercise in moral inquiry

---

[16] Even among philosophers who try to realign moral theory with common-sense tenderness towards animals, such as Bernard Rollin for instance, there is a tendency to suppose that the victim must be capable of perceiving that it is being hurt, so that consciousness of a certain level is a necessary condition for moral consideration. I think this is wrong: in the case of humans, we feel equal or greater sympathy for those who do not realize that they are victims of injustice, or who have been unwittingly wronged while drugged or brain-washed. We disapprove, and are right to disapprove, of some kinds of consensual abuse, because people may not be aware of being harmed. There is harm that is not perceived as harm and hurt that is not perceived as pain. The fact that it is not so perceived makes it no less wrong or hurtful: the unfaithful husband is not a better man for concealing his behaviour so that no one feels betrayed. The issue is whether his marriage vow is betrayed, not whether his wife feels betrayed. So too with animals, the issue is whether we do wrong, not whether they feel hurt.

and not a report of empirical data relevant to the cognitive psychology of lions or animal ethology. Admittedly, Aelian provides the Androcles story as evidence for the cognitive abilities of lions (7. 48), but it would be a mistake to imagine that his work *On the Individuality of Animals* (*Peri zōōn idiotētos*) is intended to be a contribution to scientific understanding or natural history as we understand that subject. In fact, it is clearly a work in ethics. Aelian piles up the fabulous stories of animal courage and virtue, because they will change the way in which his readers think about animals and about themselves. His prologue makes that purpose plain:

For a human being to be wise and just, to take great pains to care for its own children, to make the proper provision for its parents, to search for food for itself, take precautions against treachery, and so on for all the other gifts of nature that belong to it—perhaps there's nothing unexpected in any of that. For mankind is endowed with speech, most precious of all gifts, and has been deemed worthy of reason, which is by far the most efficient and useful. And indeed mankind also knows how to fear the gods and worship them. But for the dumb animals to partake of some kind of natural virtue, and to have been the joint recipients with mankind of many of mankind's most remarkable privileges—this is something major. (*NA*, prologue).

So humankind, blessed with reason and speech is capable of great things: that is predictable enough, nothing to write home about. But notice the way that Aelian uses the term 'privileges' (*pleonektēmata*) for those remarkable things that we might have thought were special to us. We have to be brought to see that many of the things we thought were unique and great, advantages exclusive to us, are really things that the animals share, despite their lack of things like speech and reason. That *is* something worth noticing, Aelian suggests. For it changes what we thought about ourselves, and it changes what we thought about our status *vis-à-vis* the animal kingdom.

In this way Aelian makes it explicit that his story is an invitation to the reader to reflect upon his or her moral concepts and preconceptions. Effectively, he invites us to observe that membership of the human species is irrelevant to morality—conceptually irrelevant, because justice, mercy, and kindness cannot be about species membership any more than they can be about race or colour or birth. His story shows how dependence on human language can be a hindrance to communication with other forms of intelligent life that just happen to communicate in a different way, and that the use of language does not equate with moral superiority, or moral virtue, or moral insight. And it shows that if we want to put scare quotes round terms like 'loyal', 'hospitable', and 'generous' when we describe aspects of the behaviour of beasts that correspond to the kind of behaviour in humans that would be described in those terms, it is not at all clear what the scare quotes would be doing.

The story thus invites us to throw out some of the false dogma that inhibits moral theory from acknowledging what we all know in our daily lives: that the beasts are not *outside* the fold, asking to come in, but *included* in the moral sphere of human life from the start. We have always lived with the beasts. We have always seen them as our friends, and sometimes as our foes, as a source of delight, of wonder and of awe. We have pitied the vulnerable, respected the wise, and feared the mighty. It is those who would deny that we can think like this who must accept the burden of proof.

More Lions in the Desert

The motif of the intelligent beast is not confined to the fables of pagan antiquity. In Aelian's story, Androcles encountered his lion living under an overhanging rock in the desert in North Africa. Aelian tells us that it was the Libyan desert, though Aulus Gellius implies that it was in Egypt.[17] The story must be supposed to have a dramatic date of about the first century AD Androcles, a former slave, had fled to the desert to escape from the cities (where he would have been caught and sent back to his master for punishment). His retreat to the desert anticipates the retreat of the Christian ascetics of the fourth century AD—the monks who went out to live alone or in small groups in the desert, in Egypt, Sinai, and Palestine, in the wake of the example of St Antony. Theirs was an extreme version of the ascetic life; they sought to escape as far as possible from the corruption of the city, but were unafraid of coming close to the very wildest bits of wild nature, red in tooth and claw.

If the writers of the Lives of the Desert Fathers are to be believed, these hermits and monks had a habit of meeting and sharing their lives with peculiarly perceptive wild beasts, whose intuitions about morality and true

---

[17] Aulus Gellius says he is copying from a work called *Aegyptiaca* (Egyptian Anecdotes) by Apion Plistonices.

sanctity were much superior to those of—supposedly civilized—human beings. Here too, in the incredible stories of the saints and monks of the Egyptian and Judaean deserts, we find the familiar motifs of fable, motifs familiar from our exploration of Androcles. Indeed, it is helpful to compare the two, for the literary genre is clearly similar. Just as Aelian offered his readers a way to rethink their own moral preconceptions, so the writers of the saints' Lives prompt us to reject the corrupt values of urban society and perceive both humanity and wild nature with fresh eyes. Both genres have a moral and spiritual purpose, which is well served by recounting stories about the spectacular understanding achieved by legendary saints (and the occasional virtuous beast). By reading the stories, we are encouraged to open our eyes, to come to share the vision of those who were able to relate to nature in a more authentic way.

Most striking is the reminiscence of the Androcles motif in the well-known story of Abba Gerasimos and his lion. The same story is told, almost word for word, of St Jerome (Hieronymus), and this is the one that is widely known, but the attribution to Gerasimos is probably the original.[18] In this tale a lion appears one day at the monastery gate, limping with a swollen paw. Unlike Androcles, who had initially been petrified with fear and unable to realize that the lion was trying to tell him something, Gerasimos is quite unafraid and quickly diagnoses the trouble. He gets the offending thorn removed, and the paw is duly healed. In this story Abba Gerasimos is the resident and the lion is the visitor, not the reverse as in Androcles, and so it is the grateful lion who stays to take up residence with its humane benefactor, unlike Androcles' lion who had provided generous hospitality for Androcles the refugee, in gratitude for his healing assistance. The give and take of the Androcles story, hospitality in return for healing, has been lost in this one: here *both* healing *and* hospitality are given by the saint to the lion. This explains why Gerasimos's lion adopts a partly servile role in return for its keep: it becomes a monastery worker, serving as bodyguard to the monastery donkey while the donkey is working outside the monastery precinct.

[18] Of Jerome: *Vita divi Hieronymi* (Migne, *PL* 22. 209–12). Of Abba Gerasimos: John Moschus, *Pratum Spirituale*, 107 (*PL* 74. 172–3). Both Jerome and Gerasimos had their monasteries in the wilderness of Palestine and Jordan, rather than Egypt. For maps, see Derwas Chitty, *The Desert a City*, 2nd edn. (Oxford: Mowbray, 1977), and for the claim that the lion story belongs first to Gerasimos, p. 90.

At this point the resemblance to Androcles becomes less obvious, for this time it is the donkey (not Androcles) who gets captured by passing thieves, during a brief lapse of duty on the part of its guardian. On that day the lion had foolishly allowed itself to catnap (a lapse quite out of character, given its many weeks of excellent service), and alas, it wakes to find the donkey gone. After hours of fruitless searching, the unhappy lion slinks back at nightfall to the monastery. Gerasimos hastily assumes that the lion has eaten the donkey. The poor lion, lacking language, can't explain.

Despite the divergence in the story pattern, we see here the recurrent motif of the failure of linguistic communication between lion and man. As in the Androcles version, where the lion patiently waits for the penny to drop, here too the fault seems to lie, at least in part, with the insensitivity of the human being. The abbot unjustly accuses the lion of a crime it did not commit, because he cannot understand the innocent dumb beast. Gerasimos is too quick to assume that he knows, and too stupid to understand the animal.[19]

In Gerasimos's story again, the lion is portrayed as patient and slow to anger, even when the human companion fails to understand. Gerasimos's lion does not protest at the miscarriage of justice, but obligingly accepts the punishment, which involves taking over the menial tasks formerly performed by the donkey. Doubtless the reader is expected to see this work as degrading for a lion: donkey work is for donkeys; security guard work is for lions.[20] But the lion does not complain. It just gets on with the work. However, sure enough, after some time has passed in this way, the same wicked thieves who took the donkey return the other way. The lion recognizes the donkey, attacks the caravan, and returns to the monastery leading its donkey and driving a whole troop of camels that had not previously belonged to the monastery. Now it is the turn of the monks to feel remorse, as they realize that the lion had not, after all, eaten the donkey, as they had supposed.

---

[19] On the idea that man could communicate with the beasts before the Fall, see *Jub.* 3. 27–30 (quoted in Ch. 2 above); but there the thought is that animals lost the capacity for language as a result of the Fall. The idea in these examples from Christian spirituality seems to be, rather, that we (humanity) lost something at the Fall, and that it is our disability to be unable to understand the beasts, due to corruption and sin. A perfect restoration of pre-lapsarian paradise would enable us to commune with the beasts once more, and this is what is partly achieved by the saints.

[20] This attitude is explicit in Moschus's version of the story, in which a soldier who comes to the monastery is shocked at the arrangement and gives Abba Gerasimos the money to buy a new donkey, so as to free the lion from the menial job of fetching water.

Besides the parallel that we have noticed regarding the slowness, or indeed failure, of humans to understand the beasts—because humans rely on language for finding out (here notably conceived as a weakness on the part of human beings)[21]—we can also see a parallel in the notion that humans underestimate the moral capacities of the beasts. Gerasimos's lion was more self-controlled than the monks gave it credit for. They were wrong to jump to the conclusion that it had slipped back into its beastly ways, or that it had (all too predictably) fallen into temptation. They jumped instantly to that conclusion because they misjudged the capacities of beasts, and they assumed that beasts were basically beastly and were readily tempted to be beastly. In the hagiographic context, this is a telling criticism, for the trials of the desert focus heavily on the difficulty that human beings have in resisting temptation, and how hard it is to avoid falling into beastly ways, even when they put themselves well beyond the reach of the things that would tempt them to impurity. Humans—even saintly ones—are quick to imagine that animals are beastly, but in reality the natural beasts are the human beings.

Androcles is less to blame in his story: he may be a little slow to recognize his lion in the arena, but once he recognizes it, trust is instantly restored. On the other hand, the audience at the circus and Caesar himself are incredulous when the lion and the man seem to be greeting each other as friends. Like Gerasimos and his companions, they judge the beast on the basis of their preconceptions about what lions are like. By contrast, in the Gerasimos story, the author neatly completes the plot by providing a further dramatic episode, the return of the donkey, which is the occasion for the human characters to discover their folly and to feel appropriate remorse.

In another story told by Sulpicius Severus, *Dialogues* I, chapter 14,[22] the motif of resistance to temptation so beloved of the Desert Fathers recurs. This time, however, the animal succumbs, though only after a long struggle. The story is of an old monk whose pet wolf called daily for food. One day the hermit was late back for dinner. The wolf had come as usual and waited for hours, but when the old man did not come and did not come, she had eventually gone in and stolen a loaf, leaving a tell-tale trail of crumbs. The old man eventually returns and sees what has happened. The

---

[21] On the idea that human language is a second best, inferior to the non-linguistic direct communication between bodiless souls, see Basil of Caesarea, *Homilies* 3. 23. 5–6.

[22] *PL* 20. 192D–193B.

monk is deeply hurt; but the wolf herself is equally distraught. For days she stays away, too ashamed to show her face, but finally she does appear, tail between her legs as it were. Once he is convinced that she is genuinely repentant, the old man eventually forgives the wolf, and their old habits of mutual trust are restored.

Here the animal has indeed failed, *in extremis*, to resist temptation, but the story focuses on her reaction to her failure, not the reasons for it. The tale does not support the idea of a beastly beast with no manners and no moral conscience: this wolf feels genuine remorse for what she has done. Whereas Gerasimos's lion did not do the deed, but submitted to the punishment anyway, this wolf is guilty, but punishment is irrelevant, since her intense remorse indicates a full sense of moral responsibility and shame. Perhaps the monk is a little slow to forgive: again there is a hint that he has difficulty in discovering, across the language barrier, whether the beast is genuinely showing repentance; but the motif of rediscovering mutual trust is reminiscent, once again, of the reuniting of Androcles and his lost lion in the arena.

My third example tells of the hermit Macarius of Alexandria.

Paphnutius his disciple told us this story about him—that one day a hyaena picked up her pup, which was blind, and brought it to Macarius. She knocked on the door of the enclosure with her head and came in. Macarius was sitting out in the yard. The hyaena dropped the pup at his feet. The holy man picked it up and spat on its eyes and prayed. Right away it could see. The mother suckled it and then picked it up and went off. The next day she brought the fleece of a huge sheep to the holy man. And the blessed handmaid of Christ, Melane, said to me "I acquired that fleece as a present from Macarius." (Palladius, *Lausiac History*, 18. 27 (pp. 57. 4–58. 2, Butler))

This story about Abba Macarius occurs in a number of variant versions. Here in Palladius's version the hyaena brings just one pup to Macarius; in the *Historia Monachorum in Aegypto* she lives in the adjacent cave, and she takes Macarius to her cave to see her pups, all of which were born blind, and he treats all of them.[23] Since hyaena pups would in any case be born blind, the latter version seems to have something of the just-so story to it. But in both, the main point of the story seems to be the gratitude of the hyaena, expressed

---

[23] *Historia Monachorum in Aegypto*, 21. 15. The story is closely parallel to Pliny's account of Philinus and the panther, *HN* 8. 59, where the panther takes Philinus gently by the hem of his garment, asking him to rescue her cubs from a pit into which they had fallen.

in the form of her gift of a particularly large and splendid fleece: indeed, the structure of the stories seems best to be accounted for if they are attempting to provide an aetiology for the hermit's possession of this remarkably fine fleece. In Palladius's version, Sister Melane has inherited the fleece; in the *Historia Monachorum* the story finishes by saying that 'someone still has the fleece'.

What is an ascetic doing sleeping on a massive and beautiful sheep fleece? Two worries lie behind in the story: first, the fleece is a luxury, unexpected for an ascetic such as Abba Macarius; and second, it is the skin of a dead sheep. By having the saint accept the fleece as a present from a grateful neighbour, the story excuses the apparent luxury and links it to his uncommon powers of healing and his special relationship with the wild beasts. Are the writers worried about the fact that it was obtained by killing a sheep? Palladius seems not to raise this issue, but the *Historia Monachorum* hesitates: 'The hyaena brought a huge fleece from a large sheep … and placed it at his feet. But he smiled at her, as one smiles at someone well-meaning and perceptive, took the fleece and spread it under himself'. (*Historia Monachorum in Aegypto*, 21. 15). Macarius does not rebuke the hyaena: he sees that she means well, and he accepts the fleece on those terms. She is 'perceptive', perhaps because she instinctively saw what the man would need; she has brought it as a thank you present; and she means it kindly. It is, in any case, simply a by-product of her normal way of life. Macarius does not have moral qualms about accepting it on those terms.

The story is a little different in the version of this legend which was popularized (in an English translation from a French translation from the original Coptic) by Helen Waddell in her 1934 anthology *Beasts and Saints*.[24] There Macarius is shocked by the thought that the hyaena has been out killing sheep—indeed, sheep that belong to someone else, presumably. Of course saints do not accept stolen goods, or goods that involve cruelty to animals! Macarius tells her off sharply, gives her a good talking-to about morality, and insists that he will not accept the gift until she promises to give up killing things. Eventually, despite her silence, he becomes convinced that she's promising never to eat anything that isn't dead already. He then accepts the sheepskin and sleeps on it every night till he dies.

Here again the fable smacks of the just-so story type of aetiological tale: why do hyaenas typically scavenge carrion rather than killing live beasts?

---

[24] Helen Waddell, *Beasts and Saints* (London: Constable, 1934).

Answer: because Abba Macarius taught the mother hyaena that killing was wrong. It would be easy to dismiss this variant as a sentimental elaboration of the tale, the writer attempting to address the worry about how Abba Macarius could accept the sheepskin which must have been got by immoral means, at the same time as explaining the peculiar eating habits of hyaenas. But the story is also closely parallel to one that Raimond Gaita records, from real life, of Vacek Vilkovikas, a gentle, simple-minded recluse who lived the life of a hermit on the side of a mountain not far from Gaita's childhood home in Australia.[25] The similarity of Vacek's simple way of life to that of the Desert Fathers is striking. His response to finding that Orloff, Gaita's dog, had stolen his sausages, as Gaita describes it, exactly parallels motifs in both the Coptic version of Macarius, who instructs the hyaena against the taking of life, and in Sulpicius's description of the monk and the thieving wolf that we have just looked at.

Fourthly, we may add the tale of Abba Bes and the hippopotamus, from the *Historia Monachorum*.[26] Summoned by the farmers, Abba Bes addresses the immense beast (who had been causing trouble in the vicinity) and says, 'I enjoin you in the name of Jesus Christ, not to ravage the country any more.' Whereupon the hippo disappears from the scene, as if led away by an angel. And (the writer assures us) Abba Bes did the same with a crocodile on another occasion.

Three motifs recur in these stories of the Desert Fathers. The first is the beasts' lack of verbal resources: the beasts are repeatedly either misunderstood or understood only with difficulty, even by the saint. Hence the wolf hesitates about returning to her old man for forgiveness after stealing his loaf, and he finds it hard to be sure that she is sorry; the monks punish Gerasimos's lion for a crime it did not commit; and Macarius finds it hard to tell where the hyaena is taking him and whether she knows that it is wrong to steal sheep. Notice, however, that it is never the beasts who are too stupid to understand, but always the humans; in each case the animal is well aware of what it has or hasn't done. It understands the men's instructions. It understands the moral rules. Hippo and wolf, lion and hyaena, all listen and learn. The men, on the other hand, cannot understand the beasts, even when they try to do so. And consequently they don't trust the animals to take the moral lessons to heart.

[25] Gaita, *Philosopher's Dog*, 15–18.   [26] *Historia Monachorum in Aegypto*, 4. 3.

The second motif is that of the beastly nature of the beasts: in each story the beasts either do something beastly, or they are suspected of doing something beastly. The wolf does steal the loaf; the hyaena had, it seems, killed someone's sheep; the lion, Gerasimos supposes, must surely have eaten the donkey; the hippo was causing trouble to the farmers. The expectation is that beasts naturally tend to be vicious, perhaps more so than humans. Yet, in fact, so the stories allege, that accusation is often false. It is a result of misunderstanding or mistrust on the humans' part. Even when it is not false, the fault may lie not in a beastly nature, but simply in the pressure of hunger or the animal's untrained ignorance of moral obligations. These are not vices in the way that human vices are.

The third motif to be noted is the virtue of the beasts, including their ability to recognize sanctity. This is reflected, first, in their easy trust and companionship with the saint; secondly, in their appreciation of his healing power; and thirdly, in their ready obedience to moral instruction. Abba Gerasimos's lion wouldn't dream of eating the monastery donkey, yet he accepts his undeserved disgrace with Christ-like fortitude; while the hermit's faithful wolf needs no reproof, so deep is her remorse for helping herself to his loaf uninvited.

These latter two motifs, of vice and virtue, are in tension: for even within the same story the beasts seem often to stand both for what is untrustworthy or prone to beastly immorality and also as models of innate virtue. The beasts are morally innocent despite being untrained; they illustrate a simple and natural aptitude for virtue, but their capacity for virtue is often unrecognized and frequently maligned by ordinary mortals, and even by the saints themselves, in their arrogance and moral blindness.

So are the desert stories just sentimental nonsense? Again, as with Aelian, the answer should be no. For one thing, the Desert Fathers are neither gentle nor squeamish in their relationship with the harsh environment in which they live and its inhospitable forms of wildlife. It is true that they do often show a special warmth and affinity with wild things, finding help and support from the beasts when in difficulties,[27] yet also knowing what is harmful and how to kill what would otherwise kill them. When

---

[27] Macarius again, e.g. Macarius exhausts his supply of food and water at several days' distance from his cell, on a fruitless expedition to a dried-up garden in the desert. But just in time he is sustained by a mother antelope who allows him to suckle in place of her calf, and escorts him all the way back to his cell. Palladius, *Lausiac History*, 18. 8–9 (pp. 50–1, Butler).

Abba Macarius was digging a well to irrigate some young seedlings, he got bitten by a deadly snake, Palladius tells us.[28] His response was to grab the snake in both hands and rip it apart right down its body, from the jaws down, saying, 'How dare you come to me when God has not sent you?' Here Macarius appears to take revenge upon the creature, accusing it (rightly or not, but presumably rightly—since Macarius evidently survived the experience) of trying to kill him at a time that had not been decreed by God. Similarly, an old man called Didymus, one of the monks at Nitria, was said to kill scorpions and asps with his feet, according to the *Historia Monachorum*.[29] Yet equally, on another occasion—again in Palladius's collection—Abba Macarius was filled with remorse for having taken revenge upon a mosquito that had bitten him, and as a punishment he sentenced himself to sit naked for six months in the Scete swamp, 'where the mosquitoes are like hornets and can puncture the hides even of wild boars'. There he got so bitten that he swelled up and became unrecognizable to look at. [30]

These stories are not particularly squeamish, nor are they unrealistic about the extent to which wild nature can be a menace to those who struggle for survival in harsh conditions. Perhaps they reflect a simple-minded division between animals that intend to kill and those that don't. (Macarius seems to be entitled to take revenge against the deadly snake, yet he condemns his unpremeditated squashing of the mosquito, and Didymus is admired for killing the scorpions, while Abba Theon eats only raw salad and communes with the wild gazelles and other animals that he delights in, sharing his water with them outside his cell at night.[31]) We might accuse these writers of fanciful anthropomorphism were it not that their message is as much about the vices that humans share with the beasts as it is about the virtues that animals share with mankind. For the Desert Fathers do not take mankind as the model of perfection. On the contrary, it is raw nature that shows them how to live simple, uncorrupted lives. Human corruption undermines the ideal of the simple and harmless life and replaces it with a false set of values, values which lead us to lose touch with the trust and loyalty of our fellow creatures.

---

[28] Palladius *Lausiac History*, 18. 10 (pp. 51. 5–9, Butler).
[29] *Historia Monachorum in Aegypto* 20. 12.
[30] Palladius, *Lausiac History*, 18. 4 (pp. 48. 25–49. 8, Butler).
[31] *Historia Monachorum in Aegypto*, 6. 4.

St John Cassian's Monastic Guidebook

These two motifs in the tales of the desert monks, the natural beastliness of the beasts and their propensity to simple uncomplicated virtue, also appear, in the same paradoxical relationship, in texts of spiritual direction that belong to the same context. St John Cassian, in book 8 of the *De institutis coenobiorum*, is reflecting on anger. We might expect, when he mentions the beasts,[32] that the beasts are to exemplify the fury we must avoid. But no. Instead, he observes that snakes and wild animals are innocuous when alone in their lair; they don't show their savage nature unless there is someone to hurt. So does this make them a good role model for the saint? Well, yes and no; for on the one hand, so Cassian claims, acting harmlessly in isolation doesn't count as virtue, but only reflects the lack of anyone to be nasty to; yet at the same time, he goes on, even the solitary monk is not invariably free from anger and frustration; for he easily gets furious with his tools or snaps the recalcitrant reed in anger. Thus the train of thought runs back and forth between the idea that beasts are not all bad and the idea that they are not all good: their behaviour is (a) merely natural, not motivated by virtue, yet (b) more habitual and less prone to sinfulness than is that of the human monk.

Cassian mentions the beasts again in a general summary that forms part of his discussion of melancholy. Victory in the fight against the inner passions, he says, will enable one to live at peace with wild creatures as much as with humankind. This is an excuse to mention Job 5: 23 (which, in the Septuagint, says that the wild beasts of the open spaces will be at peace with you); but again it exposes the same ambivalence: the beasts must surely be harder to live at peace with than men, for they are, are they not, naturally vicious? Yet they are also aware of sanctity and respectful of virtue, and they behave peaceably towards the true man of God. It is as though the beasts have a natural vision of true holiness within, which does not require the struggle that is typical of the human effort to reach purity and sanctity of soul.

Finally, we might turn to a brief passage from Neilos the Ascetic, writing also in the early fifth century. In his *Logos ascetikos*, chapter 61,[33] Neilos reflects on why the saints flee from the cities to become hermits. The point is, he claims, to escape the contrived wickedness of humans and live among

---

[32] John Cassian, *De Inst.* VIII. 18.   [33] *PG* 79. 793B–D.

the beasts instead. For the harm done by the beasts is, after all, nothing compared with that caused by human beings; the beasts don't teach us to sin. In fact, they respect virtue. Neilos, once again, enjoys the paradox, contrasting the corruption of human wickedness with the popularly perceived threat from wild beasts. He unpacks the motif so that the image of the beast as beastly is identified as part of the city-dweller's distortion. Thinking of the beasts as beastly is a corrupt judgement about what is truly to be feared. For it is human corruption that is most to be feared: the enemy is within.

Abba Gerasimos's lion was falsely accused of maltreating the donkey. The fault lay not in the lion, but in the failure of Gerasimos and his brethren to believe that the lion was innocent. In this injustice, and in the failure of trust that it reflected, Gerasimos and his companions fell short of sanctity. For Neilos too, the true holy man, unlike the city-dweller, will be in a position to recognize that the beasts are not vicious, but that they serve for us as models of justice. Indeed, recalling Daniel in the lion's den, Neilos claims that the beasts restored justice where human judgement had failed. The desert, then, unlike the human city, is a society in which justice is respected and nature's proper order is restored, as before the Fall.[34] Thus the desert becomes a model of heaven. The behaviour of the wild beasts is re-evaluated. We come to see it as the very reverse of what the corrupt and unenlightened city-dweller supposes. For the beasts turn out to be not the archetype of violence, but a model of sanctity, honour, and reverence.

Western philosophers have, typically, tried to promulgate those corrupt and unenlightened attitudes, the very ones from which the Desert Fathers were so keen to flee, as though they were the inevitable conclusions of rational thought. But most popular Christian piety, including not just these lives of the early saints but many others in both Western and Eastern hagiographical traditions, has agreed that the true man of God sees his fellow creatures as companions and that they return the compliment (rather more perceptively than most human agents do).

Hagiographical writing is a genre designed to mould the values of ordinary folk, to get them to look at the world under a certain description—as God's wonderful world, in which what God cares for is what counts, not

---

[34] Cf. also an earlier passage in Neilos's *Logos ascetikos*, where he offers an allegorical interpretation of a passage that superficially appears to condemn four-footed beasts, ch. 14; *PG* 79. 736C–D.

what man cares for. It does this partly by allowing us to see the world through the eyes of the saint whose life and words it purports to record. It thereby reassures and encourages the faint-hearted, by suggesting that even where the corruption of human values is so deep that true virtue is systematically punished or condemned, and where those who are most holy are most vulnerable to abuse, genuine goodness is still recognizable in nature. And, we are to see, it is nature's verdict, not the verdict of human society, that matters. So in the stories, the perception of the beasts, when they respect and love the man of God, stands for what the writer takes to be nature's own viewpoint. It tells us that, of two ways of looking at the beasts, the compassion of the saint is objectively superior, in the real order of things, to the alienation of the worldly. For it is the uncorrupted beasts who instinctively recognize what is good in the real order of things.

Perhaps the stories are sentimental, then. Perhaps they take us a leap too far in imagination, and attribute to the beasts powers of discernment that are more godlike than plausible. But the point is precisely that: for the stories are trying to give us a god's-eye view of our own arrogance and corruption. They step back from philosophy, and from every other form of human arrogance, and show that the world really looks different through the eyes of the good person. So philosophy simply wouldn't have the same starting-points once one has learnt to look at the world like that. And that explains why philosophy can never have the last word. These stories are not designed merely to entertain us with trivial imaginary fables of noble beasts and kindly old men. They are stories whose purpose is to turn beastly men into compassionate, loving individuals, to inspire us to become courageous martyrs and heroes, resistant to the corruptions of a society that is too ready to take life, along with everything else, for its own meaningless ends. They enable us to see ourselves and others with new eyes: to feel awe at the magnificence of even the smallest, humblest, and most irritating of God's creatures, and to feel horror and anguish at the extent of human depravity. Though at times, for sure, they may occasion tears of laughter, the proper response is probably tears of repentance.

7

On the Notion of Natural Rights: Defending the Voiceless and Oppressed in the Tragedies of Sophocles

Do Animals Have Rights?

Do animals have rights? Perhaps this looks like a sensible question to ask in the present climate. Some writers who seek to defend the humane treatment of animals appeal to the idea that not only humans but animals too have natural rights.[1] On the other hand, many thinkers resist such an idea, arguing either that the whole notion of natural rights is nonsense, or that it is nonsense to extend it to animals, whose interests can be adequately protected by considering the rights of humans.[2]

But what, exactly, are we asking when we consider whether animals have rights? What good can it do to declare that animals have rights? What are rights? Perhaps we need first to discover what we mean when we say of other human beings that they have a right to this or that kind of decent treatment.

In what follows I shall argue that the language of rights, when it is invoked for moral crusades, has a misleading appearance that derives from its quasi-legal terminology. This is what grounds the objection that human rights claims are just a lot of metaphysical hot air, and the observation that freely

---

[1] Among serious work on the moral status of animals, the main proponent of rights is Tom Regan (see e.g. Tom Regan, *All that Dwell Therein: Animal Rights and Environmental Ethics* (Berkeley: University of California Press, 1982) and *The Case for Animal Rights* (London: Routledge & Regan Paul, 1984). Others who find the notion of rights helpful in discussing animals include Rollin (see his *Animal Rights*, 43) and (sometimes) Clark (e.g. his *Moral Status*, 29).

[2] See esp. Peter Carruthers, *The Animals Issue* (Cambridge: Cambridge University Press, 1992); Scruton, *Animal Rights and Wrongs*; Gaita, *Philosopher's Dog*, 200–2 (quoting Simone Weil).

asserting the imaginary existence of rights in irresponsible contexts has many damaging consequences.[3] It may indeed be true that such misunderstanding of the language is damaging and can lead to cruel misrepresentation, but my claim is that these faults arise because we—society and the weak whose rights are to be protected—are getting caught out, or indeed taken in, by the confusing choice of metaphor that we are using. In this chapter I shall try to show that the currently fashionable talk of rights is a muddled, and muddling, attempt to express some perfectly reasonable and simple claims about genuine moral truths. The language of rights is the lingua franca of moral discourse in the post-Enlightenment Western world, but (I would suggest) it does not convey its meaning in a transparent way. So are we better off using it, at the risk of being misunderstood by those who read it as founded on unsupportable metaphysical mysteries? Or are we better off with the traditional language that expressed these same ideas in earlier cultures?

Standing Up for the Vulnerable and those with no Voice

Throughout history, people of moral stature have stood up for the vulnerable in situations where they are being oppressed by those without moral scruples. When we do that in the modern world, we tend to appeal to rights. We declare that those who are being oppressed have certain rights, and that those rights are being violated—a paradoxical claim, since it is precisely when the individuals have no claim to any such rights and when there is no sanction against the perpetrators of the injustice that we make those claims. It is that kind of situation, and that kind of claim that human rights exist even when they are not enforced, that I shall be investigating here. In other periods of history we do not find those claims in those words. But, I shall suggest, it is not that those other generations did not think those thoughts. Rather, the same thoughts, or something very like them, were formulated in a different way. To substantiate this claim, I propose to take a look at four scenes from plays by Sophocles, from the fifth century BC. I shall suggest that we are right to use the terminology of rights when we try to translate what is being said there into the modern idiom. I also wish to suggest that the rights in question are probably correctly described

---

[3] I shall consider some of these objections below, pp. 180–3.

as natural human rights (and not just property rights): for they include the rights of the dead to be treated with respect, rights to freedom from interference, and the right to a means of livelihood. And to forestall one possible objection, I shall suggest that where the gods enter the picture, they make precisely no difference to the structure of the moral thinking.

It is also characteristic of Sophocles to allow that obligations may conflict, and to face up to the fact that sometimes there is no course of action that does not infringe someone's rights, and that the decision about what to do (or 'which right trumps which', in the rather unattractive jargon of rights talk used today) is sometimes inscrutable or extremely painful. These facts, as we shall see, do not render the rights talk useless: rather, they show it functioning in precisely the way I am suggesting is characteristic of this language, as a way of mapping out the moral territory of absolute demands that cannot always be met. 'Ought' does not, in Sophocles, imply 'can'.

Sophocles, Philoctetes, 54–67 and 356–84: the Right to Inherit One's Father's Armour

In the *Philoctetes*, Odysseus conceives a plan to persuade Philoctetes to leave the desert island where he has been living since the Greeks abandoned him there on their way to Troy. The plan involves deceiving Philoctetes into thinking that Neoptolemus (the young son of Achilles) has been treated unjustly by the Greeks and has left in a fury. The wrong that he is supposed to have suffered is described in the following passage, where Odysseus is instructing Neoptolemus to tell lies:

ODYSSEUS. You must deceive Philoctetes when you speak to him. When he asks you who you are and where you come from, tell him you are Achilles' son—there is no need to disguise that. But say that you are sailing home, that you've grown to hate the Greeks and have left their expedition in disgust: they used prayers to get you to leave home—you were their only means of capturing Troy—but when you came, they didn't think you worthy of Achilles' armour, though you had every right to claim it (κυρίως αἰτουμένῳ); they gave it to Odysseus. You can say anything you like about me—scour your vocabulary for the worst insults you can think of. That won't hurt me!

If you don't do this, you will inflict suffering on all Greeks.

Soph. *Phil.* 54–67[4]

---

[4] Translation by Judith Affleck: Sophocles, *Philoctetes*, in *Cambridge Translations from Greek Drama*, ed. Judith Affleck (Cambridge: Cambridge University Press, 2001).

Later, at lines 356–84 we hear Neoptolemus himself addressing Philoctetes, in accordance with Odysseus's instructions, and pretending that he was wronged by the Greeks, and that he is now sailing for home, having fallen out with the Greek army:

NEOPTOLEMUS. As I disembarked, the whole army crowded around me and greeted me, swearing that it was Achilles they saw, alive again. But he was dead, and I, unhappy son, wept for him.

After a little while I approached the sons of Atreus, thinking them my friends. I asked them for my father's weapons and anything else he had. They said... they spoke without any sense of shame, 'Son of Achilles, you can take the rest of your father's things, but another man is now master of his weapons: Laertes' son, Odysseus.' With tears in my eyes I sprang up to face them, hurt and angry. 'You cad! How dare you hand my armour to someone else without consulting me?' Odysseus spoke up. He happened to be there. 'Yes, boy. And they were right to present me with those arms. I saved them and his body. I was there.' I was furious. Straight away I tore into him, every curse I knew—leaving nothing out. Did he really think he could rob me of my armour? He is not a man who angers easily, but at this, stung by my words, he replied, 'You weren't with us. You were somewhere else, and should not have been. And after this insolent talk you'll never sail home to Scyros with this armour now.' His insults ringing in my ears, I set sail for home. Robbed of what was rightfully mine (τῶν ἐμῶν), a victim of Odysseus, that vicious man of vile descent!

Soph. Phil. 356–84[5]

In both passages, the translator has used the language of rights to convey the idea that Achilles' son could expect to receive his father's arms. In Odysseus's description of the imagined scene, in the first passage, Neoptolemus 'quite properly' requests the armour, as was his right (line 63). In the second passage, Neoptolemus imagines himself calling Odysseus a cad and questioning how he could dare take the armour that was *his own* (lines 69–70) In both accounts, the listener is expected to understand that (in his view at least) the armour was effectively already his by right, and that it should not be given away to someone else, unless in some way Neoptolemus had forfeited his right to it. That scenario, in which he has forfeited his right to the armour, is what Neoptolemus imagines in his invented speech for Odysseus in the second passage. There Neoptolemus

---

[5] Translation by Judith Affleck (with minor modifications).

has Odysseus claim that he, Odysseus, had acquired a right to the arms by rescuing them, and that Neoptolemus had forfeited his right by not being part of the expedition.

Two things look slightly wrong with this passage as a case of human rights thinking, in my view. The first is that Neoptolemus himself is pictured protesting (unsuccessfully) that he has a natural right to the armour: it is a first-person claim to rights, not a third-person declaration of rights on behalf of a victim. The second is that the rights look like property rights, tied to inheritance, and in consequence they are not inalienable, but seem to be forfeited in cases where someone else has a greater claim owing to valour or loyalty to the hero. However, I think that these factors are less important than they might look. In the first place, the appearance of a first-person claim to rights is artificially produced by the fact that the whole story is a lie. The tale is designed to win the trust and support of Philoctetes. Philoctetes is a noble, upright, right-thinking individual. Under Odysseus's instruction Neoptolemus is trying to elicit in Philoctetes the classic third-person reaction to a threat to another person's basic human rights, so Neoptolemus falsely portrays himself as a youth without friends, whose rights have been violated and who has no one to stand up for him. The effect, as predicted, is to generate friendly feelings of vicarious outrage, the classic 'human rights defender' response, but to generate them *in Philoctetes*. So Neoptolemus describes an imaginary offence against himself in order to produce the third-person protest that (as I have been suggesting) we associate with this kind of thinking.

The second problem was that the rights look like inheritance and property rights. It is true that the right to hold property and not to be deprived of it by others is one of the basic human rights enshrined in the French declaration of 1789,[6] so that a threat to one's rightful ownership of property does appear to be a candidate for an offence against human rights. But it seems that we could understand threats to property rights without anything like a notion of human rights; and it is also doubtful whether the right to own property is really natural, and not just a piece of bourgeois

---

[6] Article 17.

capitalist ideology that has got carried over among the general ideological garbage of such codes of practice.[7]

However, it is not clear that in Neoptolemus's case the rights are simple inheritance rights. Neoptolemus imagines himself claiming the other personal effects of his father besides the armour, and according to the yarn that he spins, the claim is granted with respect to the other effects; there is no problem about his property rights. By contrast, with respect to the armour there is a dispute, because in respect of the armour the son's rights to inherit are in competition with some potential rights of the hero's companions who fought with him and rescued the armour from the enemy. Odysseus, so Neoptolemus pretends, also claimed a right to the armour, based not on heredity but on his conduct towards the dead hero on the battlefield. That presumed right, the right of the colleague in battle, conflicts with the son's presumed right based on heredity, and in Neoptolemus's fake story it trumps it. The dispute, imaginary though it is, is evidently supposed to be faintly realistic, and it plainly turns on who counts as the relevant heir: that is, which kind of distribution of the property would correctly accord with the need to honour the dead hero.

So the story is not about a straightforward system of property passed on from father to son. It is about how you treat the war dead, and how you treat those who risked their life fighting alongside the war hero. In Neoptolemus's case, we are not just talking about Neoptolemus having a right to the wealth his father owned. We are talking about what happens to the hero's sword and shield, his helmet and breastplate and greaves: the things of war. The presumed right of the son to inherit the family armour from his heroic father is itself clearly partly to do with honouring the dead hero, in the expectation that he would have wanted to see his son step into his shoes as a replacement for himself on the battlefield. It is also partly to do with defending the hero's orphaned, unprotected son, who will need the armour if he is to take his place as a warrior. Yet competing with that is another account of what the dead hero would have wished: namely, that his uniquely special set of armour should go to the greatest hero among the Greeks, or to the man who did most to assist him in his hour of need

---

[7] See the criticisms in Karl Marx, 'On the Jewish Question', in *Selected Writings, Early* ed. David McLellan (Oxford: Oxford University Press, 1977), 39–62.

on the battlefield, or to the man who made sure that the Trojans did not despoil the hero's body and claim the precious armour for themselves.

In this respect, I think we should say that the story is not just about Neoptolemus's right to claim his father's property, but rather about respect for the dead and correct distribution of the warrior's special effects among the various people who have acquired a right to be his favourites. This is not so much about property, as about honour, respect, and rewards for outstanding valour. There is no doubt that Neoptolemus expects Philoctetes to sympathize with him and to feel vicarious outrage at the tale of a son deprived of his father's arms, but his story of rival claims to the armour has to ring true in itself: we have to understand that Odysseus might indeed have made such claims and won—in fact, presumably we are supposed to know that Achilles' armour was indeed assigned to Odysseus, so that part of the story certainly does ring true. We are asked to picture a conflict between Neoptolemus's presumed natural right to his father's favour, and Odysseus's acquired right, based on his acts of friendship towards the dead man on the battlefield.

Sophocles, Philoctetes, 1222–36 and 1247–51: The Right to the Means of Livelihood

But even if we dismiss the example relating to Achilles' armour as an illustration of the notion of property rights, not human rights, there is more to come later in the *Philoctetes*. Odysseus's project in this play is to get hold of the famous bow of Heracles, which Philoctetes has. The Greeks have been told that they will not win at Troy unless they have that bow (and, apparently, Philoctetes as well, to wield it). It is to this end that Odysseus and Neoptolemus have come to Philoctetes' island to trick Philoctetes into boarding ship for Troy with his bow. The first ruse, in which they try to deceive Philoctetes into boarding ship with Neoptolemus under the misapprehension that he is heading home failed, because Neoptolemus lost his nerve and owned up, out of pity and remorse. Now Odysseus tries a second plan. He wants to take the bow, which Neoptolemus has been holding for Philoctetes during one of the spasms of agony that the wounded Philoctetes suffers as a result of the festering wound in his foot, and board ship with it while Philoctetes is incapacitated. Once again Neoptolemus, after being initially corrupted by Odysseus's malign influence, regains his moral sense at the last minute. Here he is running to return Philoctetes' bow to him, rather than leave the man to starve to death:

ODYSSEUS. Tell me why you've turned back? Where are you going in such a rush?

NEOPTOLEMUS. I am going to undo a mistake I made earlier.

ODYSSEUS. Your words alarm me. What mistake is this?

NEOPTOLEMUS. One I made in obedience to you and the whole army.

ODYSSEUS. What have you done that you shouldn't have?

NEOPTOLEMUS. I used shameful deception and trickery in catching him.

ODYSSEUS. Who do you mean? You're not intending some new move, are you?

NEOPTOLEMUS. Nothing new. It concerns the son of Poeas.

ODYSSEUS. What is it you are going to do? This is frightening me.

NEOPTOLEMUS. I took this bow from him. I am going to return ...

ODYSSEUS. Zeus! What are you about to say? You're not thinking of *giving* it to him?

NEOPTOLEMUS. I was wrong to take it. I have no right to keep it.[8]

ODYSSEUS. In god's name, are you saying this to provoke me?

NEOPTOLEMUS. If speaking the truth is provocation.

. . . .

ODYSSEUS. And how is it 'just' to give something back that you took under my direction?

NEOPTOLEMUS. I made a shameful mistake. I am going to try to put it right.

ODYSSEUS. And in acting like this, aren't you afraid of the Greek army?

NEOPTOLEMUS. With justice on my side, your army doesn't frighten me.

Soph. Phil. 1222–36, 1247–51[9]

Here Neoptolemus restores to Philoctetes the bow which is his only source of livelihood on the deserted island where he lives alone. We might think that Neoptolemus's concern over taking the bow is primarily motivated by a sense of Philoctetes' property rights—he's entitled to the bow because it belongs to him—together with the feeling that taking the property by deception was shameful. Perhaps those motives would be sufficient to generate the remorse expressed here; but I would suggest that the play implies a great deal more. For this passage in which Neoptolemus runs urgently from Odysseus to try to restore the bow to Philoctetes follows an extended lament by Philoctetes, after Odysseus has gone off with his bow, in which he anticipates his death due to starvation, because he can no longer hunt for food.

---

[8] αἰσχρῶς γὰρ αὐτὰ κοὐ δίκῃ λαβὼν ἔχω.   [9] Translation by Judith Affleck.

PHILOCTETES. O you stony hollow of a cave
  Now hot, now icy cold, O wretched home,
  So I was fated never to leave you
  Ever, but now you will be there
  To see me as I die.
  O, grief, grief.
  O sorry mansion, filled brim-full
  With my sad cries of pain,
  What now, what can possibly now
  Provide my daily needs?
  Unhappy as I am, whence
  Shall I chance upon some hope of finding food?
  The frightened birds wheel at me
  Through the shrill wind in the sky above;
  Yet I've no force left .... .

Soph. *Phil.* 1081–94[10]

For more than 100 lines Philoctetes continues this lament, punctured by brief exchanges with the chorus. It repeats and reworks a theme already expressed in Philoctetes' earlier speech, in the presence of Neoptolemus, which had first made Neoptolemus doubt that what he was doing could be right.[11] The main theme is the fact that Philoctetes has lost the treasured bow, which was not only his dearest friend but also his sole means of livelihood. Without it he will shortly die. In effect, he has chosen to stay and die rather than join Odysseus and Neoptolemus on the voyage to Troy.

It is clear that Sophocles means us to see that the bow was far more to Philoctetes than a piece of rather nice property he doesn't want to lose. It is vital, because it is what he depends upon for food. Add to this the fact that Philoctetes suffers from a debilitating wound, which means that his physical strength and agility are limited, and we have precisely the recipe for an appeal to human rights. Neoptolemus has taken from a sick man the sole means by which he kept himself alive; this is a man for whom Neoptolemus feels pity, a man who is entirely dependent upon the good will of his fellow human beings; it is a man who has no one to defend his rights and no means of seeing justice done. Philoctetes is wholly vulnerable, a man with no enforceable rights, and the audience is brought to see this vulnerability graphically.

---

[10] My translation.   [11] Lines 952–62.

So when Neoptolemus runs back with the bow, declaring that he has used shameful deception and trickery against a man, that he is trying to undo a wrong he has committed, that he is not afraid of Odysseus's threats when he has right on his side, and that he must return the bow to Philoctetes because he had no right to take it, we understand more in this remorse than the mere sense that it would be wrong to steal a person's property by tricking him. We understand that Neoptolemus perceives that Philoctetes is in need. Philoctetes needs the bow because it is his means of livelihood, not because it is his property. To deprive a fellow man of that basic need is an intolerable wrong, and in the attempt to make amends for his part in such an offence, Neoptolemus is prepared to give his own life, when Odysseus draws his sword against him at line 1254.

Neoptolemus is deeply committed to trying to ensure that Philoctetes has his bow. He sees it as a moral outrage that it should have been taken from him, and taken by such underhand means. We can express this by saying that Neoptolemus thinks that Philoctetes has an absolute and inalienable right to the bow, despite the fact that he is unwilling to come and help at Troy. The translations that use the language of natural rights seem to get the tone right, because the text appeals to the notion that we would think of as the right to life, or the right to one's means of livelihood. What is more, the exchange has the right structure: namely, the declaration by a third party who has nothing to gain, in this case Neoptolemus, on behalf of the weak and vulnerable victim, in this case Philoctetes. It is a declaration to the effect that some moral outrage is being perpetrated that offends against absolute moral standards.

For Philoctetes, the only means to a livelihood was, as it happens, hunting and killing animals; but although it is clear that he is understood to have the right to a means of livelihood, and in the circumstances this means that he has to hunt, this must be distinguished from the suggestion that he has a natural right to hunt, or that human beings invariably have the right to hunt. The idea that humans have a natural right to hunt animals is sometimes incautiously attributed to Aristotle.[12] But when Aristotle says

---

[12] Richard Sorabji cites the relevant passage (*Pol.* 1256^{b}10–26) many times in his *Animal Minds*, and twice he implies that he understands it to be an early case of the idea of natural or human rights (pp. 154, 157)—the latter apparently citing Myles Burnyeat's opinion expressed in a radio talk—but in other chapters, where he is not looking for antecedents of the idea of rights, he seems to me to understand the example more accurately, as an appeal to the idea of natural justice.

that hunting is a natural art, he is saying no more than he is saying when he suggests that it is natural that mammals produce milk for their offspring; nature makes things suitable for food, and it is natural for us to try to get hold of those things (and the fact that we do so is in line with what nature had in mind). Aristotle thinks that both hunting animals and making war against other human beings are natural in this way, provided the war is one in which a race naturally suited to being on top is subduing a race naturally suited to being subjugated, if they refuse to be subjugated without a war.[13]

Aristotle's notion of a just war looks fairly unattractive if we don't share his notion of natural slavery on which it depends;[14] and his notion of the natural justice in hunting looks unattractive if we don't share his assumption that nature made venison specifically for us to eat (though perhaps not just for that). But it seems clear that he is not asserting that it would be a moral outrage if a human being found himself deprived of the opportunity to hunt. Rather, his claim is that when people hunt, they are doing something that is perfectly natural, and, given the natural pecking order in nature, not unjust. The same is true of going to war when it is done in suitable circumstances, so that the result is that the better people are in charge of running the world. But this is not a right to hunt, or a right to go to war, but rather permission to do so in appropriate circumstances. Philoctetes' right, by contrast, is the right to get food, somehow. If the only available resource is game, then he will need to be permitted to hunt game. But there would be no outrage were he instead to be offered a reasonable alternative source of daily rations and banned from hunting. Neither Sophocles nor Aristotle is committed to the idea that hunting is one of the basic human rights.

Sophocles, Ajax, 1089–1114: The Right to Freedom from Interference and the Right to Decent Burial

After Ajax has dramatically killed himself on-stage, Teucer, who is Ajax's half-brother, arrives to take charge: he sees to the protection of Ajax's dependants—his captive wife Tecmessa, his son Eurysaces, and his dependent sailors and fighting men, all of whom are left unprotected and without anyone to stand up for them as a result of the hero's death. Teucer also takes responsibility for the funeral arrangements for Ajax's body.

---

[13] Arist. Pol. 1256^{b}20–5.   [14] On this theory of slavery, see appendix to Ch. 5 above.

Teucer's mother was a captive woman (a barbarian princess) taken in war, and this means that he is of servile status. Consequently, he is treated as scum by the Greek chiefs, particularly Agamemnon. But Sophocles portrays in the half-cast Teucer a character of truly noble stature, a man of genuine moral integrity and courage, by contrast with the rude and pompous leaders of the Greeks who had robbed Ajax of the armour of Achilles and so precipitated the frenzy that led to his downfall.

Ajax is dead. Menelaus, commander of the Greeks, wants to prevent the body from being buried, and he tries to give orders to Teucer and to Ajax's dependent men, forbidding them to carry out the funeral rites. Teucer is having none of it, for Menelaus has no right to interfere with the free actions of Ajax's own people. He cannot give orders about the funeral because Ajax was not under Menelaus's command.

> MENELAUS. Therefore I warn you, do not bury him, in case
>   By doing so you earn yourself a grave.
> CHORUS. Menelaus you have set out wise principles,
>   But do not yourself show disrespect to the dead.
> TEUCER. I'll never be surprised again if someone
>   Of no account does wrong, when those
>   Who seem to be of noble birth can go so far
>   Astray in what they say. Come tell me from
>   The start again. You say you brought
>   This man here as an ally of the Greeks?
>   Did he not sail here of his own accord?
>   What right[15] have you to command him? What right
>   Have you to lead the men he brought from home?
>   You came as Sparta's leader, not our master.
>   No law[16] says that you have power over him
>   Any more than he has power over you.
>   You sailed here as leader of a detachment,
>   Not commander in chief; you never led Ajax.
>   Rule your own people! Use your pompous words
>   To lecture them. But as for him, whatever you
>   Or that other general say, I will bury him
>   As is my right.[17] Your words do not scare me.
>   He did not come here to fight on your wife's

---

[15] ποῦ.   [16] θεσμός.   [17] δικαίως.

Behalf, like your overworked subjects.
No, he came because he was bound by oath,
Not for your sake—he did not care for nobodies.

Soph. Aj. 1089–1114[18]

Teucer contrasts Ajax's free action, in choosing to come to Troy, with the subservient position of the men who came under Menelaus's orders. Ajax was not subject to anyone. He came to Troy of his own accord, and he never resigned his right to decide whether to support Menelaus's project. Menelaus is therefore wrong to speak as though he brought Ajax with him, in the way that he brought his own men. Similarly, it follows that Ajax's men were not under Menelaus's command but under Ajax, and this means that Menelaus has no right to tell them what they can and cannot do. So Ajax is dead, but it does not follow that his men are now subject to orders from Menelaus.

So Teucer's speech is partly in defence of Ajax's dependants, to fight for their right to freedom and self-determination. Secondly, it is a declaration that nothing gives Menelaus a right to forbid the burial of the hero's body. It is debatable whether the word dikaiōs ('justly') in line 1110 conveys the sense of 'as is my right', as the translator has chosen to render it, or rather perhaps the sense of 'as is his due'; but either way, the general point of the passage is that Teucer is prepared to stand up for the decent treatment of his brother, and to defend the rights of Ajax—to be buried as he deserved—and the rights of his dependants—to be left unmolested to get on with the business of mourning and burying their dead. Of course, Menelaus has the resources to prevent Teucer from seeing to Ajax's burial by force, but, Teucer suggests, he does not have the moral right to do so.

Later in the play the dispute is resolved by the intervention of a rather more circumspect Odysseus, who aligns himself with Teucer and against Menelaus and Agamemnon on the matter of Ajax's entitlement to a decent burial, on the grounds that Ajax was a great hero and a brave man.

ODYSSEUS. Listen, then. In heaven's name, don't dare cast
This man out in cold blood without a burial!
You must not let violence make you hate
The man so much that you trample on justice.

---

[18] Translation by Shomit Dutta, Sophocles, *Ajax*, trans. Shomit Dutta, Cambridge Translations from Greek Drama (Cambridge: Cambridge University Press, 2001).

He was also my worst enemy in the army,
Ever since I won the arms of Achilles.
Be that as it may, I would not seek to
Dishonour Ajax by denying that
In him I saw the best of all the Greeks
Who came to Troy, apart from Achilles.
You cannot dishonour him justly;
You would harm not him, but the laws of heaven.
Even if you hate him, it is not right
To harm a noble man once he is dead.
AGAMEMNON. Are you taking his side against me?
ODYSSEUS. I am. I hated him when it was right to hate.
AGAMEMNON. So why not stamp all over him now that he's dead?

Soph. *Aj.* 1332–48.[19]

Here we see that Agamemnon is a man without scruples. He cannot get the idea that it is not acceptable just to trample all over your enemy once he's dead. By contrast, Odysseus insists that once the man is dead, even if you hated him and competed against him in life, it becomes absolutely unacceptable to take advantage of him in the unfortunate circumstances of his death. 'You would harm not him, but the laws of heaven,' he says. He is suggesting that there is a deep moral prohibition which would be broken by the failure to overcome the merely circumstantial prejudices of hatred and resentment against the man. Once a man is dead, one is required to treat him in the light of what he really was—what he was at some more fundamental level, ignoring these temporary disputes that had put him at odds with Agamemnon, Menelaus, and Odysseus.

It is true that Odysseus's estimate of what kind of treatment Ajax deserves is partly tied to his estimate of Ajax's stature as a hero: 'In him I saw the best of all the Greeks who came to Troy, apart from Achilles'; in this sense, it does not quite correspond with the idea of a *human* right to funeral rites, if we take that to mean that one should give a person a decent burial no matter who he was or how disgraced in life. Yet I think that this is fundamentally what Odysseus means, although he adds to the force of his claim by urging that Ajax has, in fact, a clear claim to a hero's burial, not just the minimal rites one would accord to any wretched human being.

---

[19] Translation by Shomit Dutta.

Sophocles, Antigone, *453–60: the Right to Burial Again*

Odysseus's claim that there are laws of heaven that demand this even-handed treatment of a person after death is closely reminiscent of the claims made by Antigone on behalf of her disgraced brother Polyneices, when Creon has forbidden funeral rites to be performed. There too, Antigone speaks of unwritten, unshakeable laws that are such that no human ruler has the right to cancel them:

> ANTIGONE. Nor did I think your edicts had such force
> that you, a mere mortal, could override
> the great unwritten, unshakable traditions of the gods.
> Those laws live, not just today or yesterday:
> they live forever from the first of time,
> and no one knows when they first appeared.
> These laws—I was not about to break them,
> not out of fear of some man's wounded pride,
> and face the retribution of the gods.
>
> Soph. *Ant.* 453–60[20]

Antigone goes on to claim, in a later speech, that once a man is dead, it no longer counts that he was a traitor rather than a loyal hero.[21] She suggests that the loyal brother Eteocles who died fighting hand to hand with Polyneices will himself, now dead, not resent the provision of funeral rites for his traitor brother, even though they were enemies in their last hours. She claims that Hades demands the same rites for all. And she speculates that whereas Creon thinks that it is offensive to give equal treatment to friend and foe, the gods below may well consider equal treatment to be the more proper procedure. All these thoughts reflect the same general response as Odysseus voiced to Agamemnon with regard to the treatment of Ajax. Antigone is not demanding that there should be the same level of public mourning and honour for her traitor brother, but just that when it comes to what is needed for decent treatment of a fellow human being, the next of kin should be allowed to get on with it in the way that is minimally decent in the circumstances, and should not be condemned for that action.

---

[20] Translation by Robert Fagles, (in Sophocles, *The Theban Plays*, ed. Robert Fagles (Harmondsworth: Penguin, 1982), modified.   [21] Soph. *Ant.* 512–23.

Even the man who had been killed by Polyneices would have the grace to grant that his sister was right to give basic burial rites to Polyneices.[22]

Teucer and Antigone stand up for the right of the dead man who has lost his life in an unworthy cause still to be treated with respect after death. In both cases, but Antigone's in particular, it is clear that the structure corresponds to what I have identified as typical of a human rights declaration. The victim whose rights have been threatened is unable to defend himself, in this case because he is dead.[23] He is the voiceless oppressed. In both cases his champion, who puts the case for proper treatment and respect, is powerless to get the right enforced, because the political and military power is concentrated on the side of the oppressor, although Antigone bypasses this by means of civil disobedience (another classic move by the defenders of natural rights under oppressive regimes).

Antigone finds herself compelled to make these moves, and to give her life in the process, despite the greatest reluctance about the heavy consequences for herself, and she grieves bitterly over the necessity to cut short her life.[24] Commentators sometimes puzzle over why Antigone is seen to feel hard done by and to grieve over the consequences of an act she undertook deliberately, knowing it was illegal and in the firm belief that it was right. In fact, Sophocles' analysis of the psychology makes good sense, for Antigone finds herself obliged to perform acts that have been made illegal by an unscrupulous regime. In an ideal world she would not have had to break the law, and she would not have had her life cut short. Hence it makes sense for her to weep over what she has done and to mourn her own sufferings, while still believing that in the circumstances she had no choice but to do the deed: no choice because she faced an absolute moral obligation.

Antigone's case also clarifies how one can find oneself forced to take up obligations to which one has never been asked to consent: in this sense it shows why moral obligations of the sort that we describe using

---

[22] Ibid. 515; cf. 899–904. Both seem to be clear that the right to burial is not something that can be forfeited due to disloyal behaviour. This makes these particularly clear cases of the kind of thinking that is typically associated with natural rights, though I do not think it is incoherent to talk of natural rights being forfeited in extreme circumstances, e.g. by those who have shown themselves unmoved and unmovable by the corresponding moral scruples—but that is because while the language is still serving a purpose it is reasonable to use it: we do not have to be bound by its apparent metaphysical underpinnings, so as to be bothered by questions of when and how people lose their natural rights.

[23] Or, if we focus on the case of Ajax's wife and fighting men, because they have no champion to protect them from the bully with the bigger army.   [24] e.g. ibid. 875–82, 891–928.

the language of human rights (and correspondingly the obligations that we have to members of our family, and to strangers in situations where we are accidental bystanders) are not covered by a positivist structure, in which one is under a legal obligation only if there has been an opportunity to assent to or dissent from an implicit contract. Antigone and Teucer are under a *natural* obligation to bury their own dead and to protect the interests of their own relatives. It is because they take those obligations seriously that we see them as individuals of heightened moral stature. In *Antigone* in particular Sophocles explores how we acquire obligations by birth which are absolutely binding and nonnegotiable even in circumstances that endanger our own lives. These obligations that we cannot refuse—indeed, that we could not think of refusing—are the flip side of the moral coin in which there are certain edicts that no human lawmaker has the right to enact.[25]

That the Significance of a Declaration of Human Rights Lies in the Declaring

In these passages we find that there are occasions when one must stand up in defence of someone who is vulnerable and unprotected, and protest against injustices perpetrated by those in positions of physical or political power. In those circumstances it is not necessarily true that there are any political or legal sanctions to restrain the powerful. It seems that Agamemnon and the rest of the Greeks have the power to deny Ajax a decent burial, even if they do not have the moral authority to do so. Is it helpful, then, to say that Agamemnon has no right to do that, even when neither Teucer nor anyone else can do anything to see to it that the dead man's rights are respected, except stand up and declare that they should be?

In a paper to the Aristotelian Society in 2003,[26] Susan James argued that asserting rights in the absence of an appropriate system for claiming them—and for enforcing that claim in practice—is a meaningless gesture.

---

[25] I have stressed obligations that come from kinship because that is the focus of *Antigone*, but equally, there are obligations that arise from one's history or one's accidental omissions in the past, such as the right to forgive or the obligation to apologize (where no one else can undertake the action on one's behalf).

[26] Susan James, 'Rights as enforceable claims', *Proceedings of the Aristotelian Society*, 103 (2003): 133–47.

Rights must be enforceable if they are to be real. Furthermore, since the conditions of enforceability are quite stringent, James argued that it is harder than we might have supposed to ensure that individuals, even under an enlightened, liberal regime, will necessarily *have* the rights we try to give them.

By suggesting that rights are enforceable claims, James was developing and strengthening a point already made by Onora O'Neill, who had suggested that if something is to count as a right, the right must be claimable, and the agent who is obliged to meet the claim must be specifiable.[27] In the absence of routes for claiming and agencies to meet the claims, rights become, in O'Neill's words, 'a bitter mockery to the poor and needy'.[28] Thus O'Neill had already questioned the usefulness of apparently empty appeals to rights, where there is no agency charged with supplying what is supposedly the recipient's right. James's paper extended that thought, by suggesting that even where an agent is specified, and is theoretically under obligation to meet the claim, practical difficulties may intervene and render the claim unenforceable. When that happens, the so-called rights are empty or meaningless, James suggests.

In a similar vein, Raymond Geuss, having elegantly mapped out the distinction between subjective and objective rights in his *History and Illusion in Politics*, claims that the notion of subjective rights so beloved of current popular theory needs to be linked to a system of enforcement.[29] Like James and O'Neill, Geuss is inclined to conclude that asserting the existence (or the 'discovery') of so-called rights where there is no provider and no sanction for failure to provide must be a nonsense. In what sense does anyone have a right to life, if death is common, unavoidable, and often inflicted by forces beyond our control and in circumstances where it would be quite useless to complain? Geuss thinks that talk of rights in such circumstances turns out to be empty: it looks as though language from familiar positivist contexts, such as legal or political institutions, has infected an alien context—nature—where the institution that could ground it is simply lacking.[30]

---

[27] Onora O'Neill, *Towards Justice and Virtue: A Constructive Account of Practical Reasoning* (Cambridge: Cambridge University Press, 1996).　　[28] Ibid. 133.

[29] Raymond Geuss, *History and Illusion in Politics* (Cambridge: Cambridge University Press, 2001).

[30] It should be noted that Geuss goes on to grant that there may be some point in the strategy of declaring rights if this has some beneficial effect on the range of things that subsequently come to be

All these contributions pursue a similar line. They suggest that talk of 'natural' or 'human' rights (and, one might add, animal rights) amounts to either wishful thinking or damaging nonsense: it involves pretending that there are rights where no such rights exist. By thinking about the examples from tragedy that I outlined above, I think we can come to see that these conclusions are only partly right and in many ways gravely wrong, and for an interesting reason. For—it seems to me—if we think, with Geuss, O'Neill, and James, that there is no point in declaring that something has a right, when in fact it has no such right, then we have missed something important about what we are doing when we make such a declaration.

It is true that talk of 'natural rights', 'human rights', 'animal rights', and so on mimics the language of legal rights. In the case of legal rights, we can discover whether someone has a certain right by determining whether the legal statutes are in force and whether they apply to people in that category. Legal rights are first granted (and that requires a suitable sovereign body charged with inventing laws), and once granted, they hold indefinitely, providing that the necessary sanctions remain in place. Checking whether the right exists thus involves checking whether the law still applies, whether the candidate has the necessary qualifications, whether the body charged with fulfilling the attendant obligations is operative, and whether the candidate has any way of claiming the right. If one of the last two conditions is missing, the right, even if it is enshrined in statute, looks to be merely nominal or empty.

In the case of the supposed natural rights, the language looks temptingly similar, and that is surely not accidental. Rights activists clearly buy into the jargon that belongs to legal rights, in order to charge others, whose actions they deplore, with apparent failures to comply with moral rules that they represent as quasi-legal obligations. They speak as though there were statutes to which we were beholden, although we were never party to their enactment; as though there were candidates whose qualification is written into their genetic code, not deliberately awarded as a privilege; and as though the body charged with supplying the entitlements were the whole human race, regardless of whether anyone is actually in a position to do anything, and despite the fact that there is no recourse to any court of

granted as genuine rights in a society. This point differs somewhat from my suggestion that the idea of declaring a right is an act of a quite different kind, with not merely instrumental value.

appeal and no sanctions for omitting to comply (other than the violence, vandalism, and sabotage that are typically associated with campaigns for so-called animal rights).

When the language of rights is taken literally, as a quasi-legal claim, it does appear to yield nonsense, and part of why it is nonsense is clearly exposed by the considerations brought to bear by the political philosophers whose work I mentioned above. But that, I think, is because we mistake the significance of the talk of human rights, or natural rights, when it enters the moral arena. We suppose that because the language of natural rights employs the same terminology as the language of legal rights, it must be doing the same job; and that job requires that rights be invented by a legally sovereign authority and that they be accompanied by suitably enforced sanctions. Yet none of this exists for natural rights, and the users of human rights language seem undeterred by the absence of legal structures and unmoved by the lack of enforcement. They do not concede that no rights exist, even though the political structures are such that it is obvious that no such rights exist.

But despite all this, there is more to be said: when the language of rights is used in moral debate, it clearly derives from a deep and authentic need to express a moral truth which the speaker thinks is binding and absolute. It appears that the language of rights is the language which serves this purpose in current usage, as evidenced by the natural way in which that language appears in contemporary translations of Sophocles. It serves a specific purpose, which no other language can currently serve: namely, to assert a claim that some moral truth is objective and absolute, and not dependent upon anyone's whim.

Perhaps it is to be regretted that we have become accustomed to use this rather strange form of expression to make (and to support) our most profoundly intuitive moral claims. Effectively we use the language of legal positivism, in which rights are human constructs, invented, granted, and enforced by some human authority, and with binding effect over only those who owe allegiance to that authority; and then we try to transfer that language to an area in which positivism makes no sense, because we seem to be trying to say the very opposite: that nature lays down the rules—which actually means that nobody makes the rules, they just exist—and that the rules are binding on everyone even if they don't see them, and that they can be denied by no human authority. Certainly the similarity to legal language easily leads to misconceptions about what is being expressed—hence the damaging and cruel effects of misuse of this language in popular thought. That is effectively what James and O'Neill are rightly seeking to reveal.

Yet there might still be a useful role for the language of rights—though perhaps not the role that one might initially have supposed, from looking at the superficial appearance of the language. The proposal that I want to put forward is this: that the significance of such rights lies (and has always lain) not in the *possession* of them (perhaps there is no such thing) but in the *declaration* of them by others. My thought is that we currently have a way to express absolute moral claims, which is not exactly the way in which they were expressed in earlier periods of history (periods that were not so shy of appealing to the absolute commandments of God). The role that was formerly played by religious language, by appeals to divine authority and justice, is (in our post-Enlightenment era) played by utterances formulated in terms of rights; and this language is the jargon standardly used when people seek to offer justification for absolute moral judgements. It seems to me that the *thoughts* that we now express in this kind of rights talk have a long history. They are not new thoughts. They are old ideas put into a funny kind of pseudo-technical speak.

It is often said that the ancients lacked the notion of a right at all, let alone the notion of 'natural rights'.[31] Several recent thinkers have stressed the extent to which these notions, as we use them, are foreign to the ancient world. Raymond Geuss suggests that the modern notion of a (subjective) right is essentially feudal in origin, but derives ultimately from Roman private law regarding property transactions.[32] Jim Griffin has also suggested (following others) that the notion of rights as we now use it is a phenomenon that belongs to the post-Enlightenment world.[33] This is

---

[31] The debate about whether the ancients had a notion of rights became prominent in the early 1990s after Margaret Thatcher, then Prime Minister of Britain, claimed (in 1989, apropos the 200th anniversary of the French Revolution) that the concept of human rights had been invented by the ancient Greeks. Sorabji (*Animal Minds*, 134–57) reviews the debate and concludes that the Stoics' theory of the community of rational beings is not a doctrine of human rights; but he does concede that the Greeks had the concept of rights (i.e. they had ways of expressing the concept for which we have the word 'right'). Here he is endorsing views expressed by Myles Burnyeat (in an article in the *TLS* in 1990 and a talk on Radio 3 in 1992; see also Burnyeat's later article: 'Did the Ancient Greeks have a concept of Human Rights?', *Polis*, 13 (1994): 1–11).

[32] Geuss, *History and Illusion*, 132–3, 135.

[33] James Griffin, 'Discrepancies between the Best Philosophical Account of Human Rights and the International Law of Human Rights', *Proceedings of the Aristotelian Society*, 101 (2001): 1–28: 2–4, citing previous discussions by Richard Tuck, *Natural Rights Theories: Their Origin and Development*

because a 'right' as he understands it must be traced to a certain notion of the human person and, in particular, the idea of human agency. Although he thinks that there are antecedents in the late medieval and early modern period,[34] Griffin suggests that the characteristic modern use, in which appeal to God-given privileges is no longer the foundation, belongs to a post-Enlightenment project. On such a view, the first use of the typically modern notion cannot antedate the thinking that asks about morals in the absence of divinely sanctioned obligations.

It seems to me that an alternative account of the historical story would place a much greater emphasis on continuity: a continuity from earlier notions that convey the idea of what *we* would call rights (not necessarily with any identifiable term corresponding exactly to our 'right'). It is not necessary to be able to point to the same legalistic language, or to find a substantive noun serving the same role as our word for a right.[35] Nor is it crucial to find a usage that makes no appeal to something like divine authority. It may be that *we* do talk in substantive terms, and this is what generates the metaphysical nonsense of looking for mysterious facts about human beings that are their rights; but in expressing ourselves in this way, we may be trying to say something that others have always said in other ways, and sometimes more transparent ways—though, equally, their appeal to substantive deities may be a metaphysical move of much the same sort as our appeal to substantive rights.

(Cambridge: Cambridge University Press, 1979), and Richard Dagger, 'Rights', in *Political Innovation and Conceptual Change*, ed. Terence Ball, James Farr, and Russell L. Hanson (Cambridge: Cambridge University Press, 1989), 298–301.

[34] Griffin cites Giovanni Pico della Mirandola (1463–94) for his claim that humans have certain privileges grounded in the inherent dignity of humans as given by God. Griffin is not alone in emphasizing the novelty of these ideas. For fuller explorations of the medieval development of the terminology of rights with an emphasis on discontinuity (the idea of a 'watershed' or 'Copernican revolution'), see John Finnis, *Natural Law and Natural Rights* (Oxford: Clarendon Press, 1980); Michel Villey, 'La genèse du droit subjectif chez Guillaume d'Occam', in *idem, Seize essais de philosophie du droit* (Paris: Dalloz, 1969), 140–78; and Tuck, *Natural Rights Theories*.

[35] Although this point is made by Sorabji (*Animal Minds*, 153), and appears to lie behind some other attempts to trace rights in the pre-medieval period (e.g. Alan Gewirth, *Reason and Morality* (Chicago: University of Chicago Press, 1978), in practice it seems that virtually all the contributions to this debate (with the possible exception of Myles Burnyeat) tend to be looking for a quasi-legal notion. That is, they seem to take it for granted that 'having a concept of natural rights' essentially involves the transfer of legal concepts or vocabulary to moral judgements (otherwise it would not constitute a concept of natural rights). If I am right that importing legal vocabulary is a modern muddle, which misrepresents the structure of the underlying thought, then we should not expect to find that legalistic turn of phrase in what is effectively the same concept (i.e. it conveys the same moral outlook, though perhaps more transparently expressed) in the ancient world.

By turning back to the texts from antiquity, and reflecting on the contexts in which we find ourselves translating certain expressions of moral indignation into the modern language of rights, we can see more clearly what we are really trying to say when we declare that someone has a right, even (or perhaps particularly) when it is plain that they have no way of seeing their rights recognized in practice. Is it not the case that rights must be declared precisely in those circumstances? To declare them in circumstances when they are already enshrined in law is surely to miss the point?

Sketching a Possible Historical Story

Continuity or discontinuity? Perhaps the question about whether the idea of natural rights is peculiarly modern is ambiguous, because it is unclear which of two questions we are asking. Are we asking whether the moral outlook typically expressed in rights language is a new outlook (one that could not be thought, let alone expressed, in the past)? Or are we asking whether the form of expression that we use to express that outlook is a new form of expression, which was not available in the past (although the moral outlook that it expresses is clearly there in earlier cultures)?

If we are asking the first kind of question, and our conclusion is that the whole outlook is indeed new, then it will be irrelevant whether there is any antecedent vocabulary that resembles the language of rights, because we shall conclude that any such resemblance is illusory, since the whole outlook that is expressed in *our* talk of rights would be missing from their misleadingly similar talk of rights. If we are asking the second kind of question, and our conclusion is that the form of expression was not available in the past, that the language of rights is new, then the conclusion tells us about nothing except the choice of words in which we convey our thoughts. It would not tell us whether the thoughts themselves were not available to be expressed, or whether there was no other language in which to express them before the language of rights.

Neither of these quests will answer the question whether the thoughts expressed in rights language are good ones, or whether the development of such a vocabulary, if it was missing before, is a more perspicuous way to express these thoughts. If the thoughts are new, and they rest upon appeal to metaphysical foundations that are missing in reality, then it seems that the moral claims collapse to nothing. But if we are only engaged in answering the second question, about the use of a new form of linguistic expression, which might express a traditional idea that was formerly expressed a different way, then the issue is merely whether the language of rights is an effective way to express that kind of moral intuition, though we might also ask more aggressively about the legitimacy of that traditional kind of moral thinking, whose metaphysical foundations (now that they are expressed as rights) begin to look somewhat vacuous.

My suggestion is that what looks like an answer to the first kind of question should really be read as an answer to the second kind of question. We discover that the language looks to be relatively recent, not exactly replicated before the Enlightenment. But the question of whether the language was there before is irrelevant to the first question, since we are interested in whether the outlook is new, not the language. My suggestion is that we are faced not with a new kind of moral view but with a new kind of language. What is new is the harnessing of the quasi-legal language of rights in an attempt to justify and prop up a traditional way of thinking that is not new at all. So the historical story will be about how the language of legal rights came to be commandeered for this task, and perhaps also about why current generations find that language, with its appeal to mysterious metaphysical entities, more satisfying for moral discourse than the earlier forms of expression that served the same purpose in the past.

Arguably, tracing the history of how precisely we got from there to here is not entirely germane to my real project of showing that the same moral outlook figures in antiquity. Nor is the history essential in order to draw conclusions about whether the current language of rights does the job well. But since I want to suggest that we should see continuity in the moral outlook, underpinning gradual change in the conceptual map, it might help to flesh out that claim across the intervening centuries. On the other hand, a detailed historical investigation would be the subject of another book. What follows here is a brief sketch, purely speculative in character.

The story might go something like this. In the feudal societies of the Middle Ages a privileged group of nobles and overlords of one sort or another had rights over the fruits of other people's labour. Those who had the hereditary rights were entitled to receive their dues from those who lacked those rights but had, instead, the duties that correlated with them: the duty to provide the nobles with the services to which such nobles were entitled. It seems that this notion of entitlement, and of specified limits to the rights of each individual to demand specific services from their tenants and specific proportions of their produce, combined with corresponding rights on the part of the tenant to till the land and to retain a specified portion for his family, is already a legal notion of rights.[36] Of course, it is not a notion of universal rights, or of inalienable rights: for only some people have the privileges, and they can lose those privileges in many ways.

It comes naturally to us to explain the feudal system in the language of 'rights' with which we are familiar. So is it not the case that our notion of universal 'rights' simply grows out of that way of thinking, regardless of whence the word itself might have appeared?[37] And is it not also true that it does so at the expense of the coherence that its parent theory clearly had?

Starting from the medieval pattern of hereditary rights and privileges, let us ask the question 'What gives a person in such a society a particular right, which another person does not have?'. Any society which grants some individuals rights over others needs to have an answer to this question, which may, of course, be a different answer for different rights. But if we look for a general answer to questions of this sort that anyone in the Middle Ages would have been able to give, it is likely that it would invoke a combination of hereditary explanations (he has the right because his father had the right, and rights are inherited) and divine justifications (he and his forebears have these rights because they were given by God, or by God's representative the king, who has a God-given right to assign privileges of this sort).

Now I take it that the Enlightenment initiated the attempt to find some other 'natural' justification for rights. Once you question the supernatural origin and legitimation of unequal rights, there seem to be two possible egalitarian responses to the question 'What gives you this right that I do not have?'. One response, from those who are opposed to the idea of

---

[36] As Dagger notes ('Rights', 299) this idea, which antedates the language of 'rights', is tied up with notions of status and the powers and privileges that come with status or social rank. But, as I shall argue below, this is surely no less true of the period in which 'rights' becomes the favoured expression; but that fact is less obvious, because the idea of privilege has been replaced by the idea of rights. 'Privilege' is a less easy word to apply where the privileges are equally distributed to all; yet there seems at first sight nothing to stop us using the word 'right' for that, even though it conveys the same idea.

[37] Although the etymological connection between subjective rights and the notion of what is objectively right is interesting (see Dagger, 'Rights', 293–4), it has more to do with why *that* term comes to serve for the idea of a subjective right than why the notion of a subjective right, or of universal subjective rights, came to be useful in moral discourse.

inherited privilege, is to claim that nothing gives you the right: in fact, there can be no such thing as a right or privilege based simply on natural classifications. By this route we reach the conclusion that any rights that exist are political, and have to be granted by a legitimate political authority. Thus, on this account, the mistake made by those who assumed inherited political privilege was to suppose that something outside human political authorities granted privileges. But in fact, so the story goes, privilege is a man-made construct, and is granted by human beings to other human beings. This is a positivist response. Any right that actually exists is a legal right, and it belongs in a legal setting, and depends upon a legally recognized law-making body, while outside the legislative community no one has any rights. This view must logically lead to the claim that there is not, and cannot be, any such thing as a 'human right', because to suppose that there are human rights, which follow simply from being born human, is to make that age-old mistake, of supposing that privileges come by birth.

The other response that appears to be available to those who deny God-given privilege is to assert that, on the contrary, everyone actually has the same rights. That is, once you remove the appeal to God's arbitrary or rational selection of some at the expense of others, it makes no sense to think of some as privileged at the expense of others. So the preferred conclusion is that everyone (every human being) has equal and identical rights by nature.[38] This seems to me to be the response that leads to the notion of universal human rights; it is surely what the French were claiming to have invented at the Revolution. And it seems to derive from suggesting that whereas in the past people supposed that only a few people had rights, at the expense of the rest, now we can recognize that, at some fundamental level, everyone is entitled to the same.

However, set in this context of my suggestions about historical origins, this suggestion begins to look seriously incoherent. For rights that were formerly seen as belonging to the few are now thought to be equally available to all; yet these rights were themselves privileges, entitling the holder to have something at the expense of others; they were the right of the overlord, for instance, to receive food and service from his peasant farmers. He had the right to receive it, while they, the underprivileged,

---

[38] By nature—i.e. not by receiving God-given prerogatives (as God's chosen favourites), but simply in virtue of their birth. This seems to be the idea expressed in the first article of the 1789 Declaration of the Rights of Man and the Citizen from the French Revolution.

had the obligation to supply it. But to give everyone rights of this sort succeeds in giving no one anything, because there is no underclass to be exploited. The rights seem empty, because there is no one obliged to meet the obligations. It is a right exercised over no one, and, not surprisingly, it cannot be exercised.

Rights that Threaten No One

At first sight it looks as if we could rescue the notion of universal natural rights from this incoherence by suggesting that the rights in question are just those that entitle the holders to certain freely available commodities, the provision of which inconveniences no one. Rather than granting some people rights to other people's possessions and services, as in the feudal system, rights are now supposed to protect the individual's access to things that belong to no one in particular, or to the things that already belong to him, or to things that can be multiplied without cost. Typical examples might be the right to freedom of expression of various sorts, freedom to practise one's preferred religion, freedom of speech, and the right to a political voice in whatever elections are held and are open to other citizen members of one's country; and it might seem that the right to life or the right to marry or rear children would be of the same sort. Giving people access to these things, it might be argued, does not mean taking them from someone else. They are not privileges that implicitly presuppose a subject population to be exploited. You can increase the number of people who enjoy these privileges without diminishing the benefit to those who had them before, and therefore there is no good reason why such rights should be unevenly distributed. Surely, then, the thinking goes, justice demands that such opportunities be extended to all. The problem about identifying the person with the obligation to provide the services appears to be solved by making the rights primarily negative in conception, focusing on freedom to do certain things; and the result is that the obligation to ensure that such freedom is not infringed will fall upon all other members of the community who might potentially be in danger of infringing them, and particularly 'the powers that be'.

However, on closer analysis, this conception of rights that exploit no one is still incoherent in two ways. One problem is that it is difficult to see what desirable commodities there could be that would genuinely fit the bill. What appear to be typical examples turn out to be deeply problematic as soon as we encounter the sort of real-life situations in which people typically find themselves deprived of the so-called right. Notoriously, of course, the right to life appears to become a right to kill another person when circumstances are such that both cannot be saved; and this is only the more extreme case of what is invariably true—that life involves using resources that could have been directed to someone else. But even the right to freedom of speech or religion is no simple matter, since others may be directly or indirectly threatened by the promulgation of propaganda and the display of attitudes that are corrupting or offensive. Thus the silencing of voices will be practised by those who perceive a threat of this sort, and to defend the rights of one group to be heard over the rights of another group to be protected from prejudice is to promote unequal privileges. In general, with any resource to which there is supposed to be a right, it remains unclear who is obliged to give up their own privileges to satisfy the needs of those who have by some misfortune fallen into circumstances in which their needs and desires are not satisfied. Even the apparently free resources cannot be guaranteed without a knock-on effect that can threaten the rights of others.

Secondly, recent human rights talk seems to have changed the meaning of the word 'right', so that it is often applied in situations where the rights attributed to individuals are rights that they are not, in fact, in a position to exercise. In the legal use of rights language, a right was a privilege that an individual had that was enshrined in the customs of the society and recognized by the political regime. That was still true of the Declarations following the American and French Revolutions, where the programme of rights was about rights built into the political institutions of a new regime. In the new language of human rights, since the Universal Declaration of 1948, by contrast, someone might be said to have an unrecognized right, where the regime under which they live does not permit them to exercise it. But this is not an actual privilege, since the person in question does not in fact have privileged access to the commodity in question. Nor does any political or social structure take responsibility for guaranteeing the opportunity to exercise a right. In fact, the entire community might deny that the supposed right was genuine. The language, therefore, does not seem to describe the facts as they are on the ground. By claiming that the individual is entitled to freedom to practise her religion, one is not stating that she actually enjoys that freedom. Rather, one is making a claim about what *ought* to happen, and making such a claim in circumstances in which it is not happening, and where others do not see that it ought to happen. It is this empty kind of right, a right that cannot be claimed and cannot be enforced, about which O'Neill, James, and Geuss were expressing scepticism in the debate reviewed above.

So, in the current moral vocabulary, an appeal to rights seems frequently to be a way of asserting that things ought to be different. It is a way of declaring that you are committed to the importance of certain things, certain moral principles. It is used in circumstances where others are not so committed, or where others fail to see the need for commitment. It is used particularly when you see an injustice that strikes at the very deepest of creaturely needs, and particularly where the victim is vulnerable, unprotected, weak, disabled, dependent, injured, isolated, juvenile, or deprived of assistance. And it is a way of stating that you uphold these particular moral values, that you regard them as absolute and binding on everyone, and that you are prepared to stand up for them against any regime or any way of life that rejects them.

The fact that rights are proclaimed on behalf of those without a voice is crucial, as I suggested in discussing the examples from tragedy above. It shows that it is nonsense to think of a right as something that comes with certain psychological advantages such as the capacity for speech or for reason, since we are more likely to need to 'defend the rights' of something that is incapable of defending itself, something that is entirely dependent upon the mercy of more able individuals—such as a child, an imbecile, or a drugged laboratory animal. I apply scare quotes to 'defend the rights' because we perceive ourselves as doing that, when in fact there are no such rights but only needs that we take to be morally decisive.

So my claim is that human rights claims are properly made by a third party, and that this is the real point of the twentieth-century attempts to formulate declarations of such rights. They are statements of moral commitment made on behalf of those who are unjustly treated, and they express, in legal language, the moral values of the onlooker, to explain the principles on which they campaign against perceived injustices. It has often seemed that the analogy with legal rights means that a victim could lay claim to rights on his or her own behalf, and this invites the popular criticism that the 'rights mentality' leads to a selfish and assertive attitude, encouraging people to focus on their sense of dissatisfaction and to devote their energies to getting what they perceive as their rights in conflict with others who are perceived to threaten them. I suspect that this corruption is inevitable. It surely follows from the confusing and inappropriate aspects of the language; but it does not reflect the moral motivation of the fashion for producing declarations of human rights, which was a move by the privileged to defend the victims of oppression.

The Pros and Cons of Natural Rights

Does it help to declare that the oppressed have rights? Who is that declaration for? I have argued that the moral significance lies in the third party, the observer, who declares 'You can't do that' in protest at the victimization or injustice perpetrated against the innocent. The cry expresses the moral outlook of the observer, and it is a protest against the moral blindness of the oppressor. If the language is understood correctly, there is no metaphysical claim and no legal claim in these words: we are not saying that a law and sanctions exist in political space. We are saying, in effect, that a law and sanctions exist in moral space: that is, the oppressor cannot do these injustices and come out scot-free, for he is morally corrupted even by contemplating such unthinkable deeds.

So when we say that the *victim* has a right, we are using a kind of transferred language. We mean that the *perpetrator* has no right, no moral right, to do something that we consider to be unacceptable. Because there are no laws or sanctions against it in political space, the victim has no means to make a claim against those structures, for they do not exist. That is precisely why we have to cry 'Foul' in a moral, not a legal, voice. The utterance of the cry does not change that. The victim still has no more legal rights after we have protested than before, unless some political and statutory rights are incidentally added as a response.[39] But if that happens, as it sometimes does, then it has nothing to do with the moral cry: it is a separate procedure to add statutory backing to enforce moral values (but notice that they will then no longer be moral principles if the reason for

---

[39] Geuss's point here, that there can be instrumental value in invoking the notion of human rights where there are no existing rights. See above n. 30 and Geuss, *History and Illusion*, 144–5.

following them has now become fear of the legal sanctions, not abhorrence of the deed). So it will be a mistake to suppose that a victim whose moral rights have been declared on her behalf could then claim those rights in the first person.

So although the cry is on behalf of the voiceless victim, it does not make the victim less vulnerable: it does not change her status as defenceless and vulnerable to moral abuse. In fact, the cry is important not for her but for two other people: the protester and the perpetrator. We can see why if we consider the use of the word 'can't' in moral discourse.[40] The cry against human rights abuses answers to the word 'can't' in the protester's moral life when she says 'I can't let that go on happening; I must do something', and it answers to the word 'can't' in the perpetrator's moral life where others find themselves saying 'You can't do that! You must see what you're doing'. These 'can't's are not legal ones, for the problem is usually that the powerful regime has no legal constraints to prevent it from committing such abuses; nor are they physical ones, for the abuse is clearly going on and is not contrary to the laws of nature. The cry about human rights appeals to the idea that there is another kind of 'can't' whose sanctions come neither from physics nor from legal constraints. This 'can't' reflects the constraints of moral integrity: you can't get away with it without the loss of moral standing. So the cry 'You have no right to do that' is intended for the perpetrator, to bring him to see the moral constraints that should move him to draw back from such horrors; and it is intended to express and put into words the moral vision which moves the bystander; to describe the moral world that she lives in, in which she find those actions horrific. In that world, the moral world of the observer, the victim is seen as the possessor of inalienable rights, rights that have been egregiously ignored in the perpetration of the violence against him. In this sense the cry is not designed to communicate anything to the victim: it is intended to give utterance to a moral vision that the bystander needs to share with those in a position of power.

In earlier generations these absolute moral constraints, the moral 'can't', were fleshed out in other kinds of substantial images, typically as an account of what God says we must do, what the gods like, or in Antigone's image of unwritten and unshakeable rules of conduct handed down from before any

---

[40] See above Ch. 1, pp. 7–9.

man-made rules got going. There is a temptation even there to assimilate them to a kind of legal structure, with the idea that the penalty for breaking them is falling into disfavour with the divine beings who have an interest in these things. There is a temptation to fill out the phrase 'You can't do that' with 'or the gods will do terrible things to you'. It is plausible to suppose that it is because that religious account of moral constraints has lost its credibility, and current generations think that they must seek a naturalistic account of morality, that the language of natural rights appeals. Where an absolute bottom line in morality is required, one that is not relativized to human perceivers or institutions and cultures, Western liberalism tries to avoid God and substitute natural rights. But in fact it is only doing exactly the same thing, replacing one set of imaginary entities, the gods, with another set of imaginary entities, rights, which produce the very same structure of moral rules, the breaking of which offends against some authority that is independent of any human judgement. In neither case does the imagery make perspicuous what the real source of the constraint is: namely, absolute moral value, for which the whims of nature, gods, or humans are all equally irrelevant.

On the other hand, the attraction of rights talk is that it captures the orientation to the victim: we want to say 'You can't do that to him/her/it', and the reason is that we think that he or she is important. This captures the structure of the motivation, the bystander's concern for the victim. But actually, when we say that the victim has a right, this isn't something in the victim. Rather, there is something offensive about the action. In addition, rights talk has a misleading universality about it. Where the ends are trivial and the suffering gross, we might actually want to say 'It is offensive to do that to this cat *just for the sake of testing a contraceptive*', where one might not wish to say that there could never be any circumstances in which the kind of misery that is here being inflicted would be justifiable. So putting the creature through such misery for the sake of frivolous gains, or to conceal other forms of moral or physical corruption endemic in human society, is the more outrageous and offensive because of the corruption that it reveals in the human value system. So, just as in the case of *human* rights, it is not only offensive that people should be massacred, but even more offensive that people should be massacred in circumstances where we have sold arms to the perpetrators to fund our comfortable lifestyle, so, equally, it is not only offensive that cats should be tortured, but the more offensive that they should be tortured for the benefit of cosmetics and drugs companies. These nuances are elided by simple talk of rights.[41]

So when we cry 'Foul', we are not saying that nature has some abhorrence for such deeds. Nature abhors a vacuum, but she does not abhor the killing of the innocent. If we say that God disapproves, that is because the only god we could choose to believe in would be one who upheld and respected moral truths. If we say that there are age-old rules, we do not mean that there is a punishment available in nature for those who break those rules. Alas no, for it is often the ones who break those rules who gain the natural advantage. Nature, sadly, favours the evil-doer over the scrupulous. There is no morality in nature. Moral offences have no damaging consequences, except the immediate effect: namely, that one has become the sort of person who has done that kind of thing. If one is not moved by that awful prospect, then rights talk will be used in vain. But rights talk is clearly popular, because those who do share a deep respect for moral value are desperately seeking some metaphor in which to capture the absolute and binding nature of that value, with respect to all kinds of action by moral beings, towards anything that one cares for.

'Anything one cares for' can include immaterial objects, works of art, natural scenery, homes, castles, architectural monuments, and the beautiful and wondrous creatures of nature, trees, rivers, and cliffs. The question whether such things have rights is a nonsense question, for rights are just the imagery we use to capture the idea that those items figure as possible recipients of abuse and mistreatment by others who have no moral judgement.[42] It could make sense to protest against the destruction of the Parthenon even if the Greek nation had been wiped off the earth, and it would make sense to protest against torturing a dead man's grieving dog, even if the owner were not there to suffer and there were no other observers to be offended. In both cases we have the same structure of a perceived absolute moral outrage committed against a voiceless victim. That is the structure that elicits talk of rights—but the oddity of talking of the rights of the Parthenon or the rights of the white cliffs of Dover suggests

---

[41] For an attempt to capture something along these lines, see Scruton, *Animal Rights and Wrongs*, 86–7.

[42] Here I do not mean that the question whether they have rights is to be answered 'no' (which is what I think Scruton and Carruthers would both claim: Scruton, *Animal Rights and Wrongs*, 66; Carruthers, *The Animals Issue*, 1). Rather that the question is misconceived, because nothing has rights in the requisite sense, and the nonsense of attributing rights to these objects shows that.

that such talk is an ill-chosen metaphor that stretches until it breaks at this point. On the other hand, the idea may be close to what was meant by primitive cultures when they said that the rivers and the trees were gods.

Do Animals Have Rights?

It follows that the question 'Do animals have rights?' cannot sensibly be asked, because rights as such do not exist; only declarations of rights exist, and they can be appropriate, based on genuine moral perception, or inappropriate, based on decadent, distorted, or sentimental values.

Yet there is nothing to rule out such a cry of protest on behalf of the victims of horrendous cruelty when those victims are animals. On the contrary, this clearly can be done coherently for animals. If declaring rights is a way of defending the defenceless, then speaking up against cruelty for the ones who lack a voice of their own is exactly where it comes into its own. The last thing we should be supposing is that it is because they lack speech that they cannot be the holders of rights—where this means that they cannot be seen as victims of outrageous mistreatment that offends our deepest moral sensibilities. It is precisely those who lack speech whom we must defend in this way.[43]

So just as there is a more urgent need to stand up for the rights of the unborn, and of infants and children, and of the disabled and imbeciles, because they are not in a position to defend themselves and are unable to resist oppression, so too there is a greater claim from animals (and equally from plants and inanimate parts of nature and the built environment) upon our vicarious moral outrage. Few of us are well placed to make such moral judgements about other adult autonomous human beings, or to intervene on the international political scene, in the way we so often try to do from the liberal West. But many of us are well placed to see when our own society ruthlessly disposes of its unborn children in incinerators, farms its gentle, grass-loving beasts in prison conditions for the sake of cheap and

---

[43] The same is true of any other supposed intellectual or mental deficiency on the part of animals, such as their inability to engage in forward planning or their lack of deliberation. For the weaker and less autonomous the victim in its dealings with the more powerful human oppressors, the more urgent the need for a vicarious champion who will uphold the cause on that creature's behalf. Bacteria, however, being stronger and better at forward planning than humans, do not usually need to have their rights defended—which goes to show that the need for rights talk occurs only in the case of those who are vulnerable and weak, as well as voiceless.

unwholesome meat, and exploits laboratory animals to test commercial drugs that are destined to prolong some ageing overweight population in their decadent lifestyle for a few extra decrepit years.

So we might wish to speak on behalf of dumb beasts and unborn children. We might find that we can't avoid it, where the 'can't' is a moral 'can't'. And we might try to use the language of rights, for want of anything else. But when we cry that someone else has rights, it doesn't change their powerlessness. What it tries to change is the moral climate: it proclaims that for all right-thinking people those objects should be objects of concern, and that the offence is on the part of those who fail to see things that way. It is a cry from the morally perceptive to try to open the eyes of those who cannot see, as Odysseus cried out against Agamemnon's assumption that he could trample on his dead enemy, and Neoptolemus cried out against Odysseus's assumption that the need to win the war at Troy justified taking Philoctetes' bow.[44]

---

[44] Note the misleading sense that one has given a reason in response to the question 'Why can't I trample all over him?' when one says that he has a right not to be trampled on. It is just as wrong to think that 'because he has a right' gives a reason as it is to think that 'because God says so' gives a reason. Maybe the morally blind person may be impressed by 'God will punish you' and do the right thing out of naïve fear. Equally, the morally confused person may think that if rights have been declared and agreed by a large consensus of people, then such rights are real, and one ought to be moved to comply. But both will be equally morally blind: unless one is moved to declare rights where they are not recognized, and to decide autonomously that one cannot do that to such a person, one is merely blindly following a popular habit. Following or adhering to declarations of rights is not virtuous, though making such declarations may be (*if* they are sound).

8

On Self-Defence and Utilitarian Calculations: Democritus of Abdera and Hermarchus of Mytilene

Earlier, in Chapter 3, we encountered Xenophanes' tale of Pythagoras and the puppy. Pythagoras protested against the beating of the puppy because, he said, he recognized the soul of a friend. To identify something 'as a friend' is, as we noticed, to see oneself as standing in a certain caring relation to it. The claim that it is a friend is not so much the *justification* or reason for regarding it as having a moral claim on oneself as an expression of one's recognition of its claim.

Nevertheless, there is a sense in which something can be friend or foe in a more factual way. A friend is someone who helps you; a foe is someone whose behaviour gets in your way. It seems to be a matter of objective fact that some creatures threaten our well-being and compete for resources that contribute to our quality of life. Slugs just do eat lettuces, and when they eat our lettuces, what is left of those lettuces, if anything, just is less good to eat. That is not something that will change as a result of changes in our values (unless we find a way of no longer wanting lettuces).

I have been presenting an argument to the effect that a humane moral response to the beasts is not grounded in any facts about what they are like, or about their interests or ours. But here it seems that we have a set of facts about the beasts: namely, whether they contribute to or damage our objective well-being, which might seem to be the grounds for determining what our moral response *should be*. It might seem reasonable to hold that we should preserve creatures that have a generally positive effect on our lives (friendly bacteria, ladybirds), wage a general war on those that make life hell (streptococci, mosquitoes, scorpions), while leaving the rest to get on with their lives provided they don't get in our way. Could we not derive a sensible guide to action, morally justified action, on the basis of this simple objective distinction between friend and foe?

In this chapter I shall explore the work of two thinkers from antiquity who took just this line, and urged the importance of killing animals where killing is necessary and justified.[1]

Democritus on the Death Penalty

Democritus is the more famous of the two early atomists, Leucippus and Democritus, who were active around the time of Socrates and the Sophists, in the second half of the fifth century BC. We possess around 300 fragmentary quotations from Democritus's numerous writings. Many of the less well-thumbed passages from these are on ethical themes. There is a set of such quotations, preserved as a group in Stobaeus's anthology,[2] which appear to be directly addressing the issue of the ethics of killing animals.[3]

Democritus invokes the notion of self-defence as the key to deciding what is justifiable. Animals can be killed, he suggests, if they pose a threat. The notion of a threat is expressed in terms of actual or intended injustice:

Concerning the killing or not killing of certain animals the matter stands thus: the man who kills those who do injustice and who wish to do injustice is not guilty—indeed to do so contributes more to the general good than not to do so. (Democritus, B 257)

Here Democritus clearly finds no problem in talking of other animals 'doing injustice' or 'wishing to do injustice', and there is no attempt to

---

[1] These thinkers hold that it is important morally that we should kill animals. Pro-vegetarian writers sometimes naïvely suppose that no one could hold that vegetarianism is morally wrong. Dombrowski, for example, argues that vegetarianism must be either morally right or supererogatory, and that anyone who does not find themselves obliged to adopt a vegetarian diet must have concluded that it is supererogatory (Dombrowski, *Vegetarianism*, 120). But this does not follow. One might hold that vegetarianism was a morally neutral decision or that it was morally wrong: both these views are compatible with taking it seriously. In this chapter we shall encounter utilitarian reasoning that leads to an obligation to eat meat. Equally, on my own account of moral sensibilities, which is not utilitarian and does not endorse the views explored in this chapter, it would be morally wrong to refuse animal products from humanely farmed beasts. See Ch. 9.   [2] Stob. *Flor.* 4. 2. 13–18.
[3] These fragments are treated by Sorabji, *Animal Minds*, 107–8, and John Procopé, 'Democritus on politics and care of the soul', *Classical Quarterly*, 39 (1989): 307–31; 311–12.

distinguish between those who do and those who don't possess a concept of justice, those who do and those who don't have the capacity to think in moral terms.[4] It appears that one can be 'just' or 'unjust' simply in terms of whether one does in fact encroach unfairly on another creature's possessions or livelihood, whether knowingly or not. And although the beasts are envisaged as 'intending to do injustice' on occasion, this clearly does not mean that they subscribe to a concept of justice and then deliberately flout it. Rather, it is simply that an animal 'wishes to do injustice' just in virtue of intending to take or eat or destroy something that it has no right to take or eat or destroy (whether it is aware of that fact or not).

Democritus's objective seems to be to place the beasts within the same moral sphere as human enemies and criminals. He encourages us to deduce our obligations to both human and animal offenders on this basis. The rules for the treatment of other animals are to follow exactly the same lines as the moral obligations with regard to fellow human beings. Indeed, this seems to be exactly what Democritus goes on to recommend, though his formulation is revealing:

It seems to me that we ought to do the same in the case of humans, exactly as has been proposed in respect of vermin and creepy-crawlies: namely to kill anyone hostile, in accordance with the traditional customs, in the entire cosmos, wherever law does not exercise constraint. The sources of constraint for each society are the local religion and treaties and oaths.[5] (Democritus, B 259)

The order in which Democritus presents his reasoning here, beginning with the rules for offending animals and then deriving the rules for human offenders, suggests that he is not citing an established use of the death penalty for human criminals in order to infer that we should extend its use to the battle against beastly enemies. Rather, he begins by establishing the rule in relation to animals, by urging us to grant that eliminating pests in the animal

---

[4] On this issue, see Sorabji, *Animal Minds*, 107–8.

[5] It is likely (but not certain) that 'as has been proposed' refers to claims made by Democritus earlier (e.g. in B 257), but the verb could also refer to established rules about such killing. 'Wherever law does not exercise constraint' may mean 'wherever we are not debarred from killing' (i.e. recognizing that homicide is contrary to sacred customs or other recognized norms in some communities) or 'wherever the local customs do not restrain the wrongdoer from committing the evil acts'; so it would follow that we have a right to impose the death penalty upon members of an alien society that fails to control its own citizens (e.g. fails to prevent them from engaging in piracy, terrorism, or war crimes) even if that society itself has laws that would prohibit the execution of the criminals. The former makes Democritus relatively mild, and relativistic, in that he allows local custom to be a binding constraint upon the administration of the death penalty, even if the perpetrator is a direct threat to human well-being.

kingdom contributes to general well-being, and is therefore recommended as good practice. He then goes on to propose that the same conclusion should apply to human enemies: we should treat them exactly like vermin.

The justice of administering death to human enemies appears, arguably, to be the more controversial of the two proposals, since it is argued for on the basis of the previous claims about animals. But perhaps it is not so much the death penalty itself that is controversial, but rather the utilitarian reasoning on which it is here founded. Democritus seeks to establish issues of justice and morality on the basis of what contributes most to the quality of human life.

It may be that the assumption of parity between humans and animals is also a novelty. Democritus is saying not just that we may, with impunity, inflict the death penalty on criminals and enemies, if we so wish. He is saying that we must do so: it is an obligation. And we must do so for exactly the same reason as we must do so to animals—namely, for the sake of improving our living conditions. Just as we cull the pests that pose a threat to our livelihood, so we must exterminate undesirable human beings. Two further fragments in the same group (B 256 and 258) stress the idea that failing to administer justice, where it is due, counts as committing injustice, just as much as doing what is forbidden. It is *obligatory*, Democritus tells us, to kill anyone and anything that unjustly causes trouble, and to do so *at any cost*. The person who performs the required killing in those circumstances reaps rewards in the estimation of their community (B 258). And anyone who kills a bandit or a robber is to be immune from punishment for the homicide, whether he did it by his own hand, or it was done on his instructions, or it happened as a result of his casting a vote.[6]

So it is just as wrong, according to Democritus, to neglect our duty, by failing to eliminate the vermin (whether human or not), as it is to do other kinds of positive injustice. 'Wrong' here appears to be a moral wrong, given the mention of justice and injustice. Yet, as we have seen, Democritus founds the moral wrong on the damage it does to our interests. There is a direct correlation between doing what is in our best interests and doing what

---

[6] Democritus, B 260. The significance of this immunity (which is more than just protection from punishment and means, rather, that the homicide should be regarded as unsullied by the act) needs to be appreciated in the context of the ancient understanding of the pollution that comes from homicide. Democritus appears to be condoning—or even recommending—vigilante pre-emptive strikes against criminals, and suggesting that they are to be treated on a par with the legal imposition of the death penalty on the orders of the official magistrates or democratic courts.

is right: indeed, what is right reaps us rewards in terms of honour, precisely because it reaps society rewards in terms of utility. The thinking resembles Protagoras's idea that the sense of moral right and wrong, and the procedures of social and political justice, serve as a survival factor for the human race.[7] But, unlike Protagoras, Democritus draws no significant line between mankind and the beasts. We do not wage war on the beasts for the benefit of the human race. Rather, we wage war on enemies and criminals: any one who threatens our well-being. If those enemies are human, we execute them or condone their murder. If they are beasts, we cull them. There is no difference, and there should be no difference, according to Democritus.

Hermarchus of Mytilene

Democritus, as we have noted, was roughly contemporary with the great Sophists of the fifth century. He was probably a bit younger than Protagoras, with whom (as we have seen) he can be fruitfully compared in respect of his ethical views. But for various reasons, to do with the prevailing fashions in the history of philosophy, we rarely juxtapose Democritus with social and political thinkers of the time, such as the Sophists. We tend more often to place him with previous contributors to the cosmological tradition in Presocratic philosophy.

As the founders of atomism, Democritus and his shadowy predecessor, Leucippus, had an afterlife in the later resurgence of atomism in the Hellenistic period. Epicurus and his followers looked back to the early atomists as one of their major sources of inspiration in developing their fundamentally materialist account of the world and of human life within it. It is perhaps not accidental, then, that something very similar, on the lines of the ethical utilitarianism that we have just discerned in Democritus's justification for the death penalty, should resurface later, in Epicurean thought, as part of a similar package designed to reduce ethics to a materialist metaphysics.

In the remainder of this chapter I shall explore some views on the correct treatment of animals offered by the Epicurean philosopher Hermarchus of Mytilene (c.325–250 BC). Hermarchus was a pupil of Epicurus at Epicurus's

---

[7] Pl. *Prt.* 320c–322d. Protagoras's version differs in so far as the participants do not themselves see their moral values as a survival factor or recommend them for that reason. For discussion of Protagoras's myth, see above, Ch. 2.

first school, founded in 310 BC in Mytilene on Lesbos, and he went with Epicurus first to Lampsacus and then to Athens, where he succeeded Epicurus as head of the School on the death of Epicurus in 270 BC.

Little of Hermarchus's work survives. The material relating to animals, together with its context in a broader explanatory account of the genealogy of morals, is preserved by Porphyry in his work on vegetarianism, *De abstinentia* (*On Abstinence from Living Things*). Porphyry, himself a Neoplatonist of the third century AD and a pupil of Plotinus, discusses Hermarchus's views, as part of his survey of earlier material related to his topic—in which he covers both those who held views congenial to his own position and some with whom he disagrees.[8] Hermarchus falls into the latter category.[9]

For his part, Porphyry held that philosophers should modify their attitude to be more sparing of animals, both because eating meat is undesirable for the philosophical life and because the evidence for animals' intelligence suggests that conventional ways of treating them are inhumane.[10] But Hermarchus's concerns were evidently rather different. He was not seeking to modify our moral intuitions. On the contrary, he was trying to shore them up by showing that they are sound and well founded. Using a genealogical aetiology, in the form of a story about early human society comparable to that used by Plato's imaginary Protagoras,[11] Hermarchus aims to show why such norms were adopted initially and to give grounds for approving them as valid.

We shall focus here on the excerpts given by Porphyry in *De abstinentia*, 1. 7–12.[12] Hermarchus's interests, in the passage that Porphyry has selected, were evidently only partly in how we ought to treat animals. Like Democritus, he rightly saw that the issue of how we treat other animals led on to the related question of how we must behave towards other human beings, and then, like many philosophers of subsequent generations, he thought that in giving answers to either or both of these questions, we presuppose

---

[8] Porphyry's project is discussed more extensively below, Ch. 9.

[9] Hermarchus's work, the content of which we know only from the excerpts preserved by Porphyry, was an attack on Empedocles. The polemical parts have been omitted by Porphyry, so we can only speculate as to what aspects of Empedocles' views were considered objectionable. A papyrus from Oxyrhynchus (*P Oxy* 3318) has recently confirmed that the title of the work was probably *Pros Empedoclea* (*Against Empedocles*), but unfortunately adds no further useful content. See Dirk Obbink, 'Hermarchus, *Against Empedocles*', *Classical Quarterly*, 38 (1988): 428–35.

[10] On these topics, see further in Ch. 9.   [11] Pl. *Prt.* 320c–322d. See above, Ch. 2.

[12] Since the attribution is secure, and Porphyry's quotations are extensive and evidently reliable, I shall refer to the material as Hermarchus, rather than Porphyry. The text is also available in A. A. Long and David N. Sedley, *The Hellenistic Philosophers*, 2 vols. (Cambridge: Cambridge University Press, 1987), 22M and N; see also Long and Sedley's brief notes *ad loc.* i. 134–6.

an answer to the more fundamental question, 'Why?'. If it is wrong to kill human beings, why is it wrong? Only if we can answer that question, it seems, can we say whether it is also wrong to kill animals for the same reason. So Hermarchus tries to expound the reasons behind morality, law, and political community, in order to explain why we have an abhorrence for killing our own kind. In his view, morality is not simply a given, or absolute, but must be explicable by reference to some intended purpose that it serves, whose results are evidently good. Only then can morality be justifiable and obligatory, he supposes.

Conscious and Unconscious Motives

Hermarchus's method of investigating the foundations of morality resembles that of Plato's Protagoras character (as we have noted) and anticipates later thinkers from Hobbes to Nietzsche and, indeed, Rawls.[13] He analyses the reasons for existing moral rules by casting back to some notional lawgivers long ago, who first laid down the rules—'the ancient lawgivers', as Porphyry calls them.[14] We need not suppose that Hermarchus has in mind a particular time in history when moral rules were formally devised. What matters is the claim that the rules are all of them invented; they did not exist from all time.[15]

It is important for Hermarchus that the laws should be invented, established deliberately, for good reason, on the basis of their contribution to purposes perceived as reasonable by an intelligent agent. It would not be helpful to consider the laws to be natural, since, for the Epicurean, nature itself cannot be purposive. Its effects are only ever either mechanical or meaningless matters of chance. Hence the notion that something was natural would not, for the Epicurean, count as a reason in favour of acting upon it or counting it as good. An artificially constructed morality would have a greater claim to be worthy of respect, particularly so if it can be shown to be systematically designed to achieve an improvement in the quality of life.

Thus rules of conduct cannot be shown to be good in virtue of being natural. Nor, of course, could they be god-given commands, since there are, for the Epicureans, no gods of a sort to engage in that kind of activity. So there is no mileage in the thought that the rules might have an inscrutable

---

[13] Porphyry uses the term 'genealogy' to describe Hermarchus's method (*Abst.* 1. 7. 1).
[14] οἱ παλαιοὶ νομοθέται (*Abst.* 1. 7. 1).   [15] *Abst.* 1. 8. 1.

purpose known only to a divine being with a greater understanding than our own. It follows, therefore, that if Hermarchus is to persuade us that it is rational to take the existing moral code seriously, it must be on the basis of reasons that we, as human observers, can recognize as worthwhile.

This is what Hermarchus undertakes to offer. The moral rules by which we live, he claims, were invented by intelligent people for the long-term benefit that they provide; they were introduced to willing subjects, who perceived that they were worthwhile and chose to follow them for their perceived value:

For none of the rules that are currently in force—the sort of rules that we hand down either in a written or in an unwritten form—none of them was imposed from the beginning; rather they were established because people accepted them. The people who introduced the rules excelled not in physical strength or tyrannical power over the people but in their intelligence. (*Abst.* 1. 8. 1–2)

In the beginning, Hermarchus says, the moral rules were not just accepted unquestioningly from authority or tradition, though they may be now. By looking to a distant past when the rules were invented, Hermarchus allows for a gap between the way people understand the rules now and the real reasons for obeying the rules. Hence it need be no objection to his theory that many people do not consciously formulate their reasons for complying in terms of a utilitarian calculus. Once the rules have become embedded, most people take them on trust, without checking whether they are yielding a net benefit: indeed, we may perceive them as harmful to our interests. But this does not alter the fact that—so Hermarchus argues—originally the rules must have been introduced precisely because they were seen to be beneficial.

In fact, Hermarchus envisages only two possible motivations for moral conformity. One is that a person sees the utilitarian value of a rule and willingly follows it for that reason; this is the motivation for morality that would have held in the original condition. The other is that one perceives the threat of punishment if one were to refuse to conform, so that one conforms out of fear of the sanctions, while failing to recognize the true reason for to following the rules. This is the motivation for morality that prevails in the current conditions. Perhaps he should have added a third possibility, one that is surely widespread: namely, that one might obey the moral precepts out of a (mistaken) belief that they matter for some other reason—that is, not for their long-term profit to the human race (which is the real reason why they matter, according to Hermarchus) but for some other non-utilitarian reason. Hermarchus makes only a passing mention, in connection with the notion of ritual impurity for homicide, of an additional religious awe, which adds to the fear of punishment in dissuading people from carelessly taking human lives.[16]

But in any case, Hermarchus rightly observes that there may be a gap between our perceived—or subjective—reasons for acting in a particular way towards our fellow human beings and the real—objective—reasons for doing so. As far as he is concerned, since the value of morality lies solely in its consequences, it does not matter at all whether most people act for the wrong reasons, e.g. out of fear or out of slavish respect for authority. As long as the ends at which morality is aimed are achieved, any motivation will do. And of course the ends, as he identifies them, are achieved perfectly well if people do the right deeds for the wrong reasons.[17] So morality functions without any difficulty, even where everyone fails to perceive the good reasons for acting upon it. And even if no one notices that it is beneficial, there could still be good objective reasons for being moral, and the world could be better for having a well-respected moral code.

Natural Inclinations and Harmful Tendencies

Surely, however, it could happen that besides the moral precepts, which (on Hermarchus's view) are designed to yield beneficial outcomes, some instincts or natural tendencies might be similarly beneficial or useful. Our habit of acting in those natural or instinctive ways might be beneficial, but not motivated by anticipation of benefits, just as (in the developed society) moral actions are advantageous but are not always motivated by the perceived advantages.

For instance, we might feel abhorrence from killing our own kind out of a kind of instinctive pity or sympathy. Might that not be an irresistible natural feeling, rather than an acquired disposition, or calculated decision?

---

[16] See the passage on the institutions of ritual purification, *Abst.* 1. 9. 3–5.

[17] The analysis will work only if morality, or moral virtue, is identified with the performance of deeds according to a code of conduct. If morality includes the motivation with which a deed is done (or if intentions are important in evaluating an agent's behaviour), then this analysis of morality breaks down, not because one couldn't give a utilitarian analysis of the value of good intentions, but because neither apparent virtue achieved through fear of sanctions nor virtuous actions done for the sake of gain would be of any moral value.

If so, the habit of sparing our own kind could surely have become an established social convention without any antique lawgiver ever having proposed it as a rule of conduct on the basis of the likely long-term benefits. Those benefits would incidentally accrue from the habit, even if the habit had just emerged from natural human instincts.

Hermarchus wants to deny that possibility. He wants to rule out the idea that natural fellow feeling played any significant role in the development of a moral injunction against killing our own kind.[18] Clearly he judges that such instinctive guides to action would be inferior to reasons based on rational deliberation of costs and benefits. Given his view of nature, which has no intentions, and hence no good purpose of its own, natural inclinations cannot be trusted as a guide to what is actually beneficial, for natural inclinations will often be random, or, indeed, counterproductive. So it would be a bad policy to follow natural inclinations in devising rules concerning what is morally acceptable. Lacking either natural teleology or divine providence, the Epicurean can appeal to nothing else in establishing that an action is commendable than its utility, its advantageous outcome.

For these reasons, Hermarchus denies that we follow our inclinations in determining what is right or wrong. Indeed, there is a risk that we might have a natural repugnance against killing other *animals*, and that disinclination, in Hermarchus's view, would clearly be harmful to human interests. Such a reluctance to kill animals would be profoundly misguided: for in fact, sparing the other animals would be the wrong thing to do—wrong, because damaging in its consequences.[19]

To establish that morality is indeed rational, Hermarchus compares the rules about murder and manslaughter.[20] Why are there laws that punish accidental killing, not just deliberate murder? Such laws, Hermarchus suggests, make no sense unless either the killing itself was causing damage,

---

[18] *Abst.* 1. 7. 1. Paul Vander Waert, 'Hermarchus and the Epicurean genealogy of morals', *Transactions of the American Philological Association*, 118 (1988): 87–106; 94, argues in favour of supposing that Hermarchus did use the term *oikeiosis*, which is normally associated with the Stoics, and that it is not an anachronistic intrusion in Porphyry's paraphrase (as suggested by Long and Sedley, *Hellenistic Philosophers*, ii. 137). But I do not think there is a puzzle to be resolved (except, trivially, the anticipation of vocabulary standardly associated with Chrysippus), for I think that Hermarchus is not endorsing the Stoic idea that fellow feeling plays a role in the origin of moral thinking, but rather dismissing it. I would punctuate (and translate) slightly differently from Long and Sedley. Roughly the thought is as follows: 'The ancient lawgivers prohibited homicide … albeit we may indeed have a certain fellow feeling and distaste for it, but (whatever the Stoics say) that was not the reason … The real reason was utilitarian calculation.' For my translation, see below, p. 219.   [19] *Abst.* 1. 12. 2.

[20] *Abst.* 1. 9. 1–3.

or there was potential damage, perhaps from the negligence encouraged by a light-hearted attitude to such deaths. So the existence of laws against accidental homicide imply that the lawgivers were interested in the detrimental effects that such occasions of death have, whether on individuals or on a society. They were not just interested in punishing evil motives as such. They were clearly interested in preventing detrimental effects.

Thus Hermarchus is committed to the view that the only good motives for adopting laws and moral rules for a particular society must be motives based on rational calculation of advantages. He assumes that this is, in fact, the basis on which our present rules were worked out. Of course, it is conceivable that not all the primitive lawgivers were in fact intelligent or good at determining the best possible rules. Hermarchus takes it for granted that we do in practice have a well-designed system of morality. Part of the basis for this confidence lies in the notion that the laws were adopted because they were respected by the people, and the people respected them because they recognized that they formulated explicitly what they had themselves been aiming at in a subconscious way.[21] We have already seen that Hermarchus rules out the idea that the rules were imposed by force on an unwilling people.[22]

The Argument about Animals

In the extract quoted in chapter 10 of Porphyry's first book, Hermarchus extends his argument about the reasons behind existing moral codes to explain the standard moral rules about how to treat animals. Assuming that we can trust Porphyry's presentation of the material, Hermarchus was trying to show that our practices in this area are consistent with our practice in caring for other human beings, and that both alike are designed to secure the well-being of human society. So, whereas we have a profound abhorrence for the killing of our own kind, when it comes to non-human animals we are prepared to kill them, at least in certain circumstances. Someone might doubt whether there could be a clear and consistent reason why the same action should be right for one creature and wrong for another.

To start with, it is a mistake to think that there could be no consistent reason, as Hermarchus points out. Just because what is admissible in one circumstance is not right in another, it does not follow that there is no

---

[21] *Abst.* 1. 7. 3; 1. 8. 2; 1.10. 4; 1. 11. 1.   [22] *Abst.* 1. 8. 2.

universal principle behind the rules.[23] Hermarchus suggests that there are two similar mistakes that people might make in this matter.[24] One is to ignore or fail to notice the universal principles, treating them (incorrectly) as something 'indifferent'—that is to say, of no moral significance.[25] The other mistake is to suppose (correctly) that some principles have universal moral significance, but to misidentify which rules have that universal status. This happens when people elevate to universal significance rules which properly apply only in certain circumstances and in relation to certain things.

What exactly is going on here? I think it is this. Hermarchus holds that there is a universal principle behind all particular precepts, and it is the idea of maximizing what is beneficial to us. If we see all the particular precepts as applications of that general rule, we shall see that there is indeed a universal aspect to morality, even where the detailed customs differ from place to place and from species to species. But the mistake of the first group—the ones who fail to recognize the general principle as a moral matter—is (here) the mistake of supposing that a general principle of pursuing what is beneficial to the human race is not a moral principle, is not in itself a matter of moral obligation (but merely indifferent).[26] These people think that pursuing what is beneficial is something that is neither good nor bad in itself. It all depends on what the circumstances are and how it is done. In that sense it is 'indifferent' in the technical (Stoic) sense. Their mistake (according to Hermarchus) lies in supposing that such a principle could not be a grounding for morality, on the grounds that it is not itself a principle that has any inherent value.

---

[23] Compare Augustine's discussion of the same error (*Conf.* 3. 7. 13).   [24] *Abst.* 1. 12. 3.

[25] It appears that Hermarchus means that people are not aware that some things that they take for granted (because they are universal in all societies) are in fact moral precepts and important for survival, and they look only at laws that differ from society to society and treat those as the crucial moral codes, the ones we have to abide by. Universal rules will thus be the unwritten customs that go unquestioned everywhere. It is not clear why Hermarchus mentions this mistake here, except in so far as he will proceed to say that most of the rules about which animals can be eaten are local customs, not fundamental moral principles. Local customs are in fact less crucial, he thinks, than the more universal, but less obvious, moral principles (e.g. perhaps the need to cull dangerous animals and to avoid murder of human beings). So a local custom about eating this or that species is not binding upon an individual in another time or place.

[26] The view (as well as the terminology) is plausibly Stoic, the point being that, for the Stoic, worldly advantage is of no moral significance, and there is a clear distinction between actions that are virtuous and actions that aim at utility. A principle of maximizing utility would be an indifferent for the Stoic. Hermarchus is maintaining that, on analysis, virtue turns out to be a matter of gaining worldly advantage, and hence that the choice of pursuing material gain, disdained by the Stoic as a matter of indifference, is in fact the foundation of morality.

The other mistake is to attribute universal significance to some moral precepts, but not the right ones. Failing to recognize the principle of maximizing benefit as such a principle, this second group of people take rules that are actually particular applications of it—say, not killing perhaps—and present them as the fundamental and universal moral principles. If you suppose that the wrongness of killing other people lies in the absolute, fundamental universal wrongness of taking life (as such a view might suggest), then you will suppose that killing anything else must be similarly wrong, for that too will break the principle that killing is wrong (which was, allegedly, the fundamental universal principle). But that, for Hermarchus, is to misidentify which principle is the universal principle. It is not—in his view—the taking of life that is absolutely wrong, but rather the doing of something detrimental or damaging to our interests. The rule against killing was just a manifestation of the deeper rule, the rule that one should avoid doing what is detrimental, that one should maximize benefit. In the case of human beings, that fundamental rule turns out to result in a rule against killing other people. But in the case of norms about how we treat animals, it has the opposite effect. So the taking of life is not (as they thought) wrong in itself, universally and everywhere; it is wrong, when it is wrong, because it does some harm to things that are important and useful in promoting our well-being.

Taking life is therefore not universally ruled out. That, according to Hermarchus, is quite correct, because it can actually be a beneficial thing to do. In such circumstances, where the taking of life contributes more to the general good than preserving life, it appears that it must be our *moral duty to kill*. Thus, if anything becomes morally *indifferent* in the Stoic sense, it is the taking of life, since it can be good or bad in different circumstances. By contrast, the pursuit of our own good is regarded as a *universal* and absolute duty.

In effect, then, the occasions on which we should or should not kill an animal are determined by the particular circumstances. Hermarchus implies that there are some general guidelines about what should be killed when:

Two things contribute in similar ways towards fearlessness: (1) that every harmful creature is unsparingly killed and (2) that what contributes to the destruction of that creature is preserved. Hence naturally the one is forbidden and the other is not ruled out. (*Abst.* 1. 11. 2)

The first rule is that we must kill what is a direct threat to us. But secondly, some things should not be killed if they contribute indirectly to our welfare by preying on the harmful ones. So we kill the enemies and preserve those who are our allies in the task of killing the enemies.

On the other hand, Hermarchus goes on, we should not then infer that killing tame and domestic animals that don't pose a violent threat is ruled out. The sense in which an animal might pose a threat has to be extended: it is more than simply a matter of whether it will attack. Killing domestic livestock and so on turns out to be justified—indeed, obligatory—because increased numbers, resulting from unchecked multiplication of such animals, would indeed pose a threat to the economic way of life on which we depend.

These arguments seem to be premised on an unstated assumption, to the effect that normally we should *not* kill, except in self-defence. But the question of whether it is right to kill an animal is not settled by whether that *individual* animal threatens us or might intend to threaten us. The threat may be from the species as a whole, as in cases where the problem is created by the excessive numbers competing with mankind for finite resources. In those cases some but not all members of the species will need to be culled.

Hermarchus does not have a problem with this conclusion, or any difficulty about how one would justify the choice of which animals to send for slaughter, because in none of this is he concerned with justice to individuals.[27] The claim that we rightly kill animals that pose a threat has nothing to do with the idea that such beasts deserve to be killed because they are hostile, ill-willed, or unruly. They may be quite tame and affectionate, but they are still perceived as a threat in respect of their effect on the quality of human life.

For there is nothing among the things that the law does permit us to kill which would not, if left to take advantage of the immunity, prove harmful to us; while, kept in the present numbers, they may provide some benefit for our life. For the sheep and the cattle and all that kind of thing, in moderation contribute certain kinds of assistance with the necessities of life, but if they became wholly abundant and exceeded the present number by a long way they would threaten our lives, on the one hand by turning to force, given that they have a nature that is well-fitted

---

[27] He observes that things might have been better had we had a relationship of justice with the animals; but that is impossible because of the impossibility of forming a contract with them (*Abst.* I. 12. 5). Notice that the idea of contract is essential to justice (agreement to fair treatment) but not to morality in general for Hermarchus. We may have some obligations (for our own good) even in the absence of any contract.

for that, and on the other hand simply by consuming the food that is put forth from the earth for us. (*Abst.* 1. 11. 3)

We may ignore the curious suggestion in the last sentence that the earth produces food for the sake of feeding us. Probably Hermarchus did not intend that implication, and in any case it is not necessary for his purpose. For he is not saying that nature produces food intended solely for us, so that it would be contrary to nature's plan that some other animals should grow so numerous that they end up consuming food intended for us. That would be a different argument, suited to a theory that espoused a teleological account of nature, according to which we might be justified in killing some animals to maintain the proper arrangements intended by nature. But for our Epicurean Hermarchus, no such purposes exist in nature. On the contrary, if we leave things to proceed in nature's own sweet way, the animals would evidently multiply without limit. We intervene precisely to prevent nature taking its course, and our duty to kill the domestic species is to promote our own purposes, not nature's. It is not nature's intention that we should have enough to eat (or that we should not have enough). Hermarchus suggests that human lawgivers invented the moral rules that permit us to kill those creatures. They made the rules like that because they saw where the best interests of humanity lay.

Anthropocentric Bias?

We might think that Hermarchus's argument looks biased. Has he not simply assumed that the interests of the animals need not be considered, while those of human beings are paramount, no matter what the cost in animal suffering? Without that assumption, surely his argument would immediately collapse?

In fact, that criticism does not hold water, at least not in a straightforward way. It is true that the justification for moral rules is founded upon the advantages for human society, and we shall come back to that. But, as regards who can be killed and why, there is no difference between mankind and the other animals. For other people do not have a right to life, any more than animals do, on Hermarchus's story. He offers the same reasons to explain why we are not supposed to kill other people as he offers to explain why we do not kill all animals. In neither case is the death of someone (or something) an offence against the victim—except that in the case of the human victim the killer might be breaking a contract or agreement to refrain from killing, to which the victim was party. That source of injustice could not apply in the case of killing an animal, since animals do not make contracts or agreements.

Hermarchus tries to free us from the idea that killing is intrinsically wrong, or that it is wrong because it hurts the victim. The sole reason why the deed is wrong (if it is wrong), he suggests, is to be found in the unfortunate consequences of the deed. Those consequences are extrinsic to the deed, such as damage to the stability of human society or deleterious effects on the quality of life. For instance, the rest of us might live in fear if murders were common and went unpunished. That consequence is enough to make murder a bad idea, even without considering the deed from the perspective of the victim.

Thus killing other people is forbidden, not because the original lawgivers did not want people to die, but because killing people would be harmful to our well-being in the long run. In just the same way, killing certain animals may also be forbidden, wherever killing them would be damaging to our well-being in the long run. And in both cases killing is permitted where the benefits are sufficient to justify it. So humans do not differ from animals in respect of whether you can kill them for your benefit, although it rarely *is* to our benefit to kill fellow human beings. This explains why there is a general moral taboo on killing our own kind. The abhorrence generated by that taboo, however, is, not a genuine reaction to the intrinsic evil of the deed but just a useful preventive, invented or reinforced by the ancient lawgivers, and helpfully enlisted by them to discourage us from doing something by which we really wouldn't benefit.

It seems to follow that if we find a circumstance in which killing our own kind does yield an increase in utility, it should be not only permissible to kill, but must actually be our duty to do so.[28] This is made explicit in relation to the beasts, but it clearly ought to apply similarly to human-kind—for example, if the numbers become too great, so that the quality of life falls too low or the available food resources are insufficient, surely it would follow that some of the people should be culled, as with animals. Similarly, the arguments in favour of exterminating a particular group of

---

[28] Compare the fragments of Democritus with which we started this chapter, which explicitly draw this conclusion. Hermarchus does not raise the issue of warfare in the text as we have it, but there are some remarks that seem to imply that the rules concerned with foreign relations will be different from the rules within one's own society. A particular community marks itself off both from the beasts and from hostile people. See esp. *Abst.* 1. 10. 3.

animals, or an individual animal, that poses a threat would imply that we are equally obliged to kill specific human groups that threaten the quality of life — say, the chronically ill or criminals. Even ethnic cleansing looks as if it could be on the cards.

Hermarchus, however, clearly does not envisage that such things are conceivably desirable. Indeed, he suggests that the sense of sacrilege and impurity that follows on any act of homicide is an essential part of the system, established by the inspired lawgivers as an effective way to get us to act in our own interests. This seems to presuppose that any act of killing one of our own kind, no matter what the circumstances, must always be detrimental to our interests. So what is the difference that makes it sometimes worthwhile to kill animals, when they are in competition with us for a livelihood, but invariably detrimental to kill a human being, no matter how much he or she may appear to pose a threat to our well-being or a drain on resources?

The pursuit of the answer to this puzzle raises a second issue about a possible anthropocentric bias in the very structure of Hermarchus's moral theory. Although he does not advocate special treatment for the human species, he does imply that the criterion for whether something is recommended practice is how it contributes to the advantage of society. But whose advantage is supposed to be involved? Is Hermarchus open-minded as to whether the advantage might accrue to the human race or to any other species? It looks as though he favours the interests of humankind, and counts as advantage only what advantages our own species. At first glance, he seems to be explaining established rules and conventions of human behaviour, by showing that they make good rational sense if they are read as contributing to a strategy for promoting the interests of our own species, *Homo sapiens*. And, we might think, that would indeed support conventions such as the general antipathy to homicide, and our moral distaste for euthanasia, ethnic cleansing, or the killing of unwanted children. But in fact, things are not so simple. If the concern was with the benefit to the *species*, strategies such as euthanasia and exposure of sickly children would not invariably count as bad, since they might yield long-term benefits. They might turn out to be superior to alternative strategies, such as any that were committed to supporting the weaker members of the species at the expense of the stronger ones. And a strategy for prolonging the species might well involve self-sacrifice on the part of the agent, if one were oneself the drain on resources that threatened the continuation of the species. Hermarchus does not seem to envisage that moral rules will include the obligation to take one's own life for the sake of others.

A second option as to what Hermarchus might have in mind as the hidden strategy of the ancient lawgivers is this. Rather than promoting the interests of the species, perhaps the lawgivers were promoting the interests of any random member of the species, when viewed by an impartial observer who values the welfare of any member equally with any other. Taken thus, Hermarchus would be saying that the ancient founders of morality sanctioned and promoted behaviour that generally favoured the well-being of any relevant person likely to be affected by the action, or the many people likely to be affected by such actions should those actions became routine. Morality, he would be saying, is a rational system set up to secure some individuals' benefit, not the benefit or continuance of the species *Homo sapiens*. Such a moral outlook would (in Hermarchus's version) still be biased in favour of human beings, since the individuals whose interests are to be upheld are, as it happens, always human individuals, not other animals or other aspects of nature. But whereas the first interpretation took it that the moral rules were for the benefit of the biological species, as opposed to its members, this reading suggests that the rules are designed to promote the happiness and well-being of the members who belong to the human moral community.

If this is what Hermarchus meant—though I shall go on to suggest that this is not the best way to read his theory—then it is not at all clear that a clear-sighted rational agent would have chosen the morally recommended action anyway, for the sake of its utilitarian benefits, as he implies. For it does not seem at all likely that our own individual preferences would necessarily coincide with the precepts of morality, if morality impartially favours the advantage of anyone who might be affected by the action. For the agent deliberating about the best course of action is not an impartial observer, and would not be thus motivated to calculate the good of all human participants equally. One particular agent might stand to gain more from the action that morality condemns, so why should he find that the rules of morality contribute to his well-being, either on the whole or on any one occasion? Thus, if we take the concern to be for individuals, it seems less likely that (as Hermarchus maintained) morality is merely recommending what was in our own best interests anyway, or that it has value as a guide to actions that deliver beneficial outcomes. We choose our actions as particular individuals within a society, not (like the imaginary moral legislators) as outsiders. Yet Hermarchus presupposes that as rational individuals we shall choose what we as individuals see is best for ourselves. Of course, that might frequently involve choosing what is best for our society, since our own individual welfare will be improved by belonging to a flourishing community in which fear and anxiety are minimized. This could account for some apparently impartial preferences turning out to be for the individual's own good. But still, it does not seem that Hermarchus can construct a universal morality in quite the way that is needed, if it is also to coincide with our rational preferences as particular individuals motivated solely by personal advantage.

Furthermore, as we have noted, this reading makes Hermarchus's view mildly speciesist in that it values the welfare of members of the human species and ignores the welfare of other animals. One possible response to that charge would be to claim that it was not arbitrary to privilege the interests of human beings, but morally right to do so, perhaps on the grounds that human beings, unlike nature as a whole, pursue ends in a purposive way. For Hermarchus, and other Epicureans, there is nothing good about promoting the natural goals of nature because nature is not actually goal-directed at all, and is not designed to produce anything good. Human goals, on the other hand, are chosen because they are good. It would follow that it makes sense to promote the purposes of humankind, and to regard that as morally good—that is, productive of good results—whereas there would be no value in promoting ends that were not directed at anything worthwhile, such as the random patterns in nature, including the desires of other species. Yet this defence appears to work only if humans correctly choose and intend what is truly good—where what is truly good is defined independently of whether we choose it.

Hermarchus does indeed hold that we do, if we think clearly, always choose to do what is for the best. Hence it follows that human purposes, properly recognized, are always directed to good ends. So we might be entitled to conclude that human purposes should be promoted as a worthy moral goal, whereas nature and the other species have no such good intentions or rationally thought-out purposes. But the defence of Hermarchus along these lines seems, ultimately, to fail. For the argument is circular. By first assuming that what promotes the human good is morally right, we can then show that the principle that one should do what promotes the human good is itself an example of something that promotes the human good and hence is morally right. But the whole argument depends on the one undemonstrated claim that promoting what is best for us humans is the correct basis of morality and the aim we should always rationally choose.

To avoid attributing to Hermarchus such a circular argument, or the associated but improbable claim that we always choose benefits impartially for members of our own kind, it seems better to explore a more intuitively plausible interpretation. Perhaps Hermarchus supposes that we each pursue primarily our own individual welfare. On this view, we are not expected to assign the interests of each and every other member of the human species an equal priority with our own. In certain circumstances, of course, one might still be inclined to serve the interests of the community, because one's own interests are best served by living in a community that has secure boundaries and excludes threats from without.[29] It follows that if one sees clearly that these are the reasons behind rules of morality and the laws against injustice, one comes to see that laws that require one to contribute to the common good, or not to kill one's fellow human beings, are actually designed for one's own long-term benefit. It is conventional to kill mosquitoes, lions, and slugs and to encourage earthworms and cats. Each of us does these things because it is conventional to do so, but it is conventional because, even if no one thinks so, it is better for *oneself* to do so.

This interpretation makes much better sense of Hermarchus's claim that we should all choose to act in the morally approved ways, on rational grounds, even without the laws and punishments that currently direct us to act thus. But now it is clear that there is nothing special about our human species. What I pursue are my own best interests, because they are my own and are what I am concerned about. I do not pursue them in virtue of my being human; nor do I favour any other human on the grounds that she is human. So it seems that Hermarchus needs no species-centred principle to support his claim that the conventional moral rules are rationally based, and that they amount to what a rational agent would choose for herself. And he does not need any speciesist principle to conclude that they prescribe killing other kinds but refraining from killing our own kind.

Why not Our Own Kind?

But can Hermarchus avoid the risk that there might be *some* human beings in *some* circumstances who are not worth preserving, just as there are

---

[29] *Abst.* I. 10. 3.

some animals like that. If there were such people, then it would follow by his reasoning that one would have a duty to kill them, as if they were pests. If, as on this model, morality does not place any special store by whether something is human or not, but considers only its use to the agent, then humans would need to be preserved for exactly the same reasons as earthworms, and killed for the same reasons as flies.

Hermarchus has two related routes to avoid this risk and preserve our intuitions about the wrongness of murder. One is that he does not rule out completely the idea that our reluctance to kill our own kind is the accidental result of a natural fellow feeling, which results from the similarity of our bodily form and our minds. '... Albeit humans may indeed also possess a certain natural affinity towards human beings due to their similarity in their shape and in their mind, which leads them to be less ready to kill that kind of animal in the way they kill one of the ones that are permitted, yet ... ' (*Abst.* I. 7. I).[30] This would be a *natural* cause, not deliberately adopted, and hence it need not actually be at all beneficial, nature being, as we have noted, entirely without purposes. So, while the conventions of morality and law are designed to see to our welfare, there may also be other motivations in play in guiding our actions, motives that go beyond what is helpful. Our reluctance to kill people may be one of those: it may go beyond what is strictly necessary. If that is so, then it is not duty but distaste that makes us refrain from killing our own kind in cases where it would otherwise be to our advantage. But since, for Hermarchus, the point of morality is to maximize our long-term benefit, it should, strictly, seek to reduce our adherence to these natural feelings of distaste for actions that would actually be worth doing. Our distaste for killing each other in these circumstances goes against our best interests. Ideally, we must suppose, morality ought to advise us to overcome our distaste and steel ourselves to kill those we should kill. So by this means Hermarchus can stick to an act-utilitarian view about morality, but explain such deceptively moral-looking motivations as the habit of sparing our own kind as non-moral motives, based on natural impulses, that are not conducive to any good end, but have not been properly eradicated.

Secondly, Hermarchus can resort to a form of rule–utilitarianism, appealing to the notion of sticking to a rule. This explanation is offered for the widespread and powerful disincentives surrounding homicide, which are

---

[30] On the reference to a 'natural affinity' (*oikeiōsis*), see above, n. 18.

encapsulated in the religious procedures for purification and other rules which apply even in cases of justified killing.

Yet the principal reason for objecting to this, and for it being declared unholy, was that it was seen to be not advantageous for the business of keeping life going in general. For although the idea started from something like that, yet there were some who saw that the rule had advantages, and did not need any other incentive to restrain them from such actions, while others were unable to see that clearly enough but refrained from killing each other too lightly due to fear of the magnitude of the penalty. Both these reasons still seem to apply. (*Abst.* 1. 7. 2–3)

Some ancient lawgivers, prompted by the natural affinity feelings, saw that homicide was generally not helpful. They also knew that it would be better for people to live by certain simple rules and habits. They then formulated a rule, such as the rule against murdering fellow human beings, and attached powerful stigmas, including religious proscriptions, to breaking it. Ordinary people in subsequent generations continue to follow the rule, but not everyone sees why the rule is useful. Many keep to the rule because of the stigma.

If everyone was able to survey the advantage and take note of it, they would not need laws. They would spontaneously take precautions against what is forbidden and act upon what is recommended. For contemplating the consequences—the benefit and the harm—would be sufficient to make them avoid the former and choose the latter. But the institution of punishment is for the benefit of those who can't see the advantage. (*Abst.* 1. 8. 4–5)

Thus the rules and laws themselves becomes beneficial as a guide for the less intelligent folk. And the law retains its value even in circumstances where the act is not, in practice, particularly harmful (as, for example, in involuntary homicide, which Hermarchus discusses at some length)[31] because it is more useful as a general guideline than one that has complicated exceptions. Hence we might, in practice, be well-advised to promote the convention that makes all homicide abhorrent, in order to ensure that we never fall by accident into actions that are truly detrimental.

As in rule-utilitarianism, Hermarchus is entitled to suggest that the rule against homicide can still be worth following, even where an individual act of homicide would otherwise have had some advantage, or was an accident which is unlikely to be repeated. Similarly for our treatment of other animals, he suggests, the ancient lawgivers devised general rules and guidelines

---

[31] *Abst.* 1. 9 (see above, pp. 208–9).

that were intended to maximize the advantages for individuals and for society in general. It may not always be obvious what the advantages are, but we can safely conform to the guidelines, knowing that they have been chosen for their general effectiveness in securing the well-being of us all.

Socrates and Hermarchus

Hermarchus's theory reduces morality to a set of strategically effective rules for maximizing the beneficial consequences to the agents as individuals and as members of a flourishing human society. One can choose to act morally because one sees the strategic advantages of acting in that way, or because one is afraid of the penalties that customarily follow upon immoral behaviour. Either way, one's own best interests are served by being good, and one will suffer disadvantages if one does wrong.

The theory seems to have the effect that no one ever chooses to do wrong while knowing that it is wrong and in full knowledge of what the consequences are. Hermarchus grants that most ordinary people, both now and in the past, do what they ought to do because they have been taught the rules and are afraid of the penalties imposed by laws and religious practices—laws and practices to which they assent.[32] But the laws which people obey out of fear are actually laws intended to ensure that they do what they ought to do, where what they ought to do is what they would reasonably want to do if they were fully aware of the consequences. We are told not to kill other human beings because actually, if we realized what harm it would cause, we wouldn't want to do so.

That seems rather like what we might think Socrates would say. For Socrates too famously said that no one who fully understands why an action is wrong would ever choose to do it. Again on Socrates' view, it may be that the laws and punishments that have grown up in human society are an attempt to persuade us to do out of fear what we would have chosen to do anyway, had we had the moral insight to see for ourselves that it was worthwhile.[33] For Hermarchus, just as for Socrates, it will be a sort

---

[32] *Abst.* 1. 7. 4.

[33] It is not clear what Socrates himself would have said about this matter. The material in Plato's *Gorgias* and *Republic* 1–2 is clearly relevant. In the *Gorgias* Polus holds that justice and morality work to our disadvantage, and that one would do better to get away with evil if one could do so. (Pl. *Grg.* 471a–475e; 476a–479d). Socrates responds by showing that it is better to be wronged than to do

of 'moral insight' that allows one to choose an action for the right reason, rather than out of fear or habit. Because self-interest grounds morality for Hermarchus, there is a sort of 'moral understanding' in the correct choice of action when it is chosen for the sake of its perceived advantages.

For Hermarchus, then, as for Socrates, the good person does what will turn out to be the best thing for herself. And for Socrates too, the reason why it could never be worthwhile to do the wrong thing is that doing wrong is disastrous for the agent.[34] For both thinkers, a right-thinking moral agent refrains from committing injustice, not because of the harm it will do to the victim but because of the harm it will do to the agent. There is, in a sense, no harm done to the victim of injustice (which is why, for Socrates, it is better to suffer wrong). For Hermarchus, as for Socrates, the harm to the victim never enters the calculation about what we ought to do.

This much seems to be common to the two versions of the idea that no one does wrong willingly, or knowingly. On the other hand, it is also important to see why Hermarchus's version seems profoundly unsatisfactory. Let us consider again the motives and reasons for moral action.

Hermarchus suggests that we ought not to kill other human beings. The reason is that it would have some damaging effects on our own prosperity. Indeed, if it were generally helpful to kill people, we would, after all, have learnt to feel that it was right to do so. He also thinks that we ought not to kill certain animals, for the same reasons.

Our response, I suggest, might be that refraining from killing each other for *those* reasons makes even refraining no kind of moral response. Hermarchus, by contrast, wants to say that it is *only* when we do it for those reasons that we truly understand our moral duty and why it is a duty. And moreover, if we do it for any other reason, such as because we care for our fellow creatures or love them, Hermarchus would say that we have not fully grasped why we ought to do it.

Hence, if someone wants to kill my cat in the course of an experiment to discover the limits of pain tolerance in animals, and I refuse to let him have the cat on the grounds that it is useful to me for catching mice, you might (quite reasonably) say that I lacked any moral scruples about killing the cat. Like the tormentor who wants to kill it, I too show only a callous habit of

wrong. Similarly, *Republic* 1 is designed to show that judicial institutions are for the good of the ruled subjects. But only if action rather than intention is the key factor in morality can obedience to laws be an adequate substitute for knowledge.   34 Pl. *Grg.* 479c.

calculating advantages. On the other hand, if I refused to hand over the cat because I did not feel that it was fair to do so, Hermarchus would say I was just succumbing to sentimental fellow feeling. To be truly moral, and to make a correct judgement about what to do, I would need an understanding of which course of action was actually more beneficial in the long run, for which my sentimental attitude towards the cat might well be counterproductive. I might need to recognize that it was indeed good for mousing, and to weigh that advantage against the benefits yielded by the experiments proposed by the cat-killing scientist. Then it might indeed turn out that *this* cat should be spared (though another, less reliable at mousing, might be sent to the lab).

Thus, for Hermarchus, responses that we would otherwise think of as moral are correct and justified only if they are warranted by explanations in terms of self-interest. The results strike us as callous and amoral. For Socrates, by contrast, quite the reverse is true. In Socrates' moral world, right choices do, as it happens, invariably further the agent's self-interest, but in a quite different way. The self-interest does not figure either as the agent's subjective reason for doing the right deed, or as the objective reason that makes it right, even though the beneficial outcome is, incidentally and essentially, a foreseeable effect (foreseeable by one who sees correctly). On Socrates' version, it is not *because* it is to my benefit that I ought to do something. I ought to do it because it is right. And because it is right, it is also the best thing for me. To do anything else would be wrong, and hence damaging to me. No one ever does wrong willingly, not because it is right to do what is to my benefit but because it is to my benefit to do what is right.

Perhaps, someone might suggest, Hermarchus's account of our moral reasoning sounds abhorrent simply because he has wrongly identified the universal moral grounding? Hermarchus assumes that what is commendable is commendable because it serves our own interests and those of our society. This is problematic, as we have seen, because he cannot show why that should be a good moral principle to hold, either individually or universally, and it seems to be that principle that is objectionable. So perhaps his project could be rescued if he were to adopt some less self-centred or species-centred principle, but retain the idea that morality is based on a practical utilitarian grounding of that sort, a factor that can be calculated by cost/benefit analysis and still be rationally accepted by those with moral understanding?[35]

---

[35] I have in mind here options such as grounding morality in the aim to promote general utility or the welfare of all sentient beings (where one does not privilege oneself or one's own society over other

I think that the comparison with Socrates suggests that such a notion would be the wrong place to look for a rescue package. The problem with Hermarchus's explanation of morality seems to lie in the very notion of seeking a reason to justify decent treatment of others. Hermarchus tries to give a reason *why* we should want to do that, as though something other than it being the decent thing to do would be more suitable to motivate us, morally. But how could there be something else that could motivate us, or count as a reason to justify such action, that would not thereby detract at once from the proper motivation, based in seeing such action as the decent thing to do? As Socrates rightly saw, it not only makes perfectly good sense to choose the right course of action willingly, precisely because it is good, but if we fail to choose it for that reason, that shows a failure to recognize the value of what is good. For something to be good is for it to have value. To choose is to choose what has value. If one fails to choose what has genuine value, or if one needs to be motivated by some other lesser value so as to choose what is genuinely choice-worthy only as a means to some other less choice-worthy end, one is simply confused or blind. It is an error, a symptom of ignorance, to choose morally decent kinds of behaviour for the sake of something else, given that nothing else can have greater value than morally decent kinds of behaviour.

It may seem tempting to think that if we commend a particular way of acting towards other kinds, and classify it as morally superior to other ways of behaving, that must be because it serves some purpose or promotes some desirable end. But that is only to push the location of real value further on, to something that we do not in fact admire or pin any special moral value on. We then have to ask why that purpose should be desirable, and although various ethical theories have tried to assert that the purpose thus identified is itself a naturally good end, the basis for that assertion always remains mysterious, whether the end envisaged is the inherent dignity of the human person or the natural value of pleasure. But even if we cite such grounds, and reinforce them with rhetoric that looks superficially plausible, when the going gets tough, we find that we have produced foundations for morality that are less secure than the value of the moral actions and good intentions that we were out to explain. For as soon as the ulterior ends

humans and other animals), or in the aim to win the approval of God (where one does the morally good thing because it is believed to be God's will, and because the result will be pleasing to God and consequently, perhaps, also beneficial to the recipients of God's favour).

appear to justify means that are not fine or noble—once they are shown to permit the torture of the innocent or the abuse of precious parts of the created world—they prove useless. For after all, the intuitive sense of what can and can't be admired is more secure than the philosophers' proposed foundations that claim to ground it.

But why should we not perceive a certain kind of response to our fellow creatures, human and otherwise, and to the natural world, as fine and proper, in and of itself? Why should we not choose to act in that way because it is good to do so, and not for the sake of something else that is (more dubiously) said to be good? Even Hermarchus, in the passage that Porphyry cites, seems to assume that, all things being equal, it is preferable not to kill, as we noticed above.[36]

So it appears that Hermarchus himself did not fully take on board his notion that only considerations of utility should count in deciding whether an action should be done. He does not in fact treat killing as morally indifferent, but assumes that it is to be avoided, and that it stands in need of justification where it is necessary for self defence. He writes as though no moral principle should be accepted unless some utilitarian reason has, once upon a time, been given to show that it is good, or can be given once all the facts have been taken into account. But he seems to provide no utilitarian reason for his preference for sparing harmless animals unless they pose a threat.

Furthermore, the comparison with Socrates suggests that Hermarchus's fundamental mistake is to ask for a reason why the things that we commend as fine count as fine and good. It is precisely when we start asking for a *further* motive, besides the fact that it is a fine thing, to justify choosing to do the right thing, that we destroy the very sense that it is a good thing. Suppose I think that killing or violence is not something I would encourage or commend. If that is because, whatever good may come out of it, the killing itself is not a nice thing, it becomes nonsense to ask myself what is my motive for avoiding it. And if I do have another motive for avoiding it, or if my society has some motive for discouraging it, we are not avoiding it because it is awful to us. In that case, we are engaged in that form of corruption that consists in doing the right deed for the wrong reason.

[36] See esp. *Abst.* 1. 11. 2–3 and 5, and the discussion above (p. 212).

9

On Eating Animals: Porphyry's Dietary Rules for Philosophers

Chaeremon the Stoic, in his account of the Egyptian priests who are, he says, regarded as philosophers by the Egyptians, explains that they have chosen temples as a place for engaging in philosophy.... Their lifestyle was frugal and simple. Some tasted no wine at all, others a very little: they accused it of causing damage to the nerves and a fullness in the head which impedes research, and of producing desire for sex. In the same way they also treated other foods with caution, and in their times of holiness ate no bread at all.... They abstained from all fish found in Egypt itself, and from quadrupeds that have solid hooves or cloven hooves or no horns, and from all flesh-eating birds. Many abstained altogether from animal foods, and all of them did in times of holiness, when they did not even eat eggs. They also refused some of the animals which had not been declared unfit: for instance they refused female cattle, and also males that were twins, spotted, or piebald, those that were deformed in shape or were accustomed to the yoke (because they were already consecrated by their labours) or resembled sacred cattle (whatever kind of similarity appeared) or were one-eyed or evoked some likeness to humans. (Porph. *Abst.* 4. 6–7)[1]

This report on the curious dietary habits of the Egyptian philosopher priests is relayed by Porphyry from a Stoic Egyptologist of the first century AD. We have already met Porphyry's treatise *On Abstinence from Animal Food*, in connection with the anti-vegetarian views of Hermarchus the Epicurean

---

[1] Translation by Gillian Clark (Porphyry, *On Abstinence from Killing Animals*, in *Ancient Commentators on Aristotle*, ed. Gillian Clark (London: Duckworth, 2000), 104–5), slightly modified.

discussed in the last chapter. It also provided some of the evidence reviewed in Chapter 3, concerning Empedocles' views on sacrifice and meat eating. Porphyry's work, which dates from the late third century AD, is a polemical review of the considerations for and against a purely vegetarian diet, ostensibly addressed to a friend and fellow philosopher called Firmus Castricius who had lapsed from his vegetarian principles—so Porphyry claims to have heard—and had started peddling sophistic arguments against vegetarianism.[2] Porphyry uses this news as an excuse to compose a treatise in four books, designed to persuade Firmus to return to vegetarian principles, and to show that all the arguments against doing so can be adequately, or more than adequately met.

The pretext of rescuing Firmus Castricius from his meat-eating errors allows Porphyry to present and discuss arguments on both sides of the debate. As a result, *De abstinentia* is a treasure store of evidence for philosophical thinking on the status of animals from the Presocratics to Porphyry's own school, Neoplatonism.

The work is in four books. In the first, Porphyry summarizes some of the more superficial arguments *against* vegetarianism, and then argues that the vegetarian diet is conducive to philosophical detachment from the bodily passions, and hence is crucial to Platonist philosophy, since the Platonist wants to become a pure intellect, living as close as possible to the intelligible world. In the second book, Porphyry considers animal sacrifice, and addresses the belief that one must kill animals in order to fulfil one's obligations to the gods. Here he insists that even if sacrifice were required, there could be no obligation to *eat* the meat from the sacrifice. Many of the arguments that he offers against sacrifice also anticipate the subject of book 3, which asks whether it is fair to kill animals, and whether the treatment of animals is such as to raise questions of justice. Porphyry argues that justice extends to other species and is not just an agreement between members of the human community. It follows that we commit injustice by killing animals for food. In the fourth book he tidies up some loose ends, including the question as to whether systematic slaughtering of animals yields net advantage on a utilitarian calculus, and whether there have been genuine communities in history that have adhered to a purely vegetarian regime and survived successfully on it. That is, he looks at whether it is,

---

[2] Porph. *Abst.* 1. 3.

in practice, a life that one can live, and whether in the process one loses more than one gains. It is from this part that our extract about the Egyptian philosopher priests at the beginning of this chapter was taken.

If the argument in book I is Porphyry's own justification for abstinence from meat eating, and not just the reasoning that he supposes will weigh most effectively with Firmus Castricius, Porphyry's primary interest in recommending the vegetarian diet is that it is 'good for the soul', particularly for the intellectual well-being of the soul.[3] Porphyry backs up his recommendation with a considerable weight of Neoplatonist psychology and metaphysics, to explain why the intellect, in its pure undescended state, is the true self, and why it is contrary to our true nature to allow ourselves to be dragged down to the sleepy world of passions and senses. Yet at the same time he is able to present these values as prudential reasons in favour of adopting vegetarianism, reasons that would appeal to a reader regardless of his philosophical position. It is, he suggests, much better for us to keep to a light, meat-free diet for a range of reasons to do with the health of both the intellect and the body.

The Argument against Luxury: In Pursuit of the Simple Life

Among the reasons in favour of a non-meat diet that Porphyry considers is the idea that eating meat is a luxury. I use the term 'luxury' here to cover a range of interconnected ideas, including the notion that meat is surplus to requirements, that it is chosen for pleasure rather than need, and that it is a mark of worldly prosperity.[4] Porphyry portrays the ideal philosophical life

---

[3] Jean Bouffartigue and Michel Patillon, 'Introduction', in *Porphyre de l'abstinence*, i (Paris: Les Belles Lettres, 1977), pp. xi–lxxxiv; p. lxvii, observe that this is the predominant argument for vegetarianism in antiquity, although it is not (as they point out) a strictly *vegetarian* principle. The recurrent 'healthy life' theme in ancient arguments against meat eating is somewhat downplayed by Dombrowski, whose interest is in recording the (rather thinner) evidence that ancient thinkers anticipated the ethical arguments against cruelty beloved of late twentieth-century Western sentiments (Dombrowski, *Vegetarianism*, 4, 41–2).

[4] Among the Greek terms that figure are ποικιλία and πολυτέλεια, though the notion is more often conveyed by a contrast with what is simple, easily procured, minimal trouble, and minimal expense. On the persistent worries about the link between pleasure and food, see Michel Foucault, *The Use of Pleasure*, trans. Robert Hurley (Harmondsworth: Penguin, 1992), pt. 2, ch. 2, discussing the Hippocratic treatises *On Regimen* and *Regimen for Health*.

as a life of minimal necessities, free of attachment to unnecessary pleasures or worldly concerns. Some sections of his treatise—book 3 in particular, but also some parts of book 2—do focus on justice, and on particular reasons why it might be just or unjust to kill animals, either for sacrifice or for food. But the general exhortation to vegetarianism in book 1 focuses on the desire of the intellectual ascetic to strip himself of all superfluous pleasures and passions.[5] Indeed, the vegetarian diet is suitable only for philosophers and not at all fitting for manual workers or athletes, as Porphyry is careful to point out.[6] In a perfect world, clearly, philosophers would abstain from all food. This is not a perfect world, however, and vegetarianism is therefore merely a realistic second best: not an ideal, but a poor substitute for total detachment.[7]

The real problem, then, is superfluous pleasure and excess of corrupting and distracting nourishment, which inhibits the pure functioning of the incorporeal intellect. But why meat in particular? Is meat the only source of superfluous pleasure? Surely some kinds of vegetable food are equally surplus to requirements and also used purely for pleasure? To guard against this challenge, Porphyry bolsters his ascetic argument with moral arguments, including arguments to show that meat eating involves injustice. Meat eating then turns out to be doubly corrupting, because it is a luxury that can be procured only by unjust means.

Thus, even though Porphyry does spend time arguing against the injustice of killing animals, it remains true that his main opposition to meat seems to be on grounds of health, not morality.[8] Equally, we should not imagine that he is opposed to luxury on altruistic grounds. It is true that one might indeed campaign against over-indulgence or superfluous pleasures on altruistic grounds, by showing that luxury is invariably obtained at the expense of other human beings who have less, or at the expense of animals, or of some natural resources. One might argue against the inequality or injustice of using such resources for one's private pleasure; but that does not seem to be what moves Porphyry. He is opposed to luxury primarily because it is damaging to ourselves.

This might seem surprising, given how much of Porphyry's work is devoted to arguing that it is unjust to kill animals. It is true that the immediate concern of De abstinentia, book 3, as we have observed, is to

---

[5] Porph. *Abst.* 1. 31–8.   [6] *Abst.* 1. 27; 2. 3.   [7] *Abst.* 1. 38.
[8] See e.g. *Abst.* 1. 52. This passage comes in a section based on Epicurean material (see below, n. 11).

show that killing and eating animals is wrong, and that it is harmful or insensitive *to animals,* given what kind of creatures animals are. Yet those conclusions, about the moral offensiveness of meat eating, are all subservient to Porphyry's principal aim, which is to show that meat eating is bad *for us.* When Porphyry tries to show that animals are intelligent or rational, for example, these issues get their importance—as indeed they commonly do for animal rights campaigners today—from the need to show that we *ought* not to kill them. Porphyry supposes, as many still do, that the issue of justice can be settled by discovering what kind of beings they are. That is why he thinks it important to establish how intelligent they are, for instance. But it remains true that discovering whether it is wrong to kill them (because they are intelligent, say) matters to Porphyry most of all because of what it means to us humans—because doing wrong is another form of damage to oneself.

There are, then, two halves to Porphyry's main argument for vegetarianism.[9] One appeals directly to the agent's welfare, recommending that we should avoid luxury for our own good; this is the focus of book 1. The other depends on recognizing animals as objects of justice and moral concern. This shows that killing them is a problem for us, so again it appeals to our own welfare indirectly, by way of the moral status of animals. This analysis is the focus of book 3.

The argument requires both halves if it is to be complete; for neither half is sufficient on its own to compel us to vegetarianism. The rejection of luxury cannot by itself justify vegetarianism, since we should need also to show that all and only animal products were excess to requirements—but it is not obvious why this should be so. Porphyry acknowledges that many other philosophical schools favour frugality, including that of Epicurus, despite his reputation as an advocate of pleasure.[10] He even borrows a substantial sequence of argument for dietary restraint from an Epicurean work.[11] Yet Epicurean frugality does not need to be meat-free, even though it serves exactly the same purpose as Porphyry's dietary abstention. One can be frugal in one's diet without necessarily choosing to avoid meat; indeed, if simplicity and ease are the criterion, it is probably simpler to

---

[9] The main argument is prosecuted in books 1 and 3. Book 2 counters an apparent difficulty (must we not sacrifice to the gods?) by showing that it is not an objection, because sacrifice need not entail eating, and book 4 addresses another possible objection (is it not damaging to human interests or impractical from a realistic point of view?).   [10] Porph. *Abst.* 1. 48. 3.

[11] *Abst.* 1. 49. 1–1. 55. 4 appear to be a close paraphrase of Epicurus or an Epicurean text (cf. Epicurus, *Key Doctrines,* 29–30).

eat meat than not to do so in most regions of the inhabited world.[12] It is obviously more difficult and troublesome to be fussy about what one eats than to accept whatever is most readily to hand, whether that be raised on the farm, shot in the forest, or fished from the sea.

In most parts of the world, even today, a great deal of complicated commercial exchange would be necessary to support a purely vegetarian economy for more than a minority of the population. The vision of simple local self-sufficiency, uncluttered by worldly concerns, as recommended by Epicurus (*apud* Porph. *Abst.* 1. 49–55), is clearly easier to realize in a traditional farming system, where producers live off whatever their own land is able to produce and do not need to engage in trade and commerce. If our concern is simply to procure an adequate diet with minimal trouble, minimal expense, and minimal sensual indulgence, there seems no reason to reject animal products. Rather, the reverse.

So opposition to luxury is not itself a vegetarian principle, if by that we mean a principle that favours a vegetable diet over one that includes meat. Indeed, it is not even clear that Porphyry has established that meat is luxurious in the requisite sense. He has certainly asserted that it is physically possible to live without it, and in that sense it is—or can be—surplus to requirements. But luxury might be problematic for two reasons: either (a) because we indulge in more than we require or (b) because we indulge in passions or pleasure. It is not always the case, however, that one eats meat *in addition* to an otherwise adequate diet. Often the diet is just sufficient with the meat included. Nor is the meat invariably taken for the sake of pleasure (as, say, truffles or globe artichokes generally are), and taking it for pleasure may be incompatible with taking it over and above an already nourishing diet. One is more likely to enjoy eating meat when one is desperately hungry, and less likely to take pleasure if one is already full. So there may be some difficulty in showing that the use of meat necessarily involves excess, either of over-indulgence or of pleasure.

To complete his argument, therefore, Porphyry has to appeal to additional supposedly negative features of a meat diet, features loosely linked to its purported connection with over-indulgence, such as the idea that it

---

[12] Notice that Porphyry suggests that it is particularly for the city-dweller that animals are more difficult to procure than vegetables (*Abst.* 2. 14). It is not entirely clear why this should be so, unless he envisages that the normal source of meat would be game and fish, easy to procure on one's country estate or at the coast.

leads to particular physical and psychological damage,[13] as well as the idea that it involves injustice. This is where the lengthy treatment of the ethics of killing animals in book 3 comes in. If injustice is committed in procuring animal products, that does not, in itself, make them a luxury, but it does make such food peculiarly unsavoury, *especially* if it is an avoidable luxury.

But surely, zoophiles might suggest, if killing animals is unjust, that actually makes such food improper in any case, whether it is a luxury or a necessity? At 3. 18 Porphyry seems to agree: 'If it so happened that we needed animal-slaughter and meat-eating for our very subsistence, like we need air and water and vegetables and fruits, without which it is impossible to live, then our nature would have been inextricably bound up with this kind of injustice.'[14] We can survive without meat, Porphyry reckons. However, if we did need meat to survive, it would still be unjust to kill and eat the beasts, but it would be an *unavoidable* injustice. Porphyry does not distinguish, here in book 3, between our physical needs on the one hand and the practical possibility on the other. In terms of our physical needs as organisms, we do not need meat; we can live on other things. In terms of the practicalities, whether we can live on other things depends on whether there are any. So when Porphyry is discussing injustice in his own voice, in book 3, he does not stop to consider the scenario in which one might face a stark choice, say between killing an animal and letting oneself—or one's child or one's dog—starve.[15] Earlier, however, in book 2, he had included material from Theophrastus about the historical origins of the use of meat, and there it was suggested that humans first turned to killing for food (and hence to sacrificing animals) when driven by famine and war.[16] And, as

---

[13] e.g. *Abst.* 1. 47.   [14] *Abst.* 3. 18. 3.

[15] Does it make a difference whether it is oneself, or a child or a dog? If the action is unkind to the victim, the moral wrong seems to vary depending on how severe the necessity is and whether one's care is for oneself or for another dependant. There is not a simple yes or no answer to whether 'we are permitted' to kill for food. On judging between the claims of different members of one's family, versus the needs of a pet, see the chapter 'For a dog?' in Gaita, *Philosopher's Dog*, 21–38. But there is a further factor, relating to whether a creature (or child) is dependent on human care and on oneself in particular, or is capable of fending for itself, a factor which crucially affects the judgement in ways that do not fully emerge in Gaita's discussion. On sentimentality, see above, Ch. 6.

[16] *Abst.* 2. 7, 2. 12. Theophrastus gives the impression that such situations arise only as a result of human wickedness, e.g. in war. This too adds rhetorical spin: the presumption is that the deed is never strictly necessary—meat eating is always an avoidable sin, not a genuine moral dilemma. But the rhetoric skates over a range of situations, since the victims of an unjust war, or deprived members in an unjust state, may find themselves reduced to a famine situation where the fault (though human) is not of their own making at all.

further material on this theme, part of book 4 is devoted to showing that the vegetarian life is indeed humanly and practically possible without major loss in the quality of life.

Still, here in book 3, it seems that Porphyry would still count it as an injustice even if killing were a practical necessity. The need for self-preservation might justify the act in one sense, but it would not make it right. So eating animals would never be better than the lesser of two evils, and doing it for the sake of pleasure would make it particularly offensive, doubly corrupting. Hence the argument that makes the objection to luxury into a strictly vegetarian thesis is the one that shows that meat eating is morally wrong.

What is the Simple Life? Vegetarianism as a Phenomenon Peculiar to Affluent Societies

Porphyry insists that eating meat is optional for philosophers like Firmus Castricius, though he concedes that a meat-free diet is unlikely to be adequate for men engaged in strenuous physical activity. However, he has no time for such people.

First then, you should understand that it isn't for every kind of human life that my discussion is going to provide advice. It isn't for the folk engaged in handymen's trades, nor those committed to exercising the body, nor for soldiers, seamen or orators, nor people who work in commerce. It's for the person who's thought about who he is, whence he came and where he ought to be trying to go. It's for the person who's laid down some principles that are far removed from the ones that go with the other walks of life: both principles about sustenance and principles in the other areas of conduct becoming to one's proper self. Not that I'd want to grumble at people who aren't like this: for after all, in normal life, one doesn't give the same advice to someone who's asleep and spends his whole life trying to get hold of the things that are conducive to sleep, if he can, as one gives to someone who's eager to be rid of sleep and who arranges all his surroundings with a view to wakefulness. (*Abst.* 1. 27)

Porphyry has no time for, and no interest in, those who have no time for, and no interest in, waking up to intellectual life and philosophy. He has no interest in the dietary needs of sportsmen and the military. For they may indeed need meat in order to carry out the tasks that they think are important. Their problem is that they think those tasks are important. There is delightful irony in Porphyry's claim that he does not have any quarrel with their choice of a completely worthless way of life. If a sleepy life is what you want, then a sleepy life is what you may have.

Porphyry is not engaged in converting society as a whole to a vegetarian economy. He is interested in explaining why philosophers must be vegetarians, for the good of their soul. But he does need to address the issue about society as a whole, in connection with his wider claim that meat is both otiose and damaging to the moral well-being of a community. This he does in book 4 with his historical and ethnographical exploration of how various societies have lived without meat or with taboos on some kinds of meat. There too, however, his main focus is on showing that a life without excess or luxury is generally less prone to war and unrest, so that material benefits accrue from the simple way of life, and that the traditional societies of the past, in which luxury was unknown, were generally happier and closer to the gods.

Porphyry's examination of these other cultures in book 4 belongs to the Classical tradition of writing about the Golden Age, an age when humans lived in easy harmony with nature and with the other animals, and war and famine were unknown. It is a fine piece of philosophical thought experiment in the 'genealogy of morals' tradition. Like Nietzsche, but unlike Hobbes—perhaps the two best-known examples of this genre in the more recent past—Porphyry sees the primitive condition as the better one, both from the point of view of genuine morality and from the point of view of our human interests and welfare. But, unlike Nietzsche (and Hobbes), he thinks of the natural morality of primitive human cultures as kindly and peaceful, not the competitive rivalry of 'live or let live'. Porphyry's vision belongs with Hesiod, Empedocles,[17] Plato,[18] with the *Jubilees* material quoted above,[19] and more generally with the idea of a Garden of Eden before the Fall.[20]

---

[17] See Empedocles, fr. 128, itself relayed by Porphyry from material in Theophrastus, as part of Porphyry's discussion of the question of justice in book 2 (*Abst.* 2. 20). On Empedocles and reincarnation, see above, Ch. 3.

[18] Plato describes a simple life without warfare in the primitive state explored in *Republic*, book 2. The first race of mortals in the *Timaeus* is also better than the subsequent generations.

[19] See Ch. 2.

[20] But contrast the material from Protagoras (the myth included in Plato's *Protagoras*) which is discussed above in Ch. 2.

Porphyry asks us to imagine what life would be like if no one had ever thought of eating meat, or making war over territory and possessions; or if there were distant places in the world where people thought more about knowledge and truth than about food and drink and sex. And he invites us to see that these would be possible worlds and possible lives: not just lives one might live, but lives one would seriously choose to live in preference to the one we live now.

Yet something is still missing. The ideals are imaginary and far removed from worldly necessities, from the human struggle to survive in harsh parts of the natural world where harvests fail and pirates raid the dwindling stores. In terms of the practical possibilities for a particular culture, meat may sometimes not be a luxury at all, but an essential means of survival. Porphyry notes that there are some circumstances in which it is genuinely impossible to survive without meat—that is, he complains about critics who cite the case of the Nomads, Troglodytes, and Ichthyophagoi as counter-examples against vegetarian propaganda.[21] In such cases, he says, the carnivorous diet is due only to necessity, because the land is so infertile that no vegetables can be grown. In effect Porphyry is anticipating the move I have been making: namely, the one that says 'Oh, but in some places people have to eat meat, or they would starve.' He does acknowledge that the vegetarian diet is not always practically possible. None the less, he thinks, this does not detract from the fact that those who can live without meat should do so.

But let us not forget the Nomads, Troglodytes, and Ichthyophagoi.[22] I think there is still a point that needs to be made about such subsistence societies. In some places, where food is scarce, one might have to eat just vegetables. In others, one might have to eat just meat or just fish. In others, one might have to eat all three in order to survive at all. It is usually only where there is plenty to eat that one can actually choose between—select from—alternative ways of sustaining an adequate intake of nourishment. So there is a link between having more than enough to eat and being in a position to choose which of a number of alternative sources of nourishment to select. It is true that occasionally there might be a choice between two

[21] Porph. *Abst.* 4. 21. 1.

[22] Troglodytes are cave-dwellers; Ichthyophagoi are fish-eaters; Nomads are tribes that graze animals and live on milk, blood, and meat. See Strabo, *Geography*, 16. 4, which locates tribes of this sort around the Arabian Gulf and towards Ethiopia.

ways of cultivating the land, in those places where the land could yield either meat or vegetable crops: then one could choose to plant vegetables for preference, if the yield from the crops would still be sufficient to sustain life; but in many cases it would not, and then there is no choice. In many cases the land (or sea) will produce whatever it is suited to growing, or it will produce nothing worth having at all. In practice, we have no real choice between meat and vegetarian diets except where there is surplus productivity, so that we can indulge in the luxury of eating some, but not all, the available types of food produced in our locality, or we can indulge in the luxury of importing extra resources from elsewhere. Hence the question 'Shall I be vegetarian?' presupposes a degree of affluence, a society or a class of society that can afford to *select* whether or not to indulge in more than the bare necessities, and to select which forms of nutrition to favour, from an abundant range of available sources.

Cranks and Intellectuals

Porphyry spent much of his life in Rome, but the predecessors whom he quotes, such as Theophrastus, Hermarchus, and Plutarch, were probably thinking of the cuisine of affluent classes in Greece, in the Classical and Roman periods, when they discussed the possibility of living without meat. Some historical and archaeological studies have tried to determine how much meat and fish figured in the diet in various parts of the ancient world.[23] The dependence on meat, cereals, or fish clearly varied according to the terrain, the quality of land in the vicinity, and proximity to the sea. Furthermore, *individuals* must have relied on a market for meat, fish, or vegetable products, depending on their main source of income. For a shepherd whose only available land is mountainous, the option of living on vegetables alone is plainly unrealistic. For a fisherman with a boat and no land, fish will be crucial for himself and his family.[24]

---

[23] See Peter Garnsey, *Famine and Food Supply in the Graeco-Roman World: Responses to Risk and Crisis* (Cambridge: Cambridge University Press, 1988); several essays in John Wilkins, David Harvey, and Mike Dobson (eds.), *Food in Antiquity* (Exeter: University of Exeter Press, 1995); and the reprinted essays in part III of Peter Garnsey, *Cities, Peasants and Food in Classical Antiquity*, ed. Walter Scheidel (Cambridge: Cambridge University Press, 1998).

[24] It is not quite clear what Porphyry's views on fish are. He makes a distinction between the method of killing fish and the method of killing animals (by implication) at *Abst.* 3. 19. 2, but he still regards it as unjust to kill the fish thus (apparently because it is not a natural but a forced death).

Furthermore, meat was not the only product of killing animals. It is hard to imagine how ancient society and technology could have functioned without the use of leather, fleeces, bone, horn, tortoiseshell, gut, and horsehair, of which the main supply must have been from animals reared and killed by man. Milk, cheese, and other dairy products depend upon a supply from domestic animals, cattle, sheep, or goats, in which the females, but not the males, are reared to maturity and give birth annually to stimulate a supply of milk. Since meat would be a systematic by-product in all these areas of production, even if it were not the principal end in view, the idea of a simple life that included dairy products but discarded the young male animals rather than eating them is economically bizarre (as it would be in modern farming).[25] So even if meat played a relatively small role in the ancient Mediterranean diet, animal husbandry must have been crucial to the lifestyle and to the economy.

But if we are tempted to think that the poorer classes may have eaten rather little meat anyway, so that it would be easy for them to take up Porphyry's theme and dispense with meat altogether, we should be missing the point. For one thing, the demand from the wealthy classes for meat, dairy products, and fish might well have been crucial to the economic livelihood of the poorer classes, living off the land or the sea, even if the latter did not themselves normally consume much of such fare. One might eat very little meat oneself, but still need to encourage others to eat a great deal. But in any case we would be missing Porphyry's point completely if we took him to be saying that the peasants' semi-vegetarian lifestyle was almost right already, and could be endorsed with only minor adjustments. On the contrary, vegetarianism was intended to be a radical statement that marked out the committed philosopher from the cultural norm. For most of Porphyry's readers—affluent intellectuals of the educated classes—it was surely supposed to be profoundly cranky. Porphyry meant them to adopt vegetarianism as a result of reflection, not by default or out of impoverished necessity.[26] In other words, we start with philosophy, not the practicalities of economics. It is philosophy which is to provide the basis for deciding what nutrition is necessary and appropriate.[27]

For the people Porphyry was addressing, the decision not to eat meat must have been a real one, not born of necessity. They must have had the

[25] For a simple explanation of how this factor bears on the morality of vegetarianism, see Scruton, *Animal Rights and Wrongs*, 80–5.   [26] Porph. *Abst.* 1. 27.
[27] *Abst.* 1. 50.

resources to eat meat if they so wished, and the choice must have amounted to a kind of statement on their part: it was not what ordinary people of their wealth and status would normally be doing. Indeed it must have required one to detach oneself even from the central community rituals surrounding the cycle of festivals and sacrifices, at which the community not only slaughtered its chosen beasts but also feasted together upon the choice bits reserved for the city and its citizens. Porphyry's treatise was intended for readers from a class for whom it would be peculiar—cranky to the point of isolation—not to eat animals that had been killed on the altars—but people for whom such an unconventional lifestyle would, nevertheless, be economically and nutritionally possible.

Porphyry was, of course, perfectly aware that he was writing for philosophers, and doubtless he was anticipating an audience drawn from the affluent elite: people whose normal diet would certainly not be confined to simple necessities. Modern discussions of vegetarianism may also assume an affluent readership, the supermarket consumers in a Western post-industrial economy. In such circumstances it might make sense to claim that people should choose not to eat meat, because vegetarian alternatives are always available to them, and meat is not essential for human well-being. That might be a possible position for someone who is accustomed to browsing the supermarket shelves in a European or North American city, before paying with a plastic card funded from a petroleum-based economy. It is not a possible position if one is addressing a traditional Welsh sheep farmer, or someone who ekes out a living from fishing in the North Sea, or a nomadic tribesman, or an Inuit seal-hunter.

Of course someone who had been convinced by the arguments in book 2 of Porphyry's treatise might think that she should say to the Inuit, or to the members of a hunter-gatherer tribe, that they were acting unjustly in killing animals for food. She might like to advise the hill farmer that his sheep were being slaughtered in a cruel way for feeding people who ought to have been eating bread and lentils. But should she not hesitate before she complains about the practice of rearing animals for meat? Does that complaint not rely upon the idea that one can *choose* whether to eat the local lambs or imported lentils from Canada? And is not that idea, that we are free to choose, premissed upon exploitation of other human beings and of the environment the world over? For it is only because there is more than enough to eat in this part of the world that we can carelessly decline the local produce and decide to eat something else. We can choose from a whole range of food imported from countries where pay is low and livelihoods are hard. And the practice of ferrying that food to our supermarkets is far more costly to the environment than is apparent in the prices that show on the supermarket shelf, so that we are obtaining our choice at the expense of the very world we live in, even to the extent of destroying the resources that traditionally supported Inuit or nomadic livelihoods. In these circumstances there are hidden moral costs to the meat-free diet, which are not just about cruelty to animals.

So what about people in the affluent West? Should they congratulate themselves on being in a better position to keep their hands clean from the slaughter of innocent blood than subsistence farmers in the Third World? At first sight it appears that they have a happier choice: they have the choice of a meat-free diet that appears to be unobjectionable, to involve no cruelty to animals or taking of innocent lives. But in fact things are not so simple: the availability of that choice of diet itself depends upon an affluent lifestyle, with a degree of luxury and surplus that is not available in the less developed half of the world. Indeed, it seems probable that it is available in the richer societies, only because they obtain their luxuries at the expense of those in the poorer parts of the world. It follows that this very affluence stems from injustice towards members of our own kind, just as the affluence of the ancient world relied upon the presence of slave labour in its midst.

Porphyry's observations about the connection between meat eating and luxury are instructive, partly because they are wrong. There is no reason to think that meat is surplus to requirements, or that it is a luxury, in the typical diet of ordinary people who live on the land and grow their own food. But Porphyry is right that there are ethical problems with luxury: about indulging in more than you need and doing so at the expense of the lives and livelihoods of others. With this in mind we should not blind ourselves to the connection between vegetarianism and luxury in our own society, and to the need to reflect more broadly on the practical implications, rather than merely the theoretical ones, of proposed alternative lifestyles. Is a vegetarian way of life, lived from within a society that privileges the individual's right to choose whatever he or she fancies regardless of the cost to others, morally superior to the traditional way of securing a simple and authentic human livelihood, in compassionate partnership with the natural productivity of whatever local environment constitutes our home?

Picky eating, whether it is for the sake of one's heart or for the health of one's soul, or driven by sentimental images of pretty white lambs gambolling beside their mothers or the watery gaze of dark-eyed calves, is a privilege of the affluent society. Porphyry's arguments for the offensiveness of luxury, telling though they are, do not lend support to modern Western vegetarian propaganda (as one might naïvely suppose). For in the modern world it is precisely luxury—the overproduction of offensive and wasteful surplus at the cost of grossly inhumane farming conditions, worldwide exploitation of human resources and permanent damage to the environment—that allows us to disdain the traditional local home produce, honourably raised by compassionate farmers who live on the land and care for their flocks, in favour of artificially processed factory-made veggie burgers that look either cheaper, tastier, or more 'cruelty-free' in their sterile shrink-wrapped packets.

Conclusion

This has been a book about what we think animals are, how we perceive ourselves as like or unlike them, and about the humane attitude towards animals and other natural things. In looking back at the ancient texts of dead philosophers and old poets, I have tried not merely to ask what they had to say on these subjects—what they said about what makes us what we are and what makes animals different; nor to inquire simply into the historical explanations, for why they did, or did not, think of animals as somehow very much the same or very much different from ourselves. I have also tried to ask whether they were right to think like that, and what we can learn from their reflections in these areas. For the questions are not of merely academic interest: we need to know now. We need to know what we ought to think and how we ought to respond.

Yet the questions are not straightforward questions. The complexity is not merely in the difficulty that we have with reconstructing what people of distant times and cultures were trying to say, and understanding what assumptions they took for granted. Those are indeed difficulties, and we may not readily identify what is going on at first reading. Some of what I have tried to do here is to present those ancient texts in a sympathetic way, to allow us to feel with them and not just to find them alien.

The issue is more complicated, however, because when we come to consider the nature of the beasts, and the nature of the human being, we discover that any description of the world, any account of how things are with respect to the differences between ourselves and other kinds, already reflects the moral stance we take towards the world and towards our fellow creatures.[1] It is not that the moral stance follows from the biological and psychological

---

[1] I have tried throughout this book to avoid falling into the trap of supposing that we can talk generally of 'the way we treat animals' as though there were a 'we' and as though there were 'animals' and as though there was one way in which we treat such things. But the problems with that way of talking go beyond the objections raised by Beardsmore, 'If a lion could talk ...', 46 (against Peter Singer and other contributors to the animals debate), as I hope to have shown, given that the lines we draw for our moral map are drawn in the imagination and in the cultural habits of our society, not merely in taxonomic practices and in biological textbooks.

inquiries, but rather that the decision about what counts as a relevant biological fact follows from the moral stance. The two are bound up together. We cannot first ask whether Aristotle was right to see continuity in the psychological functions of animal and human souls, and then (having settled how things are in nature) draw conclusions from nature to decide the correct moral treatment of the other species. For the question whether he was right to see continuity is already a moral question: given that we can focus on continuity or on discontinuities, how should the natural scientist draw his boundaries?

If the moral grounds are to be responsive to work in the sciences, then the scientists' perceptions and categories must be scrutinized for their evaluative assumptions. And then we find that there is no such thing as a value-free scientific account of the world. Science itself may be callous or sentimental, humane or amoral, even when it describes, not only when it prescribes. And to seek to be amoral is not a way of excusing oneself from the obligation to see the world from a moral perspective. It is already to opt out of that, which is a moral abdication.

Modern theories of natural rights appear to appeal to laws of nature, and hence it looks as though (to be valid) they must be responsive to objectively given facts of biology or physics. If one takes them at face value, it appears that we could check the moral status of an object by checking its natural capacities. Then one should be able to read off moral judgements about right and wrong action by comparing the rules of nature with the rules of human conduct: if the conduct matches what the natural facts prescribe, then the conduct is irreproachable; if it does not, it is reprehensible. But in reality, we cannot do anything of the sort. Natural facts cannot prescribe, or condemn, action as morally justified or otherwise. That is not because of a problem in bridging the fact/value divide, but rather because there are no natural facts from which to read off the prescription. We see the facts from our moral perspective, so we cannot read off an obligatory perspective from any non-perspectival, given facts. To see the facts as relevant, we need a stance towards them. We need to assess whether they are facts that count for us, whether they are relevant to our moral take on the question.

So we need to think, and we are obliged to act and to react, in a world that we see under a certain description. We have to ask whether our description of the world is better than the alternatives, or whether we have something to learn.

Our quest, in this book, has not been merely to piece together some account of what Aristotle and the rest had to say about the nature of reality and our place in it, alongside the plants and other creatures with souls; nor merely to make those accounts of our souls and theirs impinge upon our own difficulties with regard to the justification of our attitudes and responses to other kinds. I have also tried to show how these questions force us to think about where moral justification could come from, and to show that such a question cannot be answered if we continue to believe that moral obligations are determined by the moral status of the object. For the moral status of the object is a product of our own imagination, and (it seems to follow) it is up to us to imagine moral status wherever we have the will to find it. Then, once we see that, we also see that there remains the question where we ought to have the will to see it.

So, I have suggested, the question does not stop there, with the observation that the humane attitude is one perspective among many. We should not go on to conclude that while some take a callous attitude, others (with equal justification) are sentimental—and the humane is just one of those ungrounded responses, a way of seeing other kinds governed by a kind of fellow feeling for which no objective justification can be sought. Rather, I have suggested, the mistake was to look for justification in the facts of nature and biology—as though the fact that the humane response is right, and the others ones are wrong, is because the humane response is right (truth telling) about the realities of nature as they are shown by objective science, and the other responses are wrong about them. No. My point is that we need another way in which to judge whether a response is right or not—morally right, that is. That question is not answered by whether it reports facts out there in a value-free world, for every response can choose the facts that support its judgements. We need to assess the moral worth of the attitude that such a response expresses; for sometimes it is a finer thing to see and dwell upon some facts and to fail to see and refuse to dwell upon others. That measure of fineness is given not in the facts on which one dwells, but in the worthiness of the attitude that chooses to see them.

In this way I have tried to show that moral truth exists. It is true that the humane response is the one that we (so long as we are not corrupted) can recognize and admire, and that when it occurs, it identifies a person as a moral agent sensitive to genuine goodness. That is true independently of whether we can actually identify any such agents in our contemporary society (or in the past); for it is possible for an entire society to fall into corruption—to become steeped in sentimentality, or to endorse the grudging values of economic man and forfeit its imagination in the interests of commerce. We should not define true virtue by what a society can conceive as right. But it will remain true that where the truth is lacking, the society is lacking what it needs if it is to be a humane society. Such a society, I suggest, stands in need of help, because there is no worse disaster than to lose one's grip on that kind of reality—least of all under the illusion that one will best regain one's grip on reality by abstracting from the imagination and pursuing a callous form of amoral scientific investigation.

It is often supposed that we have rather recently outgrown the attitudes of pre-Enlightenment societies, and become more friendly in our attitude towards other human beings (especially those of other races and colours than our own), and towards the weak and vulnerable in our own society. Sometimes it is suggested that the next most obvious step is to grow out of our supposed prejudices against other animals, as though they too were based on an arbitrary misperception, which could be cured by a clearer understanding of what kind of creatures we are. My aim has been to show that the supposedly benighted societies of former times have not invariably been so blind as we foolishly suppose, and that we would be quite mistaken to assume that what aids our development towards a more humane outlook is the supposed discoveries and proofs of the Enlightenment project.

What does help us to see that folk of other creeds and colours are more like us than they are unlike us? When the Pharisee asked 'Who is my neighbour?', Jesus gave him a story about a Samaritan. Five centuries earlier Sophocles portrayed Teucer as a noble character maligned for his foreign birth by the leaders of the Greeks. It seems to me that we still cannot do better than to engineer a change in attitude by retelling the great stories of long ago: for it is from stories and poetry above all that we learn love, sensitivity, fellow feeling, and the vicarious anger that cries out against the oppression of the weak.

Bibliography

The Apocryphal Old Testament, trans. H. D. F. Sparks. Oxford: Oxford University Press, 1984.

Aristotle, *On the Heavens*, ed. W. K. C. Guthrie. London: Heinemann, 1971.

Baggini, Julian, 'Degrees of concern'. *Philosophers' Magazine*, 23 (3rd Quarter 2003): 38–9.

Beardsmore, Richard W., 'If a lion could talk ... ' In *Wittgenstein and the Philosophy of Culture*, ed. K. S. Johannessen and T. Nordenstam, 41–59. Vienna: Hölder-Pickler-Tempsky, 1996.

Bouffartigue, Jean, and Michel Patillon, 'Introduction'. In *Porphyre de l'abstinence*, i, pp. xi–lxxxiv. Paris: Les Belles Lettres, 1977.

Burnyeat, Myles F., 'Did the Ancient Greeks have a concept of Human Rights?'. *Polis*, 13 (1994): 1–11.

—— 'Is an Aristotelian philosophy of mind still credible? A draft'. In *Essays on Aristotle's* De anima, ed. Martha C. Nussbaum and Amélie O. Rorty, 15–26. Oxford: Clarendon Press, 1992.

Carruthers, Peter, *The Animals Issue*. Cambridge: Cambridge University Press, 1992.

Cassian, John, *The Monastic Institutes*, trans. Jerome Bertram. London: The Saint Austin Press, 1999.

—— *The Institutes*, trans. Boniface Ramsey. New York: Newman Press, 2000.

Caston, Victor, 'Aristotle and the problem of intentionality'. *Philosophy and Phenomenological Research*, 58 (1998): 249–98.

Charles, David, *Aristotle on Meaning and Essence*. Oxford: Clarendon Press, 2000.

Chitty, Derwas, *The Desert a City*, 2nd edn. Oxford: Mowbray, 1977.

Chomsky, Noam, *Language and Mind*. New York: Harcourt Brace and World, 1968.

Clark, Stephen R. L., *The Moral Status of Animals*. Oxford: Oxford University Press, 1977.

—— 'The reality of shared emotion'. In *Animals and their Moral Standing*, 121–38. London: Routledge, 1997.

Coetzee, J. M., *Elizabeth Costello*. London: Random House, 2003.

—— *The Lives of Animals*, ed. Amy Gutmann. Princeton: Princeton University Press, 1999.

Dagger, Richard, 'Rights'. In *Political Innovation and Conceptual Change*, ed. Terence Ball, James Farr, and Russell L. Hanson, 292–308. Cambridge: Cambridge University Press, 1989.

Davidson, Donald, 'Rational Animals'. *Dialectica*, 36 (1982): 318–27; repr. in E. Lepore and B. P. McLaughlin (eds.), *Actions and Events: Perspectives on the Philosophy of Donald Davidson*, 473–80. Oxford: Oxford University Press, 1985.

———— 'Thought and talk'. In *Mind and Language*, ed. S. Guttenplan, 7–23. Oxford: Oxford University Press, 1975.

Descartes, René, *Œuvres de Descartes*, ed. Ch. Adam and P. Tannery. Paris: Vrin/C N R S, 1964–76.

Diamond, Cora, 'Eating meat and eating people'. *Philosophy*, 53 (1978): 465–79; repr. in *The Realistic Spirit*, 319–34.

———— *The Realistic Spirit: Representation and Mind*. Cambridge, Mass.: MIT Press, 1991.

Dombrowski, Daniel A., *Not Even a Sparrow Falls: The Philosophy of Stephen R. L. Clark*. East Lansing, Mich.: Michigan State University Press, 2000.

———— *Vegetarianism: The Philosophy behind the Ethical Diet*. Wellingborough: Thorson's Publishers, 1985.

Donagan, Alan, *The Theory of Morality*. Chicago: University of Chicago Press, 1977.

Dupré, John, 'Conversations with apes: reflections on the scientific study of language'. In *Humans and Other Animals*, 236–56.

———— *Humans and Other Animals*. Oxford: Clarendon Press, 2002.

———— 'Is "natural kind" a natural kind term?'. *Monist*, 85 (2002): 29–49; repr. in Dupré, *Humans and Other Animals*, 103–23.

———— 'The mental lives of non-human animals'. In *Humans and Other Animals*, 217–35.

Farrar, Cynthia, *The Origins of Democratic Thinking*. Cambridge: Cambridge University Press, 1988.

Finnis, John, *Natural Law and Natural Rights*. Oxford: Clarendon Press, 1980.

Foucault, Michel, *The Use of Pleasure*, trans. Robert Hurley. ii. Harmondsworth: Penguin, 1992.

Freeland, Cynthia, 'Aristotle on perception, appetition and self-motion'. In *Self Motion from Aristotle to Newton*, ed. Mary Louise Gill and James G. Lennox, 35–63. Princeton: Princeton University Press, 1994.

Gaita, Raimond, *Good and Evil: An Absolute Conception*. Basingstoke: Macmillan, 1991.

———— *The Philosopher's Dog*. London and New York: Routledge, 2002.

Garnsey, Peter, *Cities, Peasants and Food in Classical Antiquity*, ed. Walter Scheidel. Cambridge: Cambridge University Press, 1998.

———— *Famine and Food Supply in the Graeco-Roman World: Responses to Risk and Crisis*. Cambridge: Cambridge University Press, 1988.

———— *Ideas of Slavery from Aristotle to Augustine*. Cambridge: Cambridge University Press, 1996.

Geuss, Raymond, *History and Illusion in Politics*. Cambridge: Cambridge University Press, 2001.

Gewirth, Alan, *Reason and Morality*. Chicago: University of Chicago Press, 1978.

Gotthelf, Allan, 'Aristotle's conception of final causality'. In *Philosophical Issues in Aristotle's Biology*, ed. Allan Gotthelf and James G. Lennox, 204–42. Cambridge: Cambridge University Press, 1987.

Griffin, James, 'Discrepancies between the best philosophical account of human rights and the international law of human rights'. *Proceedings of the Aristotelian Society*, 101 (2001): 1–28.

Guthrie, W. K. C., *A History of Greek Philosophy*, vi: *Aristotle: An Encounter*, Cambridge: Cambridge University Press, 1981.

Hamlyn, David W., *Aristotle's De anima Books II and III*, ed. J. L. Ackrill, Clarendon Aristotle Series. Oxford: Clarendon Press, 1968.

Historia Monachorum in Aegypto, ed. A. J. Festugière, Subsidia Hagiographica 34. Brussell: Societé de Bollandistes, 1961.

James, Susan, 'Rights as enforceable claims'. *Proceedings of the Aristotelian Society*, 103 (2003): 133–47.

Jefferson, Mark, 'What is wrong with sentimentality?'. *Mind*, 92 (1983): 519–29.

Jubilees or the Little Genesis: Ethiopic Version, ed. R. H. Charles. Oxford: Oxford University Press, 1895.

Labarrière, Jean Louis, 'Des deux introductions de la *phantasia* dans le *de anima*, III, 3'. *Kairos*, 9 (1997): 141–68.

The Lives of the Desert Fathers, trans. Norman Russell, with an introduction by Benedicta Ward, SLG. London: Mowbray, 1981.

Lloyd, Geoffrey E. R., 'Right and left in Greek Philosophy'. In *Methods and Problems in Greek Philosophy*, 27–48. Cambridge: Cambridge University Press, 1991.

Long, A. A., and David N. Sedley, *The Hellenistic Philosophers*, 2 vols. Cambridge: Cambridge University Press, 1987.

Maguire, Joseph P., 'Protagoras ... or Plato? II: The *Protagoras*'. *Phronesis*, 22 (1977): 103–22.

_____ *Selected Writings*, ed. David McLellan. Oxford: Oxford University Press, 1972.

Marx, Karl, 'On the Jewish Question'. In Marx, *Selected Writings*, ed. David McLellan (Oxford: Oxford University Press, 1971), 39–62.

Matthews, Gareth B., '*De anima* 2.2–4 and the meaning of *life*'. In *Essays on Aristotle's* De anima, ed. Martha C. Nussbaum and Amélie O. Rorty, 185–94. Oxford: Clarendon Press, 1992.

Midgley, Mary, *Beast and Man*. London: Methuen, 1978.

_____ 'Brutality and sentimentality'. *Philosophy*, 54 (1979): 385–9.

Modrak, Deborah, *Aristotle: The Power of Perception*. Chicago: University of Chicago Press, 1987.

Nussbaum, Martha C., *Upheavals of Thought: The Intelligence of Emotions*. Cambridge: Cambridge University Press, 2001.

―――― (ed.), *Aristotle's* De motu animalium (Edition and Commentary). Princeton: Princeton University Press, 1978.

―――― and Hilary Putnam, 'Changing Aristotle's mind'. In *Essays on Aristotle's* De anima, ed. Martha C. Nussbaum and Amélie O. Rorty, 27–56. Oxford: Clarendon Press, 1992.

―――― and Amélie O. Rorty (eds.), *Essays on Aristotle's* De anima. Oxford: Clarendon Press, 1992.

O'Neill, Onora, *Towards Justice and Virtue: A Constructive Account of Practical Reasoning*. Cambridge: Cambridge University Press, 1996.

Obbink, Dirk, 'Hermarchus, *Against Empedocles*'. *Classical Quarterly*, 38 (1988): 428–35.

Osborne, Catherine, 'Ancient vegetarianism'. In *Food in Antiquity*, ed. John Wilkins, David Harvey, and Michael Dobson, 214–24. Exeter: University of Exeter Press, 1995.

―――― 'Aristotle *De anima* 3.2: how do we perceive that we see and hear?'. *Classical Quarterly*, 33 (1983): 401–11.

―――― 'Aristotle on the fantastic abilities of animals'. *Oxford Studies in Ancient Philosophy*, 19 (2000): 253–85.

―――― 'Boundaries in nature: eating with animals in the fifth century BC.' *Bulletin of the Institute of Classical Studies*, 37 (1990): 15–30.

―――― *Eros Unveiled: Plato and the God of Love*. Oxford: Oxford University Press, 1994.

―――― 'Perceiving particulars and recollecting the Forms in the *Phaedo*'. *Proceedings of the Aristotelian Society*, 95 (1995): 211–33.

―――― *Rethinking Early Greek Philosophy*. London: Duckworth, 1987.

―――― 'Sin and moral responsibility in Empedocles's cosmic cycle'. In *The Empedoclean Κόσμος: Structure, Process and the Question of Cyclicity*, ed. Apostolos L. Pierris, 283–308. Patras: Institute for Philosophical Research Patras, 2005.

―――― 'Socrates in the Platonic Dialogues'. *Philosophical Investigations*, 29 (2006): 1–21.

Palladius, *Lausiac History*, ed. C. Butler, ii: Introduction and Text, Texts and Studies 6. Cambridge: Cambridge University Press, 1904.

―――― *Lausiac History*, trans. W. K. Lowther Clarke, Translations of Christian Literature series I. London: SPCK and Macmillan, 1918.

Perry, Ben Edwin, *Aesopica*. Urbana, Ill.: University of Illinois Press, 1952.

Porphyry, *On Abstinence from Killing Animals* (*De abstinentia*), trans. Gillian Clark, Ancient Commentators on Aristotle. London: Duckworth, 2000.

Procopé, John, 'Democritus on politics and care of the soul'. *Classical Quarterly*, 39 (1989): 307–31.

Putnam, Hilary, 'Philosophy and our mental life'. In *Mind, Language and Reality: Philosophical Papers*, ii. 291–303. Cambridge: Cambridge University Press, 1975.

Raz, Joseph, *The Practice of Value*, ed. R. Jay Wallace, The Berkeley Tanner Lectures. Oxford: Oxford University Press, 2003.

Regan, Tom, *All that Dwell Therein: Animal Rights and Environmental Ethics*. Berkeley: University of California Press, 1982.

—— *The Case for Animal Rights*. London: Routledge and Kegan Paul, 1984.

Richardson Lear, Gabriel, *Happy Lives and the Highest Good: An Essay on Aristotle's Nicomachean Ethics*. Princeton: Princeton University Press, 2004.

Rollin, Bernard E., *Animal Rights and Human Morality*. Buffalo: Prometheus Books, 1981.

Schofield, Malcolm, 'Aristotle on the imagination'. In *Articles on Aristotle*, ed. J. Barnes, M. Schofield, and R. Sorabji, iv. 103–32. London: Duckworth, 1979.

Schopenhauer, Arthur, *On the Basis of Morality*, trans. E. F. J. Payne, with an introduction by Richard Taylor. Indianapolis: Bobbs-Merrill, 1965.

Scott, Dominic, *Recollection and Experience*. Cambridge: Cambridge University Press, 1995.

Scruton, Roger, *Animal Rights and Wrongs*. London: Demos, 1996.

Sedley, David N., 'Is Aristotle's teleology anthropocentric?' *Phronesis*, 36 (1991): 176–96.

Segal, Alex, 'Goodness beyond speech'. *Philosophical Investigations*, 27 (2004): 201–21.

Sharples, Robert W., "Responsibility and the possibility of more than one course of action: a note on Aristotle *De caelo* II.12'. *Bulletin of the Institute of Classical Studies*, 23 (1976): 69–72.

Solomon, Robert C., *In Defense of Sentimentality: The Passionate Life*. Oxford: Oxford University Press, 2004.

Sophocles, *Ajax*, trans. Shomit Dutta, Cambridge Translations from Greek Drama. Cambridge: Cambridge University Press, 2001.

—— *Philoctetes*, trans. Judith Affleck, Cambridge Translations from Greek Drama. Cambridge: Cambridge University Press, 2001.

—— *The Theban Plays*, trans. Robert Fagles, with an introduction by Bernard Knox. Harmondsworth: Penguin, 1982.

Sorabji, Richard, *Animal Minds and Human Morals: The Origins of the Western Debate*. London: Duckworth, 1993.

Sorabji, Richard, *Aristotle on Memory*, 2nd edn. London: Duckworth, 2004.

—— 'Body and soul in Aristotle'. *Philosophy*, 49 (1974): 63–89; repr. in *Articles on Aristotle*, ed. J. Barnes, M. Schofield, and R. Sorabji, iv. 42–64. London: Duckworth, 1979.

—— *Emotion and Peace of Mind: From Stoic Agitation to Christian Temptation.* Oxford: Oxford University Press, 2000.

—— 'Intentionality and physiological processes'. In *Essays on Aristotle's De anima*, ed. Martha C. Nussbaum and Amélie O. Rorty, 195–225. Oxford: Oxford University Press, 1992.

—— *The Philosophy of the Commentators: A Source Book*, i: *Psychology*. London: Duckworth, 2004.

Tanner, Michael, 'Sentimentality'. *Proceedings of the Aristotelian Society*, 77 (1976–7): 127–47.

Taylor, Paul, *Respect for Nature: A Theory of Environmental Ethics*. Princeton: Princeton University Press, 1986.

Theophrastus, *Sources for his Life, Writings, Thought and Influence*, ed. William Fortenbaugh, Pamela Huby, Robert W. Sharples, and Dimitri Gutas. Leiden: Brill, 1993.

Tuck, Richard, *Natural Rights Theories: Their Origin and Development*. Cambridge: Cambridge University Press, 1979.

Vander Waert, Paul, 'Hermarchus and the Epicurean genealogy of morals'. *Transactions of the American Philological Association*, 118 (1988): 87–106.

Villey, Michel, 'La genèse du droit subjectif chez Guillaume d'Occam'. In *Seize essais de philosophie du droit*, 140–78. Paris: Dalloz, 1969.

Waddell, Helen, *Beasts and Saints*. London: Constable, 1934.

Wagenknecht, David, *Blake's Night: William Blake and the Idea of Pastoral*. Cambridge, Mass.: Harvard University Press, 1973.

Wardy, Robert, 'Aristotelian rainfall or the lore of averages'. *Phronesis*, 38 (1993): 18–30.

Wedin, Michael V., *Mind and Imagination in Aristotle*. New Haven: Yale University Press, 1988.

Weil, Simone, *Lectures on Philosophy*, trans. Hugh Price. Cambridge: Cambridge University Press, 1978.

Wilkes, K. V., '*Psuchê* versus mind'. In *Essays on Aristotle's De anima*, ed. Martha C. Nussbaum and Amélie O. Rorty, 109–28. Oxford: Clarendon Press, 1992.

Wilkins, John, David Harvey, and Mike Dobson (eds.), *Food in Antiquity*. Exeter: University of Exeter Press, 1995.

Wittgenstein, Ludwig, *Philosophische Untersuchungen* (*Philosophical Investigations*), with a translation by G. E. M. Anscombe. Oxford: Basil Blackwell, 1953.

Index Locorum

General Index